RABIN

RABIN

OUR LIFE, HIS LEGACY

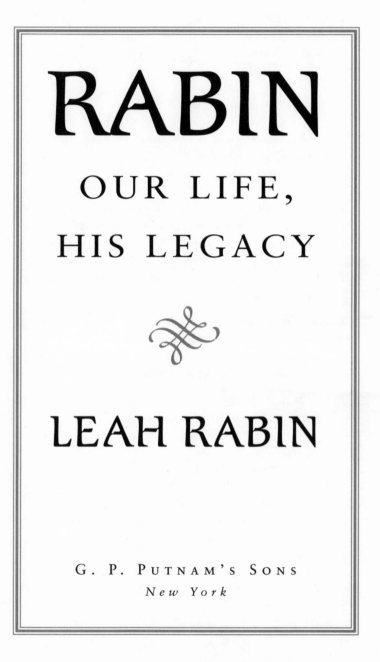

LEAH RABIN

G. P. PUTNAM'S SONS
New York

G. P. Putnam's Sons
Publishers Since 1838
200 Madison Avenue
New York, NY 10016

Grateful acknowledgment is made to the following people for the
permission to reprint their works: Yehuda Amichai, "God Has Pity on
Kindergarten Children" (translated by Assia Gutmann); Hayim Hefer,
"Makama"; Rabbi Stanley Rabinowitz; Lt. Gen. Amnon Lipkin-
Shahak; Tzvi Shahak for his daughter Bat-Chen's poem "A Letter to
Rabin"; and Meir Shalev.

Excerpts from Yitzhak Rabin's *The Rabin Memoirs* (second edition,
1994) are courtesy of its publisher, Steimatzky Ltd.

Library of Congress Cataloging-in-Publication Data

Rabin, Lea.
    Rabin : our life, his legacy / by Leah Rabin.
      p. cm.
    Includes index.
    ISBN 0-399-14217-7 (hardcover)
    1. Rabin, Yitzhak, 1922–95. 2. Rabin, Lea. 3. Prime ministers—
Israel—Biography. 4. Generals—Israel—Biography. 5. Prime
ministers' spouses—Israel—Biography. 6. Generals' spouses—
Israel—Biography. 7. Rabin, Yitzhak, 1922–95—Assassination.
I. Title.
DS126.6.R32R34   1997   96-36743 CIP
956.94'04'092—dc20

Printed in the United States of America
10 9 8 7 6 5 4 3 2 1
This book is printed on acid-free paper. ∞

BOOK DESIGN BY DEBORAH KERNER

ACKNOWLEDGMENTS

This book was written over the past year while I was trying to cope with the murder of my husband. It is, in a sense, my personal memorial to the man I have loved all my life, with whom I shared a blessed and privileged existence for nearly fifty years. I have tried to do justice to a man who was larger than life and yet so very human. . . .

There is nothing I want more, nothing more meaningful for me to do, than to leave this book as a testament to his life—to our life together.

I pray for his pure and wonderful soul and I pray that he will be remembered and understood as he deserves to be.

A number of people assisted me in the publication of this book whom I wish to thank.

First, I am deeply grateful to Putnam president Phyllis Grann's deep conviction in this book and her belief that the legacy of Yitzhak Rabin urgently deserved to be recorded. Publisher Neil Nyren skillfully oversaw the book's publication and clearly demonstrated why he is regarded as such an authority in the publishing world. Julie Grau was a constant driving force for the project and directed all aspects of the book's development. Julie is a masterful editor—discerning, exacting, and gifted in her perception of human details. Besides that, she is such a warm and engaging person to work with!

I cannot overlook the contributions of others at Putnam—especially Nicole Wan, Julie's reliable editorial assistant, Scott Fitterman, who coordinated the receipt and printing of the various drafts, and David Koral, our copyeditor.

At Williams & Connolly, Bob Barnett and Peter Kahn deserve my deepest appreciation for creating and sustaining all the intricate relationships that go into the making of a book like this. Bob Barnett is regarded as the premier representative for an author in the world of publishing today, and I can certainly understand why. He brought me together with Phyllis and Putnam, and saw to it that the whole publication process was handled with the utmost professionalism.

Bob's colleague Peter Kahn merits unbounded praise for his extraordinary dedication. Peter's expertise in coordinating the diverse team of people—throughout the world—needed to realize this project has been remarkable. Not only did he serve as a sort of command center in advancing every stage of the book's progress, he was a diligent and astute reader of various drafts and was a trusted sounding board for me on matters of both style and content. Judy Nigro, Peter's administrative assistant, kept close tabs on the endless details that accompanied the project.

Ron Beyma assisted me in all aspects of the writing and preparation of this book. He was introduced to me by my publishers as a skilled writer, a careful researcher, and an astute student of history and politics. I discovered a very compassionate, sensitive, and caring individual who, through the process of writing this book with me, discovered worlds and people previously unknown to him—Israel's amazing history, the culture and religion of the Jewish people, the complicated web of Middle East politics, not to mention Yitzhak's life and my own, and the many, many people who have been a part of our life. This book could not have been completed without the virtuoso weaving that Ron Beyma has so marvelously accomplished. I can wholeheartedly say that through our months of working together, I have acquired a true friend whom I honor and respect.

Julian Ozanne, formerly of the *Financial Times* Jerusalem Bureau, did a diligent and thorough job of checking the accuracy of the book's many details.

In Israel, Meir Ahronson was of great help in making available many of the photographs used in the book. Niva Lanir's role as researcher and consultant was much appreciated. She helped to shape the messages that deserved priority in the book, and also contributed engaging recollections of Yitzhak.

I wish to thank the talented precision translators who rendered important texts into English—Louis Williams and Katia Citrin. Louis did an especially remarkable job of providing sensitive and thoughtful translations under very tight deadlines. Thanks are also in order for Ettie Annetta, who helped on several occasions when we needed important tapes duplicated. As always, I extend deepest gratitude to my trusted, diligent, and conscientious administrative assistant, Ayala Zilberman, who has helped me in countless ways, countless times.

This book is meant to be a personal account, and not a definitive history, but I would be remiss in not mentioning several works that have been referenced in preparing *Rabin,* including Howard M. Sachar's *A History of Israel,* Robert Slater's *Rabin of Israel,* David Makovsky's *Making Peace with the P.L.O.,* and, of course, my late husband's own memoirs.

I would also like to acknowledge those people who have kindly permitted me to include their creative works in this book. Yehuda Amichai, Arik Einstein, Hayim Hefer, Meir Shalev, Amnon Lipkin-Shahak, and the family of Bat-Chen Shahak. Each has uniquely captured an aspect of Yitzhak's life and provoked reflection on the tragedy of his death.

I would also like to express my gratitude to those who generously shared their insights and gave of their time for this book. I must first and foremost thank former Israeli ambassador to the United States Itamar Rabinovich, who gave so much attention and assistance in the final review of the manuscript. Because of the tremendous demands on their calendars, I wish to thank former secretary of state Henry Kissinger, Ambassador Martin Indyk, U.S. Special Middle East Coordinator Dennis Ross, and Chairman Yasir Arafat.

Heartfelt thanks also are extended to Dr. Gabi Barabash, Norman and Diane Bernstein, Yossi Genosar, Ya'acov Heifetz, Amos Horev, Ben Kingsley, Rabbi Stanley Rabinowitz, Mrs. Moshe Safdi, Shimon Sheves, Dr. Ephraim Sneh, Danny Yatom, and Dov Weissglas. Eitan Haber was extremely helpful both in providing copies of my husband's speeches and in contributing significant background information for the book.

The real place of honor in these acknowledgments must go to my family—my son, Yuval, my grandchildren Jonathan, Noa, and Michael, my son-in-law, Avi Pelossof, but foremost to my daughter, Dalia, my closest and most trusted friend, whose steady encouragement and unwavering love and support were so vital during this most difficult time of my life. I love you all with all my heart.

To Yitzhak
To Dalia and Yuval
To Jonathan, Noa, and Michael

CONTENTS

RABIN

A LAST KISS

∞

Yitzhak, my dearest—

It is raining today, and the rain is pelting Mount Herzl and the flowers that cover your grave, dousing the candles that surround it.

And we are here at home—without you. Alone, alone, alone. You are no more. They took you from me, from us. And never again will you be in our beautiful home that you loved so much, with me, with the children, to whom you were such a loving father and a warm, good, caring grandfather. You were everything to them that a child or grandchild needed you to be—despite being always, always so busy with your work.

It is very difficult to get up each morning—without you, to sit down at the breakfast table—without you, and to know that from now on this is how it will be forever. You will never again be here, and I will be here with you—and without you.

I have so much to tell you, my dear beloved Yitzhak, so much about how I cherish the past we shared together and of the present and the future that respects your legacy.

∞

"There she is!" they yelled as I pulled into the driveway beneath our apartment. I was alone in the car, without a security guard.

"After the next election, you and your husband will hang from your heels in the town square like Mussolini and his mistress. This is what we are going to do to you," someone in the crowd shouted. "Just you wait."

Mussolini.

Some of the demonstrators outside our apartment building even compared us to Nicolae and Elena Ceauşescu of Romania, perhaps the most reviled despotic twosome of modern times. A friend visiting that Friday afternoon counted the people from our eighth-floor window with her forefinger. Forty-seven . . . forty-eight . . . forty-nine. Just as we suspected. Had there been fifty, the demonstrators would have needed a permit. Yitzhak and I heard this invective, these comparisons with fascism almost daily, as the peace process gained momentum.

At a demonstration a month earlier in Jerusalem, Benjamin Netanyahu stood on a terrace in Zion Square making a speech, while nearby an image of Yitzhak in a Nazi uniform dangled before a television camera. This was more of the same. The demonstrators across the street that Friday, November 3, 1995, yelled their trash until about six o'clock, when Yitzhak came home. They were waiting for him and left not long after he arrived.

Why were there never supporters of the peace process out there, making their presence known? Why were they unwilling to assert themselves, to make their voices heard just as strongly? Yitzhak ignored what the mob said about him that Friday, just as he had brushed their insults off on Fridays past. That Shabbat eve was a quiet night at home, although I remember his anger when I told him what they were now chanting about the two of us.

Months earlier we'd begun to see posters on the street, branding Yitzhak a traitor and murderer. You could see them on every street corner, on pylons and poles and lampposts. Pictures showing Yitzhak wearing a kaffiyeh, the Arab headdress Yasir Arafat wears. Leaving Jerusalem one day without Yitzhak, I asked the driver to stop the car at an intersection. The driver and I got out and tore down those horrible posters.

∞ *"Ishti,* I think I have a slight infection in my eye, and I don't believe I should play tennis today." These were the very first words Yitzhak spoke to me the next morning. It was a bright, clear, sunny Saturday.

"Would you like me to call you a doctor?" I asked.

"You have one?" He was surprised. Saturday morning in Tel Aviv is like Sunday morning in New York or Madrid. I told Yitzhak I would try to track down an eye specialist, and luckily I was able to reach Dr. Gutman, a fine ophthalmologist who had once treated our daughter, Dalia.

A doctor was to begin this day. With tragic symmetry, a doctor's pronouncement was to end it, too. And, with it, the heart of my life.

The doctor said he would be at our home in ten minutes. When Yitzhak complained about the irritation in his eye, I took a look and saw a flush of pinkness, a slight infection.

Yitzhak was always a zealot about his health. It had to be perfect. No wonder the routine of vigorous tennis each Saturday morning was so important to him. When his health wasn't flawless, believe me, you heard about it. He wasn't driven by fear or worry about himself, nor did he draw joy out of complaining. Yitzhak simply had a moral conviction that he had to be in perfect condition to carry out his job. He permitted himself no less.

I remember how Yitzhak had hurt his rib on one of his last trips to the United States. Traveling on a commercial El Al flight, he got out of his seat and must have been a little dizzy from the half of a sleeping pill he would take on overseas flights. He tripped over the base of a seat and banged his chest as he fell. For weeks after the rib was sore. Yitzhak cursed the pain and wondered why it wasn't getting better. I tried to explain to him that this was a slow-healing injury, but he was nonetheless impatient about it.

Fortunately I was with him on that trip, but I was always concerned when he would make those flights alone because my self-protective mechanisms are much stronger than his. When I am sleeping and get cold, I instinctively cover myself. Once asleep, he could be freezing and still not realize that he needed a cover. When he flew without me, I would worry that there would be no one there to cover him and that he would arrive at his destination with a bad cold, as he often did.

Covers, bullet-proof vests. Self-protection, slight or serious. They were not Yitzhak's thing, not his natural instinct. A reliance on the expert advice of doctors on the one hand and a rejection of personal defenses on the other. This was a fundamental paradox in Yitzhak's character.

That Saturday night, November 4, Yitzhak was to speak at a massive rally in support of the peace initiative at Kikar Malchei Yisrael—the Kings of Israel Square, an expansive open space in front of Tel Aviv's City Hall. Planning for the rally had begun several weeks before. Yitzhak wasn't sure it was a good idea. He was concerned that not enough people might attend the rally. The journalist and communications adviser Niva Lanir, a close friend of ours and a trusted aide during his years as defense minister in the National Unity governments of the 1980s, called to discuss the upcoming election campaign. She was also involved in organizing the rally. Yitzhak asked if she thought a significant number of people would turn out. She said they would, but he still wasn't sure. He called Shlomo "Chich" Lahat—a former mayor of Tel Aviv and a major force behind the rally—who reassured him. "Don't worry, Yitzhak," he said. "The crowd will be very large." It truly needed to be: a weak showing would be read as a lack of confidence in the peace process, a sign that people weren't all that enthusiastic. If it wasn't going to be an overwhelming success, Yitzhak would rather not have had it at all. That was his dilemma: Should we take a chance on the rally? He wasn't eager to put the peace process to a popularity test.

At midday, we went to an outdoor luncheon at a friend's home in Herzliyah Pituach. Yitzhak talked to many people and had a good time at the gathering. Our friends noted how very relaxed he was, despite the concern I knew was on his mind. We arrived back home at about half past two. Yitzhak took his customary Saturday-afternoon nap, the only extra sleep he allowed himself during the week. As usual, I zealously guarded the telephone, cutting short the rings to protect this precious rest time for him. Whereas I intercepted the phone calls during his nap, Yitzhak would schedule personal meetings for later in the afternoon. After he got up and before the visits began, Yitzhak did what he often did on a Saturday afternoon. Perched on the edge of our bed, he shined his shoes with the passion that only a military man could muster. Comfortable, worn shoes were his favorites—venerable old friends. We would be on our way out to a reception, and I would say in exasperation, "You're not going to wear *those!*"

And the stoic answer back was usually, "Give . . . me . . . a . . . break." Only a special occasion or a particular wish to please me made him give in to wearing a pair of better shoes, and then he invariably would say, "Look, I'm wearing these shoes tonight just to please you."

Every Saturday, Yitzhak allotted time for consultations with leaders from government and industry, who would brief him on key issues. This Saturday was no exception. In the afternoon, there was a meeting with Martin Schlaf, a friend from Vienna. Haim Ramon, a leading member of the Labor Party and the head of Histadrut, the collective council of labor unions in Israel, was the last to visit that day—one half hour before we left for the rally.

In a rush to arrive on time, a plainclothes security person, Yoram Rubin, met us in the hallway outside our front door. The three of us squeezed into one of our apartment house's two tiny elevators at about seven-thirty in the evening. It would take roughly fifteen minutes to get to the square on a Saturday night. The rally organizers had asked Yitzhak to be there by eight, and he was always prompt. The official car—an armored silver Cadillac, which security had provided him the year before—pulled up in front of our apartment house. It was quiet outside—just the sounds of cars coming to life at the end of Shabbat. No demonstrators stood in the vacant lot across from us.

Yitzhak had no special love for the Cadillac. After it arrived in

Israel, our press immediately jumped on it. "Ahh-hahh! Now Rabin needs to travel in a *Cadillac!* Why doesn't the prime minister set an example with a more modest car?" they grumbled. Yitzhak avoided using the Cadillac as much as he could, unless there were strict orders from the security authorities that a particular trip required the sturdily armored car. You could feel the extra effort when the car had to accelerate from a stop because of the additional weight.

Recently someone had managed to pry off the Cadillac's hood emblem. The message was brazen and clear: *If we can get to your car, we can get to you.* Tonight security asked that we use the Cadillac because of the expected crowds. In addition to the driver, Menachem Damti, Yoram Rubin sat in the front seat. Yitzhak and I sat in the back, with the short curtains on the car's back windows open for a good view of the clear, early-evening sky. A second car with two security people followed us. That was the standard convoy and the full extent of routine travel security for Yitzhak.

En route to the rally, Yoram turned around, arching his neck over his arm, and reported in a subdued voice, "Yitzhak, I want you to know there is a serious warning that a suicidal Islamic terrorist may try to infiltrate the crowd tonight." It was a measure of the man that his security people and all those who worked closely with him called him by his first name. Yitzhak didn't flinch at all from Yoram's report. Another false alarm, he must have thought. He was more concerned about the size of the rally—and the endorsement that its success might signify for the peace process. I could always tell the difference between Yitzhak being "cool in the face of a crisis" or Yitzhak dismissing a threat or a warning. This was the latter. His mind was on other things.

Not me. The words "suicidal Islamic terrorist" sent a shiver down my spine, though I tried not to let it show. God forbid this should happen now, I thought. Not tonight. *Especially* not tonight. I never let go of my fear that something awful might occur, but I allowed it to drift to the back of my mind: You're going to a peace rally, you have a fleeting vision of what could happen, and then you file it away.

This kind of threat was our daily routine. What, after all, could we do about it? Yes, all the security measures had been taken. There were guards standing on the roofs all around the Kikar. People entering the square were checked, but can you really check 200,000 people? No way. Who could stop the infiltration of one maniac who was promised a welcome in heaven by forty virgins as a reward for his terrorism?

While I shared Yitzhak's concerns about the turnout, I was looking forward to the rally. When we arrived, we were bowled over. An immense, warm, happy crowd, buzzing with magical enthusiasm. You literally couldn't see the end of the people.

From the instant we arrived, Yitzhak was caught up by the joy of the moment. The banners, the posters, the rush of happiness. Nothing we had ever experienced could match this. It was like a wonderful carnival. Signs bobbed in the air. The crowd yelled, "Rabin, we love you!" For a while the mood overcame me, but I kept my eyes on the crowd most of the time. The demonstrators from the day before didn't worry me now. They were loud-mouthed extremists with no sense of decency, but not life threatening. I scanned the crowd, but what would I be looking for?

Everyone who helped organize this rally was on the stage. It was to be a "victory rally" after signing Oslo II—an historic agreement between Israel and the PLO providing for a partial Israeli military withdrawal from the Occupied Territories, an extension of Palestinian self-rule, and the first democratic Palestinian elections—and a counterdemonstration to the Zion Square rally a month earlier. We were so very grateful to its organizers and to such dignitaries as Egyptian ambassador Bassiouni and representatives from Jordan and Morocco, who made a point of being there. I approached people whom I knew had worked hard for this achievement to let them know how much I appreciated their efforts, and how much it meant to Yitzhak.

I walked around the folding chairs and wooden benches set up on the stage. I spoke with Jean Frydman and Dov Lautman, both of whom had donated a substantial amount of money to hold this rally. Jean was a veteran of the French Resistance. When Yitzhak came in, Jean escorted him to the front of the stage, and the crowd roared. I stayed behind and talked with Chich Lahat, the main organizer, who coordinated the support of friends and reserve officers. Chich's wife, Ziva, decided she would mix with the crowd and take a reading of the atmosphere in the square. Ten minutes before the end of the rally, Ziva came up to us and said, "You have no idea how much they love Rabin."

Yitzhak called me over to stand by him in the front row at the edge of the stage overhanging the plaza. Below us, in the square, young people were climbing into the fountain, totally drenching themselves with water, in an effort to move closer to the stage, chanting, "Rabin! Rabin! Rabin!" We were overwhelmed by the ecstatic youths before us.

The wife of a reporter from the newspaper *Ha'aretz* approached me and asked if Yitzhak was wearing a bullet-proof vest. I was stunned by her question. Yitzhak would have thought it incredibly inappropriate to wear a bullet-proof vest on an occasion such as this.

"Bullet-proof vest?" I said to her, astonished. "What are you talking about? Are we in the Third World? It's out of the question. This is Israel." After all, the slogan of the rally was "Yes to peace, no to violence."

The speeches began; Shimon Peres started talking at about twenty past eight. Yitzhak was the last speaker.

Before starting his speech, Yitzhak hugged Shimon Peres. It had happened before, but this seemed a crowning moment of their partnership over the last years. Yitzhak didn't often display affection in public. The crowd loved it. When Yitzhak addressed the crowd, he thanked everyone for rallying for peace and against violence.

"Violence," he said in words I shall never forget, "is undermining the foundation of Israeli democracy." He spoke with passion and determination. I watched Yitzhak, I watched the crowd. But Yitzhak's total concentration was focused on the words he was speaking: "I have been a military man for twenty-seven years. I fought as long as there was no chance for peace. I believe there is a chance now, a great chance, and we must take advantage of it for the sake of those who are here and those who are not, and there are many."

His speech got a thunderous reception. When the singer Miri Aloni stepped between Yitzhak and Shimon Peres with microphones in both her hands, I knew Yitzhak would be expected to sing. Contrary to many reports, it wasn't the first time he had sung at a public rally. He joined in the national anthem, "Hatikvah," when it was played at public ceremonies. But it is true that singing was not his favorite activity. Song sheets for "The Song of Peace"—an anthem from the late sixties—were handed out, and somebody gave one to him. Yitzhak did his best to follow along, and though singing wasn't his natural instinct, I could tell he sang "The Song of Peace" as a happy man. He was moved by the outpouring of support, of love.

After the song, the rally concluded with the singing of "Hatikvah." Yitzhak and I were about to leave, when I suddenly remembered we hadn't said good-bye to Chich, so we returned to thank him, and Yitzhak gave him a big hug. As Yitzhak and I headed for the stairs, we were trying to stay close to each other, but we were besieged by people in the crowd who gathered around us.

People called out to me: "Leah, take good care of him!" They said it again and again and again.

With a slightly exasperated smile, I opened my hands and said, "I'm doing the best I can."

When I saw Bennie, one of the security officials, with his walkie-talkie in hand, the Islamic bomber came to mind. A threat that happily never materialized. Bennie was pressing his earphone against the side of his head. I said to him, "Thank God, everything went so well."

"*So far,*" he answered in a wary voice. The tension apparent on his face said, As long as you are still here, I cannot begin to relax.

Yitzhak and I headed toward the car. I started down the stairs behind the stage on my husband's right. The crowd continued to press close, and Yitzhak stepped ahead of me. Cars waited in a queue in the parking lot behind the square. Shimon Peres had con-

sidered waiting to talk with Yitzhak, I later learned, but decided to
go ahead. Menachem, our driver, was waiting to help me into the
car. I was still on the stairs as Yitzhak moved to get in the car.

"Where's Leah?" Those were the last words that Yitzhak uttered before the gunshots. The next few seconds will forever remain a blur. On that terrible night, when the first bang was heard,
Yitzhak looked back, as though he were thinking, Just a minute,
what is going on here? and then I saw him drop down as others
piled on top of him. I thought, and later so strongly wanted to believe, that he was thrown down as an act of protection.

I heard three short bangs. Could they have been firecrackers?
Noisemakers?

Suddenly, I was standing alone. I could hear the crowd buzzing,
and someone shouting, "It wasn't real!" Then a second security
guard thrust me into the front seat of the next car in the queue.
This was the security car that had followed us to the rally. The
silver Cadillac had already sped off—with Yitzhak, the driver
Menachem Damti, and the security guard Yoram Rubin.

Doors slammed. The car I was in lunged forward, and the
crowd swirled around us as we pulled away. Where were we
headed? *What in the world was happening?*

We broke free of the crowds and raced down the street. The car
barreled through all the traffic lights. I couldn't see the Cadillac or
any other security cars. The driver slapped the flashing blue light
on the hood and flipped on the siren.

I don't believe that the security people knew where they were
heading. From the moment they pushed me into the car, I asked
again and again, "What happened?" and each time they answered,
"It wasn't for real."

"*What* wasn't for real?" No answer. Was security repeating
what we all heard someone in the crowd yell or something that an
official with accurate information was telling them through their
earpieces? Okay, I told myself, we're in the middle of some sort of
emergency. I am in the hands of the security people. My job is to
let them do their job.

We drove like crazy. The car raced around like something out of a Clint Eastwood movie—rumbling over railroad tracks, careening over sidewalk curbs, through red stoplights with its siren blaring. The security guards were subdued, intense, and clearly under orders to do what they were doing.

Then we were speeding out of town. Back came the image of the security guards piling on top of Yitzhak. There had been a threat and they had protected him from it. The last time I saw Yitzhak before the guards toppled him, he looked fine.

We were supposed to go to a post-rally party near Zahala at the home of friends, and I thought the security people were probably speeding me there to meet Yitzhak. I wanted nothing more in the world than to get there, jump out of the car, and run up to Yitzhak and ask him what the hell had happened.

Then I realized that we were headed in the opposite direction. "Why are we going this way?" I asked. "This is the *wrong* way." No answer.

"Where is Yitzhak?" The words rushed out of my mouth. *"If it wasn't real, where is Yitzhak?"*

"In the other car," they said.

"Where?"

"Behind us."

"What car?" I couldn't see any car. "What car?" I asked again. They finally admitted, "We don't know."

It struck me as odd that they weren't chattering into their mobile phones or radios. Today, I suspect that they were under instructions to keep our location secret.

"Where are we going?" I asked.

"We are headed to Shabak headquarters," I was told.

We pulled up in front of Shabak, or General Security Service, Israel's equivalent to the FBI. The offices are located about ten minutes from our home. The structure is enormous in size—though deliberately unimpressive and nondescript. I was taken into an austere room, asked to sit at the desk, which had a phone on it, and told to wait. "When we know anything, we'll tell you," one of the agents said.

The minutes dragged on and I started to suspect that the bullets were not blanks. Several agents, all of them young men, darted in and out. "What happened to him?" I kept asking.

"Be calm; when we know something, we'll tell you," they said. They weren't cold or rude to me. They just didn't have any information. I was sure they would tell me when they had hard facts. I had been used to waiting for specifics in a crisis before. When I would see something on the news that looked like a tough mob or security scuffling with demonstrators, I would call Yitzhak up and he would say, "It's nothing." This time I didn't know what to do. I didn't know whom to believe. And I didn't know where Yitzhak was to call him.

At least there was this much information: someone had fired a pistol at Yitzhak. I telephoned our daughter, Dalia, from the Shabak headquarters. "Dalia," I said, "someone shot at your father, but they say it wasn't real, that they fired blanks."

"Where is he?" she asked.

"I don't know."

"And where are you?" Dalia asked.

"I'm at Shabak headquarters."

"We're leaving immediately," Dalia said.

"Come quickly," I told her, and hung up.

The minutes passed and my anxiety and dread increased, but still I was hopeful. If Yitzhak had been hit, I thought, perhaps it was just a slight wound.

Then I overheard a cryptic exchange among the Shabak staff just two sentences long: "One was severely injured. The other one only slightly."

"Where is he?" I asked in a desperate way that demanded an answer.

"They took him to Ichilov Hospital," they finally admitted. The severely injured one was Yitzhak, I could tell. It had now been twenty minutes since I arrived at Shabak headquarters, and I could sense the panic rising around me. Something very terrible had happened. I demanded, "You take me to the hospital immediately."

If Yitzhak had been the one who was slightly wounded, they would have said so . . . and they said nothing. Before we left for the hospital, I overheard another remark about one being shot in the vertebrae. Were they leaving it up to me to draw the conclusion for myself? The horror that I should have to pray that it was *the other one* who was seriously wounded! I hoped that, if it was indeed Yitzhak, he would not be paralyzed. My mobile, dynamic husband couldn't be permanently crippled or brain damaged.

By the time Dalia and her family arrived at Shabak headquarters, I was already on my way to Ichilov. The trip to the hospital was a nightmare. What do you think in those moments? What are your hopes? What do you wish for? Please, God, help him . . . help me.

When I arrived at the hospital, I saw instantly just how serious the situation was. Professor Gabi Barabash, the head of Ichilov, met me at the entrance. I asked Dr. Barabash what the chances were. He looked at me, and his big, penetrating eyes expressed despair rather than hope, though no one dared give voice to hopelessness. At that instant I not only felt my heart sink, I could also sense myself starting to slip away from the moment into a surreal awareness, though I was still filled with very real dread, and very real hope. Wasn't a miracle always possible?

Someone led me to an unoccupied patients' room containing two beds, both covered with green hospital sheets. There was a nightstand to the right of the bed I sat on. A phone was perched on a little bench at the far end of this long and narrow room. Dalia rushed into the room, and I started to cry.

We waited for Dr. Barabash to hurry back with reports. I was told Dr. Yoram Kugler, head of the trauma unit, and Dr. Motti Gutman, a member of the emergency room team, were working feverishly in the operating room. They had removed the spleen and inserted a chest drain. Later I learned Yitzhak had received more than twenty units of blood.

In a short time, Shimon Peres and many others arrived at the hospital, including Chief of Staff Amnon Lipkin-Shahak, Shimon Sheves—the former chief aide who was organizing Yitzhak's reelection campaign, Labor Minister Ora Namir, and President Ezer Weizman. Members of the Knesset and a growing stream of other officials. One by one they trickled in. President Bill Clinton called and spoke with me and U.S. ambassador to Israel, Martin Indyk, offering words of encouragement and friendship.

There was still a chance he would pull through. So we were told and so we wanted to believe.

It was then that I learned that the gunman was caught, and that he was a Jew. I was appalled, disgusted. I was outraged. Instantly my mind switched gears from the supposed Islamic terrorist and I could think only of the demonstrators across the street from our home. How could they?

After all the drastic medical measures, the doctors reported that they had managed to stabilize his blood pressure. "We have hope," Dr. Barabash said. Ora Namir kept saying, "I'm telling you he is strong. He will overcome."

They told me that in the car speeding to the hospital, trying to calm the security officer and the driver, Yitzhak had said, "It hurts, but not too much," before he lost consciousness. Little aggravations—like an inflamed eye or a bruised rib—might have troubled him, but when times were truly grave, Yitzhak was brave and tough and still considerate of others in the most uncommon way imaginable.

Maybe five minutes passed. Dr. Barabash returned. Yitzhak's condition had deteriorated. Those were the words that put us on notice.

Dr. Barabash came back one last time. His eyes told the whole story. I didn't need the words.

It was over.

I turned weeping to Tel Aviv mayor, Ronni Milo, and said, "They should have shot me instead of Yitzhak."

I insisted on seeing Yitzhak. I remember walking twenty or thirty meters down the corridor. My granddaughter, Noa, says the room was cold. Perhaps. I didn't notice. I noticed only the coldness of his skin and feeling so bewildered that I was now supposed to leave. All the efforts at the hospital had been valiant but futile. Yitzhak was actually dead two minutes after the shooting when he collapsed in the car, the bloodstained copy of the "Song of Peace" folded in his pocket. After the bullet punctured his aorta, air began to flow to the brain. First, irreversible brain damage. Then clinical death, even though the doctors tried to massage his heart for nearly an hour. Had he been wearing a bullet-proof vest, he might still be alive today.

∞

My darling Abba'le, you were lying there covered and they uncovered your face. I gave you a last kiss. You were so, so cold and so pale. At least I was able to kiss you one last time. I kiss you good-bye but you are already in another world—you don't know what they did to you—you don't know you were murdered—you don't and you will never know—and we? We also don't quite know the whole meaning of what was done to you—why you were taken away from us forever. And then . . . we were urged to leave the hospital, to go back home without you, to the home which we had left a couple of hours earlier, like any other Saturday night, this time for the wonderful rally where you were so excited and so happy.

CHAPTER
2

SHALOM, CHAVER

We came home in the early hours of Sunday morning. Hundreds of people had gathered outside, standing and waiting. The car drove up to the back entrance of our apartment building—an entrance we never used—because there were so many people in front. The security guard walked us through the service entrance, past the garbage bins. Even though the crowd meant well, security didn't want us to face such a gathering after the ordeal at the hospital.

My children and I went upstairs, all of us together, all of us grappling with our loss. Close friends joined us in the living room, but I can't recall exactly who was there that early Sunday morning, nor what was said. We sat in the living room for quite a while— maybe another two hours. I don't remember saying much, I just listened.

As I sat quietly, trying to still my reeling mind, a terrifying realization came to me, unbidden: as I was in the midst of the most devastating personal tragedy imaginable, the nation had just been pitched into a catastrophe unparalleled in its history. In a trick of memory, a strange image persisted in blazing through my state of shock and pain. . . .

∞

...*A couple walks down the Tel Aviv beach at about ten o'clock on a June night in 1933. It is within days of my first setting foot in Palestine as a little girl. Two men approach the couple. One of the men raises a torch. The other points a pistol and shoots the husband while the wife looks on in horror. The assailants flee in a flash. The man is rushed to the hospital and dies because he has lost so much blood....*

∞

Chaim Arlosoroff was a thirty-four-year-old Labor movement leader and the *bête noire* of the right-wing Revisionists. They accused him of consorting with the Nazis. This young politician, who also was head of the political department in Palestine's Jewish Agency had, in fact, just traveled to Germany and was active in trying to get Jewish people and property out of that country. Although the murderer was never identified, three ultra-nationalist Revisionists were accused. Two were acquitted. One, Avraham Stavsky, was convicted, but his conviction was ultimately overturned.

Yitzhak and I discussed Arlosoroff many times. He thought that Arlosoroff was a rising young star and would likely have played an important role in the struggle for independence. Yitzhak was fairly certain Stavsky was the assassin. It was a common assumption; we all had good reason to believe it. It was left in the air, but we all had good reason to believe it happened that way. No matter who killed Arlosoroff, the Revisionists had created a climate that provoked his death. They spread vicious rumors and promoted articles contending he was a Nazi collaborator.

Arlosoroff may have been my one truly lucid thought that night. Friends tell me that I sat in the chair I always sit in. I know that the people around me were plunged into thinking about the funeral arrangements. You couldn't "open a book" and figure out what to do. The assassination of an Israeli prime minister had never happened before. Yitzhak was at the hospital. The coffin would go to Jerusalem tomorrow morning. Danny Yatom, Yitzhak's trusted military aide, said the funeral would be delayed until Monday, when President Clinton and other world leaders would arrive. People talked, and I said "Okay." Burial would be on Mount Herzl. "Okay." But *why* did it happen? We would go to Jerusalem for the lying in state in front of the Knesset tomorrow. "Okay." But I still don't understand. . . .

The very thought of sleep seemed impossible, but the doctor gave me something mild at about four o'clock. Eventually exhaustion took hold. Dalia, Noa, and I all collapsed onto the same bed—but that night was passed in something like an unconscious numbness rather than sleep.

The very first words I uttered when I awoke were, "Something terrible happened last night, didn't it?" At first I thought it might have been Dalia because she had recently had a brush with a serious illness. Then I remembered: *Yitzhak.*

In the light of day, I recalled an incident that had taken place two weeks earlier at the Wingate Institute, a sports academy near Netanya. Yitzhak was attending a festival there and his visit was disrupted by a raucous group of extreme right-wing Jews. One man at the event unexpectedly ended up on the speaker's platform along with Yitzhak. I heard reports on the radio that suggested Yitzhak had been attacked. I telephoned him anxiously and asked him what had happened. Yitzhak played it down. "One guy tried to come up to me," he said, "it wasn't as bad as they made it sound."

Later I saw the coverage on TV and watched a security guard actually lift this guy up and set him down away from Yitzhak. Security had removed him like a bundle. It made me uneasy. For someone to be able to get so close to Yitzhak should have been taken as a warning. If you asked Yitzhak if he had felt threatened he would have said, "Absolutely not. I don't think that anybody would seriously want to hurt me." He was constantly asked in TV interviews about people saying they would get him. He would brush the threats off with the words, "Come on."

How different last night. No noisy disruption, just a punk lingering in the shadows of the car park. They say he lurked there for more than a half hour. He chatted with the police. A harmless fellow Jew, waiting for a glimpse of the prime minister. He listened to Yitzhak singing the "Song of Peace" over the loudspeakers. He looked like a guy who wanted to shake Yitzhak's hand. Maybe he was even a Shin Bet agent in disguise. After all, a thousand security agents and police officers combed the square. A thousand protectors, and Yitzhak still lies dead in Ichilov Hospital. Until the nightmare happened, nobody took the threats seriously, nobody could believe deep down in his heart that a Jew could murder the prime minister.

But we learned that Yitzhak's murderer had stalked him before. There were accounts that he may have received some rudimentary security training while working briefly with Jewish groups in the former Soviet Union. Some think it was there that he learned the tactic of yelling that he was firing blanks while shooting live bullets. Whether he yelled out that they were blanks or an accomplice did, to this day we still do not know, and what difference does it make, after all?

The murderer had confessed to three earlier attempts to kill my husband in 1995. On January 22, he was ready to strike at the Yad Vashem Holocaust memorial. But Yitzhak did not appear there as planned to commemorate the fiftieth anniversary of the liberation of Auschwitz—having to respond to a suicide bombing at a bus station in Beit Lid that killed twenty-nine of our soldiers. His second attempt was at a Moroccan folklore festival on April 22 at Nof Yerushalayim hall in Jerusalem—but he couldn't get past the security guards without an invitation. On September 11, when a highway interchange was dedicated at Kfar Shmaryahu, he tried again but could not penetrate the mass of people.

I shake my head now that I know the murder could have happened sooner. This was a calculated series of events—a work of cunning and premeditation. The sheer persistence of this plot brought back the words of the poet Leah Goldberg: "The imagination of the victim is always inferior to the imagination of the killer." Who would have imagined that a Jew was methodically stalking the prime minister of Israel?

On November 4, the murderer's fourth attempt in less than a year proved successful. Yitzhak's *chef de bureau,* his right-hand man, Eitan Haber, announced my husband's death to the media from the hospital. Israel first learned that Yitzhak was dead from the TV news anchor Haim Yavin at eleven-fifteen on Saturday night—a little more than an hour and a half after the assassin's attack.

Sunday morning I saw the papers with their headlines and pictures. I looked at them . . . and then I could look at them no longer and threw them aside. I have no doubt about what Yitzhak would have said: "It happened. So what can you do about it?" What *could* we do? All that was left was to honor him, his memory, his legacy, his unique personality. And as my son, Yuval, later put it in a memorial speech, to pursue "this way of peace and security; to take this road together—so that my father's sacrifice will not have been in vain."

In the car to Jerusalem on Sunday morning, all was quiet. There wasn't much to say. We were all in shock: it still seemed like a very bad dream. The coffin lay in state at the Knesset, the Israeli parliament. We sat near Yitzhak for an hour as people—mostly government officials and Knesset members—passed through the long line. One by one, they came and shook our hands, expressing their sympathy, in a state of disbelief. Some I would rather not have received, but these are unavoidable situations.

Seeing that coffin, draped in the blue-and-white flag of Israel with its bold Star of David, atop the black bier . . . seeing it for the first time on the square outside of the Knesset was, for me, an awful confrontation with an inconceivable reality.

∞

One and a quarter million people filed past your coffin in twenty-four hours. You in a coffin! You, who could never be stopped for a moment, forever interred in a coffin.

We sat opposite the bier. How awful that was. There were so many visitors from near and far: the cabinet, the Knesset

members, and we—the children and I—close to you, and
only you were missing because you were there inside the cof-
fin. How simply awful!

People stood hours in line just to pass by and pay their
last respects, to be there beside you, to say a last good-bye.
You are no longer and you do not know how great the pain
is, how great the disbelief is among our people. You cannot
know how towering my feeling of loss is . . . towering. You
cast a giant shadow over us, and now the vacuum you left is
so terrible and so shocking for the entire country, the entire
world—and me.

∞

I had no sense of my personal responsibilities. I was consumed
by sadness. My children felt the same sense of loss as I; he was
such a strong figure in their lives.

Many hundreds of people were waiting outside our house when
we returned, and I decided on the spur of that difficult moment to
speak to them. So many people were there. I could see them pressing down the street. Cameras and microphones bobbed everywhere as the press sought to bring what we were feeling to the
nation and the world. Choking back my tears, I said to the crowd,
"Two bullets killed this great, wonderful man. . . . It's a pity that
you all weren't here when there were demonstrators on the other
side of the street calling him a traitor and a murderer. It's too bad
that you didn't come then. But you are here now and that also
encourages me, my children, and my grandchildren that you are
honoring his memory in this wonderful and respectful way, and
that you want peace. Thank you very much for being here. I value
this and love you in his name."

I wasn't angry. I was honest. I hurt beyond belief. And I know
that they, too, hurt.

The voice of the many, many who were supporting the peace
process and all that Yitzhak tried to do, had not been heard. It was
not heard when there were violent demonstrations and threats.

When they called Yitzhak a traitor, a murderer, a Nazi. Perhaps believing the truth was self-evident, the majority that was so silent had abandoned the streets to the voices of violence and hatred. But Yitzhak did not complain because he was so busy pushing forward, uphill, to reach peace. The silent majority trusted Yitzhak and believed that, so capable was he, he could do it alone.

∞ Eighty-seven heads of state landed at Ben-Gurion Airport. Throughout Sunday and early Monday, the plane engines reverberated like distant roars of grief, with leaders arriving from all corners of the globe to pay their last respects, to honor a man who had become a profound symbol of peace.

President Bill Clinton, King Hussein, and former presidents George Bush and Jimmy Carter attended the funeral. The ailing President Reagan could not be there but sent former secretary of state George Shultz as his representative. John Major and Helmut Kohl . . . Jacques Chirac and Václav Havel . . . Hosni Mubarak, Viktor Chernomyrdin, and Boutros Boutros-Ghali. Most wore yarmulkes. King Hussein wore a traditional Jordanian red-checkered kaffiyeh. Throughout the crowd of mourners were blue baseball caps (distributed by the women of the IDF), knitted *kipot* of Orthodox Jews, and Druze turbans.

The funeral was an unforgettable procession of modern history, news reports proclaimed, but I could scarcely notice it. My son Yuval's arm around my shoulder bolstered my ability to stand and to withstand . . . just as my grandson Jonathan, dressed in his khaki fatigues and bright red beret, helped support his grieving mother, Dalia. The funeral began with a ceremony in front of the Knesset and then the long convoy started out to Mount Herzl.

∞

There was a wail of sirens in your memory! The wail that always freezes the blood—on the eve of Holocaust Remembrance Day, on the eve of Memorial Day for the Fallen—was now sounded for you. Two minutes of silence across the land. I stood at attention—can it be in your memory?

Then we accompanied you on your last journey. We drove in the cortege behind your coffin. Is it possible to grasp this? The coffin was carried in a command car and the children and I were behind it. Again and again I ask—is it Yitzhak? Is it possible?

∞

Thousands of people stood along the route, mute, sobbing.

So many times, I had accompanied Yitzhak to Har Herzl for memorial services. Eighteen thousand Israelis have died in wars since our state was founded in 1948. Israel has many Arlingtons, but Mount Herzl is our Arlington of Arlingtons. It contains the graves of Levi Eshkol, Golda Meir, and many of the giants who founded the state of Israel. Mount Herzl, an elevation overlooking Jerusalem, gained its name as the burial site for Theodor Herzl, the founder of modern Zionism, who had died in Europe in 1905 and whose remains were transported to Israel in 1949.

Here on the ridge six generals laid my husband to rest.

President Clinton's eulogy echoed perfectly the noble and moving tenor of the ceremony. With such deep respect, global comradery, and the pain of personal loss, he spoke. His words touched me deeply. "Leah, I know that too many times in the life of this country you were called upon to comfort and console the mothers and the fathers, the husbands and the wives, the sons and the daughters who lost their loved ones to violence and vengeance. You gave them strength. Now we are here and millions of people all around the world in all humility and honor offer you our strength. May God comfort you among all the mourners of Zion and Jerusalem."

When he said, "Though we no longer hear his deep and booming voice, it is he who has brought us together again here in word and deed for peace," he brought home our personal loss so poignantly. "Your prime minister was a martyr for peace, but he was a victim of hate": so perceptively the president saw the forces that had cut Yitzhak down and the irreplaceable leadership he provided. "Legend has it that in every generation of Jews from time immemorial, a just leader emerged to protect his people and show them the way to safety. Prime Minister Rabin was such a leader." And then came his parting words, *"Oseh shalom bimromav hu ya'aseh shalom aleinu ve'al kol Yisrael, ve imru amen."* He who creates peace in the heavens may he create peace for us all and for all of Israel and let us say amen.

"Shalom, chaver"—good-bye, friend—were President Clinton's words of farewell.

So moving, too, were King Hussein's words: "My sister, Mrs. Leah Rabin, my friends, I had never thought the moment would come like this when I would grieve the loss of a brother, a colleague, and a friend—a man, a soldier whom we respected as he respected us.

"You lived as a soldier," His Highness continued, "you died as a soldier of peace, and I believe it is time for all of us to come out, openly, and to speak our piece, here today and for all the times to come. . . . Let's hope and pray that God will give us all guidance each in his respective position to do what he can for the better future that Yitzhak Rabin sought with determination and courage. . . .

"When my time comes," the king said, "I hope it will be like my grandfather's and like Yitzhak Rabin's." This bold comment reflected the personal history of the Hashemite family. In July 1951, when he was just sixteen, King Hussein saw his grandfather, King Abdullah, gunned down at the Al-Aqsa mosque in Jerusalem by an Arab assassin who feared the king was trying to make peace between the Arabs and Israel. Yitzhak's funeral was the first time since his grandfather's death that King Hussein had set foot in Jerusalem.

Our granddaughter Noa's moving words brought us—the family—back to our personal loss. In her eulogy—a eulogy that Yitzhak's aide Shimon Sheves asked her to write and which her mother, Dalia, encouraged her to deliver—she gave voice to the enormity of the family's desolation. "Excuse me for not talking about peace," she began. "I want to speak about my grandfather. . . . People talk about a national catastrophe, but how can you console a whole people or make them part of your own private sorrow when Grandmother never stops crying and we are mute, conscious of the huge emptiness left by your death?" She spoke of our regret when she said, "You never forsook others, and now they have forsaken you." He was our torch, as Noa so beautifully said. She remembered our *Abba'le* so tenderly, so vividly. "Your meaningful half smile, that which is no more, frozen with your death. . . . With little choice I bid you farewell, my hero, and ask you to rest in peace, and think of us and miss us because we down here love you so very much. And the angels who are looking after you now, I ask you to take good care of him. He deserves your protection. Grandfather, we shall always love you."

Again and again my mind revisits the sight of Noa delivering her eulogy with such great love and warmth and tears that came only when she could hold them back no longer—stoic and brave she was, as her grandfather would have wanted.

Our son, Yuval, recited Kaddish. The word is Aramaic and literally means "holy." It is the traditional prayer said, in this case, by the son at the funeral of his father.

After the burial service, the horror of watching the coffin disappear forever into the earth. Everyone filed past us. I shook hands, I kissed them as they came to console us, sharing our unspeakable pain. There were so very, very many of them, with such grief and so many tears.

Senator Edward Kennedy and his son, Congressman Patrick Kennedy, sprinkled earth from the Arlington grave sites of the senator's brothers Robert and John.

Many people likened Yitzhak's death and funeral to President Kennedy's in 1963. America loved John Kennedy for what he represented: hope, potential, possibility. The world stood still in shock and horror when he was assassinated. President Kennedy had too little time to realize his great promise.

Israel, on the other hand, loved Yitzhak for what he had achieved. Yitzhak had the chance to prove himself both as soldier and peacemaker, a trusted and pragmatic leader and a visionary. God blessed his long life with achievements. He always felt that his second term as prime minister was a privilege, providing him with the chance to do what truly needed to be done, equipped as he was then with the experience of many years.

For so many of the children of our nation, Yitzhak was like their own grandfather. To adults, their father. To the seniors, their friend or brother. So many letters I read begin, "I don't remember having cried so much over the death of my own father . . ." Our daughter, Dalia, captured this spirit when she addressed these words to her departed father on the seventh day of mourning: "You were a father who was always there: You were everyone's father; a warm and loving presence—without words; a presence of wisdom, a presence of security—so much security and strength. . . . They all write: you were everyone's father."

As prime minister, Yitzhak was always traveling throughout our small country. Chances were good that you would have seen him in person. He was very visible. He was the most important national figure to the children—a hero from their history books and their leader in the present.

After Yitzhak's funeral, we drove back home. The *shiva* had begun. For seven days and seven nights the entire nation, immobilized, eulogized my husband, and the world joined in. For seven days life in Israel stopped. Shops, offices, and businesses were closed. Shop windows displayed Yitzhak's picture draped with black ribbon. It was an undeclared period of personal mourning for an unbroken week. Undeclared but unmistakable. We, his family, could not grieve as a typical family could—in private, searching moments. This entire time was extra-dimensional. At times of enormous shock, my natural instinct—a survival reflex—has always been to detach myself, to view myself from afar. That's where I was when the *shiva* began. There . . . and also somewhere else.

An endless line of mourners wound its way up to our apartment house, starting early in the morning and continuing until late at night. They shook my hand. They kissed me. *"Toda raba,"* thank you, I said again and again. They cried with me. They cried for me. It was all so unreal.

I received people I had never met and some I had not seen for many years, friends from the old days. They were all searching for a way to accept this horrible reality. Perhaps they hoped, through a handshake with me and with the children, to make contact with him and try to understand. . . . And yet there were many who never made it, who couldn't get near our home because of the throngs of people.

Endless bundles of mail were carried to our house. Letters, songs, poems arrived by mail, by fax, or were collected from various sites—the square, the cemetery, or in front of our house. There were beautiful pictures which are now displayed throughout our home. The house is full of portraits of Yitzhak; they look out at us from every corner.

During the *shiva,* a number of Israeli Arabs from small towns and villages came to the house. They traveled in groups. They stood in line and came into our living room—expressing their condolences with enormous sorrow. "We have lost our brother, our leader, our father," so many of them told me.

Flowers and more flowers. At his grave. At the murder site. At the entrance to our home. Candles flickered everywhere. The light from the candles outside at night was so intense it lit up our living room—eight stories up. The whole street was coated with wax from the burning candles. But it was not only to our home that mourners came, stunned, hurting, and weeping. Day and night, Kikar Malchei Yisrael drew them: children and adults alike, crying, singing, lighting thousands of candles.

I was told that I seemed to radiate a tragic composure during the lying-in-state and the funeral. Actually I was reeling in an orbit of sorrow. I completely lacked any sense of direction. It was my encounters with the news media that helped shape whatever focus I had. Israeli television approached me on Monday, the day of the funeral. By the third and fourth day, journalists from all over the world made their requests. During the seven days I was interviewed by CNN, CBS, NBC, Israel's Channel Two, Egyptian TV, and many others. I believe these media appearances dignified Yitzhak's memory. (With the exception of an appearance on Ted Koppel's *Nightline*—what a disappointment, Yitzhak and I had known him for years—where the audience representation in an Israeli "town hall" meeting was outrageously stacked to favor the opinions of the right-wing and ultra-Orthodox.)

When I spoke, I tried to think of how Yitzhak would have handled the situation. If somehow Yitzhak could have talked about his own death, he would not have spent his time accusing individuals or been paralyzed by fear. His natural instinct would have been to analyze why it happened and to determine what we as a nation were going to do about it now. This would have been his agenda and it quite naturally became my own. The tragedy had to hold a lesson for all of us.

To my great surprise, my presence alone held comfort for many who seemed relieved to have an image, a single person on whom to focus their grief. "Be strong, be well, we need you," they told me. I saw and still see myself chiefly as a symbol. I chose to speak out because it was both instinctual and what, I believe, Yitzhak would have wanted.

I expressed my belief that unbridled incitement gave birth to this deadly creature that eventually killed Yitzhak in cold blood. I made no effort to conceal my bitterness about the elevated and negative political rhetoric. People needed to focus on the climate that made the murder possible. Our grandson Jonathan summed the environment up in a single sentence, "The murderer was just a revolver."

I also sensed an obligation to defend our security people for their vigilance in protecting Yitzhak. They would have been willing to give their lives on Yitzhak's behalf. Unless I said this again and again, people wouldn't have believed I was sincere. My comments were shaped by a combination of self-protection and merited defense for those who were caught in a tragedy—our tragedy as well as theirs.

I needed to sense some beam of light in this tragic moment. We were in a crisis, ensnared by a national and personal disaster. At a crossroads, you must choose to go forward in a new direction. This new direction had to be a strengthening of the peace initiative. Perhaps this tragedy occurred in part in the absence of loud, vocal support for peace. The demonstrations covered by the media were those by opponents to the peace process. That silent majority could afford to be silent no more. As a nation we had to recognize that indifferent silence could be as dangerous as volatile words.

∞ The *shiva* had solemn and remarkable moments.

During the seven days, an unexpected visitor came to our home in Tel Aviv. He had never been there before. He wore an overcoat, sunglasses, and a hat. When he entered our living room, he called me "sister" and kissed me on the head three times. He had traveled under the cloak of great secrecy to Tel Aviv, expressly to see me and the children.

The man was, of course, Yasir Arafat, and he was accompanied by his closest aides, Mahmoud Abbas (Abu Mazen) and Ahmed Qurei (Abu Ala'a). It was Arafat's first time in the state of Israel.

Security considerations had made it impossible for Arafat to attend the funeral. This was understandable. But it was during this visit to our home that I truly discovered the warm and authentic side to this human being behind the political facade. My children and a couple of friends joined me in our living room. He kissed each of the children after he kissed me. It was as though we'd never had a disagreement with our Palestinian neighbor, as if we were continuing a dialogue that had never known argument.

Yasir Arafat described how he had telephoned Yitzhak's aide Yossi Genosar after he'd heard of the attempt on Yitzhak's life. Over and over, Arafat said to Genosar, "Please tell me some good news. Make me feel calm." Between one and two A.M. on the Sunday morning following the murder, Yasir Arafat's wife, Sua, had called me directly to express her horror.

Arafat described how shocked he was by the murder and how

desolate he felt at losing his partner in the peace process. During the night of the murder, he recounted how he spent those terrible hours. He was shattered by Yitzhak's death.

We talked about his family. When his daughter Zahiva was born in July 1995, I sent the family a silver dove mobile to hang over the crib. "I don't have time to see her," Arafat complained. "I don't get home until two in the morning."

"But this is the time little babies wake up!" Tali Shahak, wife of our chief of staff, told him.

During Arafat's visit, President Clinton called, and I told him about my guest and how moved I was. Within hours, photos of Chairman Arafat in our living room appeared in newspapers throughout the world, documenting the respectful relations these two former enemies had forged.

∞

Yitzhak, my dear husband,

On the seventh day, I return to the cemetery, to your grave, and there is nothing more difficult than facing it, and knowing that it is where you now are, and that for eternity this is the only place you will ever be. You disappeared from us—and you are forever gone.

The grave is covered with flowers and surrounding it are hundreds, maybe thousands, of extinguished candles. I walk around it all, refusing to believe, unable to grasp.

∞

We stood and we cried. The prayer of "El Male Rachamim"— God Full of Mercy—and the Kaddish that was once more recited by our son, Yuval. Again we bid farewell, and began the ritual of the shaking of hands, embraces, and kisses with friends and loved ones standing by us. Farewell, Yitzhak—we are departing, but you will remain, for eternity.

∞ We have risen from the *shiva*. I have literally "risen" from the seven days in which I sat in the same chair, in the same corner, receiving the thousands of mourners that have passed before me. When I got up, my feelings resembled the song written about me by the entertainer Arik Einstein, within seven days of the murder: "She rinses her face, she puts on her smiles, and she steps into life. She grits her teeth, hides her tears, makes up her eyes, and returns to the living." Yet I am still so far from returning to the living. . . .

On the seventh day of the *shiva*, a rally commemorated Yitzhak's death in the very same place where he lost his life. Once again masses of people crowded the square and all the streets around it. Yet how silent. A week before there were signs, songs, and great rejoicing. Now only sadness and mourning lingered. A towering billboard nearby carried Yitzhak's picture and the words "You have started the song. We must finish it."

They came to be with Yitzhak . . . and my words had to reach them through him. To make sure my remarks would be worthy, I read the speech in advance to the children and to Yitzhak's aides Shimon Sheves and Eitan Haber for their advice and approval. These words would be broadcast around the world, and the responsibility weighed on me. Don't allow yourself to cry, I said to myself, don't permit yourself to break down.

Shalom, chaverim,

Here he stood but one week ago. Here, in those moments, he was a happy man, and from here he went to his death. And now, with your permission, I want to talk to him— something I can no longer do in this world.

Since that tragic moment, the hundreds of thousands, the millions who came. . . . And the journey that followed. How terrible. I rode with our children and grandchildren, behind your coffin. And the funeral—to which eighty of the world's nations came to pay their last respects. Yitzhak, turn your eyes and see how they have gathered together here.

And since then—this immense, gigantic, stupendous ι   ʳ

ing to you, to what you were for them. This love, a little of which you may have sensed, but the magnitude of which you could never have imagined. They come, and they come—and still they come. A whole country in deep mourning for a week now. A whole country has stood still and is weeping. They continue to come to your grave day and night, and have covered you in flowers. They light candles and leave letters—addressed to you.

And within the house we—the children and grandchildren, and your sister, Rachel—are drowning in letters and telegrams. Thousands come to console and be consoled, and to part from you—Jews and Muslims, Christians and Druze and Circassians, children and youth and old people, and more letters and drawings from all over the country.

Yitzhak, can you believe it? Please believe me, something has happened here the likes of which neither this country, nor possibly the world, has seen before. The shock of the murder has reverberated beyond the frontiers of this land, and people are mourning you across the Middle East and over the face of this planet.

I'm asked where I get the strength from, and the answer is—from you. From you, Yitzhak, for I was in the shadow of your immense strength for many years. And today, as I talk with you, I know that only this way would you like to see me—strong. And the current of this love that reaches out to us is yours, but it must be answered with gratitude—and I am here to thank them, all of them.

I want to tell you that your security men have also come. They weep, and we try to hearten them, and we tell them: Yitzhak functioned all those years with total faith in you. He didn't think for a moment that something could happen to him because you were protecting him. And I was also calm, for they protected you. And today I swear to them on all that's holy that I will never have any recriminations toward them over what happened. And from my instincts, and my familiarity with you, I know that you would tell them the same things, if only you could. It happened, and your guards did everything, and we shall always believe in them, because they are so wonderful. Each and every one of them is wonderful, dedicated, and dear to us.

Yitzhak, you know me, and you know that I'm always looking at the half-filled glass not the half-empty one. And that's why I want to believe that this terrible tragedy which has befallen me, us, all of us, this monstrous price that you and we have paid, was not a vain sacrifice. For we have risen from that nightmare to a different world, a world that relied on you, for which you signified what was good and right, and for whom you were a source of hope. For they knew that you were the hope for peace and for a better society.

But they relied on you too much, and let you fight alone—alone in the turret—and were too silent in the face of the writing on the wall, of the shrieked insults and the horrifying incitement that you chose to ignore. And they were silent. And it was only that last evening, here in Kikar Malchei Yisrael, that a crowd of many thousands came to show support for you and for your long and difficult road to peace. And you were encouraged and happy.

And now our wonderful youth know, as do the children and this entire country, that there can be no more silence. Now the voice of reason and right will be heard. Now the silent majority will become a majority no longer silent. A majority that will strengthen those who follow your road to peace.

Following my instincts, without of course the chance to talk with you, I phoned Shimon Peres, and I told him: "You started the journey together. Be of stout heart! My children and I, the government and all to whom peace is dear, will help you. I turn to you, Shimon Peres, to continue leading the nation of Israel to peace in the spirit that was Yitzhak."

Shalom, chaver. Dear and beloved chaver. Father of my

children, grandfather of my grandchildren, father and grandfather to so many wonderful children and youth. I'm not parting from you, but you may rest in peace—for you will live on with us forever.

Our daughter, Dalia, also spoke, and her farewell touched me most deeply. We desperately wanted to believe this grim reality was all an illusion. "OK, Daddy, we get the idea. You can come back now," she would say privately in our home. At the seventh-day ceremony she described the hollowness we all felt:

Seven days and seven nights since the great blow. Three pistol shots in the peace-loving city square—and chaos. And since then, as though an act of Genesis, we arise from the dust, marshal our strength, try to force our gaze forward— to the other, strange and alien, cold and terror-filled world that closes in on us in all its black shades.

Seven days and nights of mourning. In a pain that we cannot yet touch. And I speak to you. Speak to you a lot. Mostly at night, in our big, soft bed that always held all of us. Speak more than ever before, for you were not a father for soul-searching talk or daily chitchat. And I tell you how great and strong our mother is, how you would be so proud of her.

You were always, and ever will be, the father for everything, a great man. Always present with boundless kindness, warmth, and love. No words. Hugs, a look, a kiss. Lots of kisses. A presence of wisdom and the last word. A presence of safety—so much security and strength. And I am so full of you, our beloved.

And the words are so small, empty, and helpless. And the sensations fill every cranny of the body, and again and again that terrible pain. Untouchable. Everything is so fragile. So breakable.

And we stand facing the rising waves of the love of kindergarten children and their tears, and I sit and wonder:

*how is it that you were so much ours, our good and beauti-
ful father. Yet they all write. You were everybody's father.*

*And I held a hardened feeling that stuck with me for
years, that they were too blind to see, that their senses were
unable to distinguish how great and wonderful you were. I
now know that it was not that way at all.*

*They felt. They knew. They saw. That immense warmth
reaches out to them, to the children in kindergartens and
schools, to all who have a soul. And I have no consolation.*

*The whole world came. And the whole world stood in si-
lence. And the world wept with us. They knew that you were
the intelligence and the hope. And you were the great dam
against wrongdoing, the first and last address against distor-
tion and injustice. The keeper of the seal.*

*My precious father, this is the first time in my forty-five
years that you have broken a promise to me. You promised
that nothing would happen to you. I have lost that primal
sense that, beside you, no wrong could befall us. I have lost
you, and I refuse to accept it, to digest it.*

*My precious father, it is only seven days, and the road is
so hard before me.*

∞ Yitzhak's murder affected Jewish life around the world. Joyous
events were canceled or postponed. Almost all the decisions made
were handled with taste and thoughtfulness. One was not. A
planned fund-raising dinner for Bar-Ilan University in New York,
scheduled for a week after Yitzhak's murder, was postponed until
January 1996. When the dinner took place, a brochure was placed
at each guest donor's seat. Two weeks after the dinner, the contents
of that brochure came to light in Israel. The university sponsors
had added to the front of the brochure a picture of my husband accepting an honorary degree in 1993. But inside there were no less
than *twelve* photographs of the murderer, selected because he was
a model student of the university.

Israel Segal, an Israeli television journalist, broke the story in
February. Minimal action was taken in response and no apologies

were made. Bar-Ilan claimed it was a technical mistake, an over-sight. They apparently assumed no one would notice. They fired the woman who handled public relations for them in New York.

After the news broadcast, the rector of the university, Shlomo Eckstein, and the president, Professor Moshe Kave, wrote a letter asking to visit my home and asserting that the entire university should not be stigmatized because of the actions of a single student. A single student? Not so single, I think; he has many admirers in our society—even schoolgirls who write him adoring letters.

It is my belief that Yitzhak was murdered by a conspiracy. Whether the act itself was the result of a conspiracy, I don't know, and I'm not sure that it matters. He was certainly the victim of an intellectual conspiracy—a conspiracy every bit as calculating and lethal. A core of extremist rabbis, not teachers, at Bar-Ilan University were among those who inspired attitudes that led to the murder, and these people share the blame for the murder because the murderer believed he was fulfilling a holy mission sanctioned by them—that the "holy land" of Judea and Samaria is more holy than the life of the prime minister who was willing to compromise on this land for peace.

Nevertheless, I invited President Kave and Rector Eckstein to my home along with four students from the school's Labor faction. I wanted to listen to their views under my roof. The president dominated the meeting, devoting half of it to the story of the brochure, denying that the photographs were intentionally included, asserting that their addition to the brochure was an oversight, and would never have been done willfully. When the students spoke, the president appeared intolerant, even aggressive toward them. He seemed defensive.

My son, Yuval, who was also present, turned to President Kave and said, "May I ask you a question? Do you think it is just coincidental that my father was murdered by a student of Bar-Ilan?" He could have come from any other university, the president responded. My view: No coincidence whatsoever. This weed was raised on their poisoned soil.

∞ We observed the tradition of the *shloshim*, a period of remembrance and a stage of mourning held for thirty days after the death of a loved one. National grief prevailed throughout this period. People still streamed in lines to the cemetery, lighting candles, writing endless letters and creating drawings—the need to express their grief was so profound.

On the thirtieth day, we—the family—returned to the cemetery.

∞

This day too has come. Thirty days and nights of the ongoing nightmare have passed. Endless stacks of letters must be answered, requests from the world over for plans to commemorate you, and more and more telephone calls as well as visitors who did not manage to come during the shiva. *These thirty days and nights passed in a flash, but when I think what happened before these thirty days, it seems as if it were all two thousand light-years away.*

Nothing will ever again be as it was before November 4, the day you were taken from me, from the children, from the nation that has not yet stopped eulogizing you and crying over your death.

Once again our family is in a motorcade: we drive to the cemetery. The grave site has been neatly arranged, for the time being, until the tombstone is completed. Yitzhak, your grave is covered with flowers, candles, letters, and a tennis racket, plus two cans of balls. Our friend and tennis partner, Raphy Weiner, who loved you so much, put it there.

A child has left a stuffed teddy bear, her dearest possession in life.

I am with you—opposite your grave—and opposite the cameras. That awful combination. The entire world is witness to our tears but it is impossible to stand in that place and not cry.

The eulogies were delivered by Shimon Peres and Chief of Staff Amnon Lipkin-Shahak. Amnon's words tore into our

hearts. He seems to me to be following so truly in your foot-
steps. He can appreciate your deep bond with the soldiers
and the army, the project that was your life's love.

Again we take leave of you, from the grave, still in disbe-
lief,

So very many tears, Yitzhak.

∞

Our friend Niva Lanir spent weeks organizing a ceremony
at Binyanei Ha'Uma, a large conference center in Jerusalem, marking the conclusion of *shloshim.*

The ceremony included a most beautiful film about Yitzhak's
life and sections of the 8-mm films that Yitzhak took in the years
he was so keen on photography: picnics on Shabbat with the children, and personal and family pictures from Washington.

Shlomo Artzi and Boaz Sharabi—popular Israeli performers—
sang. The poet Yehuda Amichai and the writer Meir Shalev read
passages in Yitzhak's memory. Amichai read his poem "God Has
Pity on Kindergarten Children":

God has pity on children in kindergartens,
He pities schoolchildren—less.
But adults he pities not at all.

He abandons them,
and sometimes they have to crawl on all fours
in the roasting sand
to reach the dressing station,
and they are streaming with blood.

But perhaps
He will have pity on those who love truly
and take care of them
and shade them,
like a tree over the sleeper on the public bench.

Perhaps even we will spend on them
our last pennies of kindness
inherited from mother,

so that their own happiness will protect us
now and on other days.

Then Meir Shalev spoke:

What remains after the pretty words, the soul-searching,
the conciliation, the legacy, the unity? Simple truths re-
main—contempt and anger and pain. The words that no
imaginary unity can expunge. Neither rift, nor civil war.
Anger and contempt—yes. Anger over the soil from which
the murderer sprung. Contempt for the ideas that cloak
murder.

And the longing remains. Longing for the man we failed
to praise enough to his face. For a forthright and honest
man. Though we may not have agreed with all his opinions
and actions, we knew that this was the inner man, his pu-
rity—and this was of value.

And the yearning for the man who did not lock himself
inside the fortified battlements of his opinions. Who at an
advanced age, when beliefs are carved in stone and ideas
freeze, and men no longer stray from well-trodden paths—
suddenly, with great momentum, leapt from the furrows of
his life onto a new path. And the roots of the turnaround,
for those who remember, were already planted in the young
Yitzhak Rabin, who, in his speech on Mount Scopus after
the Six-Day War, said that we Jews are unable to rejoice as
conquerors and victors. That was what he said—and here
there arose a Jew and murdered his spirit.

And the longing for a man who was also a member of a
generation that fades away before our eyes. A different and
wonderful generation—that of the Palmach. A generation
the exact opposite of parasites, shirkers. No pomp and cir-

cumstance, no extremism or demagoguery, nothing messianic. A generation that mocked its eulogizers. But, yes, the Silver Salver. And, yes, such a comradeship, such a shower of adoration, seems still to fall on the living brothers, who cover their faces, and on the dead who cover no more. And how terrible the laughter of fate. To all the crowns adorning Yitzhak Rabin had to be added the most horrible and unnecessary of all—that of the last fatality of the Palmach. And from here on, another longing—for ourselves, for that same part of forthrightness and honesty, values and courage— which is being extinguished in our souls.

And the hardest longing of all, the longing of family. The yearning of love from which there is no shelter. The longing of a wife, the yearning of a sister, the craving of a son and daughter, the longing of a close friend, a grandson, a granddaughter. The pining from an empty bed, an orphan chair at the table, the yearning for a caress, the photo album, the longings spread over memories. Here stood a husband, there sat a father, here a brother, and there fell a grandfather.

And what now? The memory, the last kiss of the dead. And thus, in memories, he wreaked his vengeance. Not in wars between brothers, not in the capture of divided tribes. But with the old weapon, the tried and trusty weapon of Jews—a very long and very sharp memory. We, who remember the snapping dogs of our history, we will remember this murder, too. We will remember who was murdered. We will remember who murdered. We will remember for what and why. We shall not forget. . . .

CHAPTER
3

A JEWISH
HOMELAND

I came into this world a *Yecke*, a German Jew, on April 8, 1928, in Königsberg. This northern seaport was then in East Prussia and so part of Germany, although East Prussia was physically severed from the rest of Germany by the Polish Corridor. After World War II, Königsberg was renamed Kaliningrad and became part of Russia. I have never visited this city since I left it as a child and have no particular desire to do so. For me, there are no longer any roots in that town or in Germany.

In Königsberg, my father—Fima Schlossberg—was a dry-goods merchant. One of my earliest memories was his broadly smiling face arching down over me as a youngster and asking, "Leah, shall we go and count the lentils today?"

From my earliest recollections, I would today describe our family as upper middle class—well-to-do, in fact. Our apartment, in a three-story building across from a large and inviting park, had many rooms arrayed off a long corridor. But I spent most of my time in the house tucked away in a single room with the *Kinderfräulein*, a nursemaid governess, seeing very little of my parents. When I was very young, I remember them more in evening dress than in everyday clothes—since they would stop and visit me on their way out to the theater or a concert. As was typical for Jewish children at the time, I didn't go to kindergarten. Instead, *Kinder-*

fräulein Trüdel and I would go walking together in all kinds of weather to the park or the zoo, and on visits to my Jewish girl-friends, each accompanied by her nanny. I enjoyed being outside and at a very young age learned to ski and to ice-skate.

Then something totally beyond the realm of my comprehension happened.

On January 31, 1933, when I was almost five, Adolf Hitler became chancellor of Germany.

What was most frightening about Hitler's ascent to power? Had you asked my father, he would have said, that he was elected. Hitler represented the will of the German people, and what could a Jewish family expect in Germany with such a lunatic ruling the country? My father was a decisive man, and early on he read the writing on the wall. (Others, alas, did not. The Kristallnacht pogrom was still five years in the future.)

My father packed a suitcase the day after Hitler's election and took a train to Trieste. From there, he sailed to Palestine and prepared the way for us to settle there. My mother, my older sister, Aviva, our German nursemaid, Trüdel, and I took the train to Riga that same night. We had family in Latvia, and we remained with them until all the arrangements in Palestine were finalized. My father joined us in Riga for Passover. He had leased the Palatine Hotel in Tel Aviv—a bold step, a totally new business experience for him, and our first home in the new land. We returned to Königsberg until June to pack and say our good-byes and then we sailed for Palestine.

Family friends said I was a polite, well-behaved child back in Germany, a child who said evening prayers on bended knee and followed my governess's commands to a tee. A governess who tucked my elbows into my waist at the table and took the temperature of my bath water with a thermometer. My dear Trüdel and I last hugged each other in a tearful parting at the train station in Königsberg. My father predicted that I was bound to become a more mischievous child in Palestine: "Just wait until there will be no German nanny any longer." The "liberation" began with high-spirited games on the deck of the ship to Palestine.

When our ship docked in Jaffa on June 5, the stifling summer heat that greeted us was unforgettable. Shouts in every language reverberated throughout the harbor as small boats bobbed alongside ready to ferry us to shore.

Without warning, someone flung me—a proper five-year-old little girl—overboard into the hands of a giant Arab longshoreman. My hat sailed into the water and I yelled, "Where is my hat? My hat!" My doll landed safely beside me in the boat, but my hat was gone . . . and, far worse, I had no idea where my parents were. I was sure I would never see them again, even though we were soon reunited, as the immigration physicians administered painful anti-typhoid injections.

The pungent, babbling Jaffa wharf . . .

The dusty road to Tel Aviv . . .

Veiled women, camels, endless sand . . . it was all so exotic.

Then our new home. I took an instant liking to the Palatine Hotel. Coming from the boiling Jaffa port, the cool marble hallway felt like a blessed refuge. Shiny stone floors, soft recessed lighting, and intricate Persian carpets gave the Palatine's lobby a soothing Oriental touch—especially in the summer, when the heat blazed outside.

At the hotel, two handsome, ebony waiters from the Sudan—Tewfik and Ahmad—became my pals, even though we had no common tongue, and exploring the long hallways of the hotel on my own gave me a further sense of adventure and freedom. We lived at the hotel for six months, while my father went out of his mind dealing with a little girl playing ball and jumping rope in the foyers and hallways. I didn't know where to put myself.

Hebrew came slowly, learned from a new nursemaid and playmates, and I stubbornly refused to use it until I was confident I was in command of it. Gradually I was left on my own to explore the world, and in time Tel Aviv became a vast playground for me. So much construction was under way, there were always sandpiles and excavations for jumping, hiding in, and climbing.

Watermelon, corn on the cob, ices on a stick. The seashore and the tea salons.

It was a wonderful childhood in "sandy" little Tel Aviv.

Still, my parents brought an important part of Central Europe with them to Palestine. Although they had all the touches of *Yeckes,* my parents were born in Russia. Their parents moved to Germany when they were very young—my father's to Königsberg and my mother's to Danzig.

Papa was a great admirer of culture in general and German culture in particular, and these passions were strongly woven into the fabric of our everyday life. My parents had traveled a lot when they lived in Germany and would always talk about their visits and experiences. On a regular basis, they would visit the stages and galleries of Berlin and come back with enthusiastic reports. My parents were fervent fans of theater, opera, and movies. The names of great theater people and singers—Tito Gobbi, Lotte Lenya, Bertolt Brecht, Helena Thimig—were constantly in the air in our house. While their outlooks and tastes ran very deep, my parents didn't have much opportunity to travel back to Europe— certainly not for pleasure—after they emigrated to Palestine.

Still, Europe never really died in my father's heart. My parents never owned expensive original art. We had some prints from the Sistine Chapel and copies of the old masters. A print of Manet's *Olympia* hung in our living room. The only original painting was a landscape of a tiny French harbor, which once hung in the Palatine Hotel and is now in my sister Aviva's home.

When we were growing up in Tel Aviv, Papa used to read us poems by Goethe and Heine in the original German on Saturday mornings. When he arrived in Palestine, he was far from fluent in Hebrew, but Papa quickly became a regular theatergoer in Tel Aviv, thoroughly enjoying it. Every Saturday night my parents went to the old Tel Aviv Museum for chamber music concerts. They subscribed to the orchestral concerts immediately after their inception. Toscanini conducted the premiere concert of the Palestine Symphony (later the Israel Philharmonic) on what used to be a big fairgrounds in 1936. They played in a shed with a corrugated tin roof. When it rained, it beat on the roof with the rattle of a hundred snare drums, legend says. It leaked. Still it was glorious!

Through my parents I absorbed an extensive cultural foundation: art, music, theater, literature, and, after some adjustment, opera as well. I remember one particular night as a youngster of about eight or nine. I hated to be left alone in the house. My parents were obviously dressed to go out.

"Where are you going?" I asked.

"To the concert . . ."

"What are they playing?" I asked impatiently.

"Beethoven's Seventh Symphony."

"But you heard it already! Why do you have to go *again?*"

My father's cultural passion somehow did not conflict with either his early commitment to Zionism or his hatred for his life in Germany as a young man—understandable given the prejudices Jews faced there. Papa was a committed Zionist from the age of fifteen, when he joined one of the Herzl groups that sprang up to carry the torch ignited by Theodor Herzl, the Austrian journalist who articulated the vision of a Jewish state.

During his first trip in 1927, Papa bought property in Palestine. A house in Jerusalem . . . an orange grove in the area of Benyamina . . . Small holdings here and there. But their later usefulness was great. After we moved to Palestine in 1933, things were tougher. When we were short on money, he would sell a piece of property. My parents—like so many other European immigrants to Palestine—were professional people. They appreciated culture and fine living. But somehow they didn't seem to mind hoeing yams on a kibbutz or whacking the bell on the reception desk for a porter to fetch the luggage. After all, they were doing these things in beloved Palestine.

For my father, Palestine was his one and only destiny. Papa was the second of four children. Both his sisters—Esther, a spinster pediatrician, and Nettie, whose father-in-law, Leon Kellner, had been a good friend of Herzl—moved to Palestine in the early 1920s. His older brother, David, was a gifted though insecure scholar. An excellent speaker, he worked for a Zionist organization in Berlin. He fled Germany for Palestine only after Kristallnacht in 1938. Penniless when he got off the boat, David was supported by my father, as were many others in and out of our family.

Papa had a great influence on me. I loved him and was very much loved by him. My candor is a trait I inherited from him. He was an outspoken, honest person—sometimes sharp. My mother—Gusta, short for Augusta—was more tolerant and soft-spoken. I was also very close to her, feeling totally secure and assured of the love both my parents had for me. Silver-framed photos of them occupy a place of honor on the sideboard by our dining room table. He is so vibrant and passionate about life. His keen wit and bold mind are evident in his features. The dark hair and strong, sturdy face speak robustness. My mother, on the other hand, is a study in softness, with wispy locks of hair surrounding her exquisite, gentle, angelic features. In Tel Aviv, she was known for her charm, her beauty, and her youthful appearance. When she died, she was forty-eight. During her last illness, her doctor had playfully noted her age as thirty-six on her bed chart and one easily could have believed it. My daughter, Dalia, has inherited some of my mother's features, very definitely her youthfulness.

Belying her looks, mother had a tough and resilient core. She could swim skillfully across the ocean breakers and would be up at dawn to pump and light the Primus pressure stove that scalded the laundry. After my parents came to Palestine, my mother was normally cheerful and smiling, coping well with a totally unknown and difficult situation. When finances were strapped, she managed. I remember her upholstering chairs or stitching new covers for the eiderdown comforters. She had no preparation or training for any craft work such as this. However, when she felt that something needed to be done and there wasn't enough money to order it, she went ahead and did it herself. Gusta Schlossberg was a true pragmatist, who made the best of every situation.

With the part-time aid of my mother, the constant help of an Egyptian assistant manager, and several other staff members, Papa ran the hotel and enjoyed it very much. Here and there, mishaps doubtless happened. One traveler anticipating a long stay asked if the Palatine ran a kosher kitchen. "Yes, I believe it is," my father answered, although at that time, it really wasn't. "That's too bad," the would-be guest sighed. "My doctor has prescribed a thick slice of smoked *schinken* [ham] every day."

While Tel Aviv's fanciest hotels are on the coast today, they were then in the center of the city. No exception, the Palatine was the most posh hotel in Tel Aviv at the time. It catered to an elegant clientele, gala weddings, and distinguished foreign visitors. The Palatine set trends and decreed custom. One time, the mayor, Meir Dizengoff, hosted the empress of Ethiopia to lunch in a private salon off the main dining room. Everyone peeked out from behind their menus or over their napkins just to get a glimpse of them as they walked by. Asparagus was the first course, and the mayor dug in with a fork and knife. But the empress elegantly lifted an asparagus spear off her plate by hand and started nibbling on it. Down went the mayor's fork and knife as he, too, finished off the first course with his fingers.

Living in the hotel was never intended as a long-term arrangement. When our crates of furniture arrived from Germany (including a precious case of a dozen dolls I was so fond of), they were unpacked into our new apartment. It took only about ten minutes to reach the hotel by car from our new home. While the hotel was fun, there *was* one reason I was glad we moved. Next to the hotel sat a fire station. If the sirens went off and I was alone in my room, I became hysterical and ran into the corridor yelling. To this day, I panic when I hear a siren—on the street, on Independence Day . . . anywhere, anytime.

Even though we didn't live there any longer, special occasions brought me back to the Palatine. For the feast of Purim, Jewish children dress up in costumes, much like those of Halloween or Mardi Gras. Each year the high-spirited procession—with the mayor riding a horse at its very head—would wind its way down the street in front of the hotel, where the terraces were jammed with spectators. When I was about seven, my mother made me a beautiful Purim costume as a lift boy—bottle green with a pillbox hat, *Palatine* in gold letters embroidered across its front. I was even supposed to operate the elevator. However, I had to give up my new job rather quickly because English was the closest thing to a common tongue for the hotel guests and I couldn't speak it. It was a very cute outfit, although every year I yearned to dress up as Queen Esther, the famous heroine of the holiday. My mother generally wanted me to be something amusing.

Within the hotel, the atmosphere was one of cosmopolitan peace. In Palestine itself, one wasn't so sure. During the late thirties, Arabs and Jews coexisted peacefully—much of the time. But the two groups never really mixed or resided in the same locales. Arab Jaffa and Jewish Tel Aviv were neighboring cities. In Jerusalem, the ethnic quarters were separated much as they are today. When we drove to Benyamina to see my Aunt Nettie, we passed through the mysteriously silent Arab villages and cities, and I was always a little uncomfortable. But my father was never concerned and would jump out and cheerfully ask for directions in halting Arabic. Then the Arab riots started in 1936 as the Jewish presence in Palestine grew, and travel was less a casual journey and more a calculated risk.

Papa left the hotel business after the riots began and Jaffa was burning, convinced that tourism to Tel Aviv was in great jeopardy. He joined a company called Ha'Avara (which means "transfer" in Hebrew). His firm helped German Jews transfer their money through purchasing German building supplies and raw materials, which were then shipped to Palestine. When the refugees later arrived in Palestine, they were reimbursed for the money they had expended. It was a brilliant conduit for transferring funds, but it all stopped in 1939, when the war broke out.

The heat was unbearable in Tel Aviv, and my parents suffered from it enormously. We got our first electric refrigerator in 1936. Air conditioning didn't exist at the time—certainly not in Palestine. In the blistering summer, people often slept on the balconies; I used to sleep on the floor. Every couple of years, we moved from one flat to another. I think my parents hoped that the next one might be a little better ventilated than the last, but all our moves did was to trace an arc around Rothschild Boulevard. My father always liked convertible cars, which enabled him to get some evening breezes against his face as he drove.

The hardships may have been great and the changes big. Not for a fraction of a second, however, did my parents look back with nostalgia and regret at having left Germany. Nazi Germany was becoming more and more of a threat, and they were just happy to have left in time.

I'm sure part of their resolve was aided by the unflinching discipline of their everyday life. True to his European upbringing, my father insisted that we eat our meals in the dining room. In those days, there were no kitchen eating nooks. In the dining room, the table would be set quite formally three times a day—with linen damask tablecloths and napkins. My mother came with only one china service—a very nice Rosenthal one—and one sterling silver flatware set. We also had a sterling silver coffee ensemble. These were used three times a day. The standards always remained the same, whether we had guests or not.

Discipline was surely one element. The warmth and friendship of the people around my parents was another. My parents were always surrounded by friends. The style of entertainment was more informal than today—with people dropping by for coffee, cake, and conversation in the evenings—and no difference at all between an evening when the family was alone and one when visitors came. I was always interested in listening to these discussions. The dialogue was serious, even profound with very little small talk. The conversations tended toward political and economic topics, such as the possible value of Dead Sea potash or the latest political controversy—often with a passionate expression of views. This crowd of friends that now included my parents was immensely involved and cared greatly for the development of the new Jewish homeland, which was not yet then a state.

Every *aliyah*, or wave of immigration, has been laughed at to some extent for their quaint customs, but none more than the *Yeckes*. The German Jews were often and in many ways the butt of jokes. It took the adults such a long time to master the language, and they never shook off the very noticeable German accent. It wasn't just the language, but the tortured politeness of such well-behaved and meticulously trained people, with men doffing their hats when they said hello and the endless stream of *"Danke schön"* and *"Bitte schön."* Eastern Europeans found this behavior very funny.

Conversing in Hebrew was easier for my father than my mother. Throughout her life, she had enormous difficulties with Hebrew. Even though my father engaged a private tutor to coach them both two evenings a week, the motivation to master the language eluded her. My father's determination paid off in slow, hard-earned stages. First mastery of a Hebrew newspaper. Then classics, including Mendele Mocher Sefarim and S. Y. Agnon. But most of all, it was my father's commitment to converse with others in Hebrew that gave him this skill. While he became perfectly accomplished in Hebrew, my mother—for all her virtues and charm—could never really master a single spoken sentence.

School jump-started my own Hebrew skills enormously, as one would expect. My primary education began at the age of six in the privately run Balfour School. The Balfour School was very bourgeois. My parents hated it, deriding it as a private business, bereft of values and preoccupied with making money.

Still, school meant more than just skills and rudiments, it also nurtured the beginnings of political and social awareness for me among my peers, even those at the stuffy Balfour School. School was an important gateway for me into the broader Jewish society of Palestine. Papa was never a socialist, but instead a General Zionist—a moderate—as was typical for fellow immigrants of his wave. Still, he had a great admiration for Pinhas Sapir and Levi Eshkol—later prime minister—and other founders of Mapai, the workers' party.

Following in the footsteps of my sister, Aviva, seven years my senior, I joined HaShomer HaTzair (a socialist Zionist youth movement) in the eighth grade. I embraced its uniform of blue skirts or shorts with blue blouses. We had compulsory meetings twice during the week and on Friday and Saturday evenings. We hiked throughout Palestine. We debated ideology. We savored the history of labor movements, monumental revolutions, and—of course—Zionism. And on Friday, I remember dearest of all, we sang together, often deep into the night.

Late in August 1939 my parents visited Europe. My father was on a business trip in the Balkans—one of several he made. Mother was en route to visit her parents, who were in Milan. My sister and I had been entrusted to the care of a housekeeper and her husband: the two of us were to join my parents two weeks later in Milan. Shortly before my mother left, my father was convinced the conflict would be delayed.

COME STOP THERE WILL BE NO WAR STOP, he telegrammed Mother, meaning, I am sure, that there would be no war in the immediate future.

War was declared as my mother's ship was sailing across the Mediterranean. When she arrived in Genoa, she learned that if she went to Milan, the borders might be closed and she would not be able to get out of Italy. So she left for Budapest to meet Papa, but she could hardly have expected the drastic events that would befall her parents afterward. My grandparents moved to Bergamo after Milan was bombed by the Allies. My grandmother died there of heart failure and my grandfather was later taken to Auschwitz. Although she didn't know it at the time, Mother would never see her parents again.

Did my mother or father ever urge her parents to flee Europe with the change in political circumstances there? I don't know; she might have. The complexion of things had changed. Mussolini was more favorably disposed to the Jews than other European leaders for a long time. By 1940, when Italy became an active Nazi ally, it was surely too late to do anything.

Aviva and I were afraid we would be separated from our parents for the duration of the war in Europe. I was only eleven, but I vividly remember people hoarding everything: cooking oil, toilet paper, and sacks of flour and sugar in the expectation that the war would reach us. All that the two of us had were two boat tickets and a little cash. My sister was more pessimistic than I, but we were both elated when three weeks later a cable finally arrived from my parents: TAKING THE ORIENT EXPRESS TO GREECE, AND A BOAT FROM THERE.

But the threat was not confined to Europe, as I learned first-hand on a scorching day in September 1940. On the way to visit a cousin with a friend of mine, we had walked down to the number 6 bus stop at the corner of King George and Dizengoff Streets. We stopped for a lemonade. Then the bus came. Should we finish the lemonade or hop on the bus? We opted for the bus.

One could hear the faint whir of airplanes in the distance. Within two minutes bombs slammed into that intersection. The lemonade kiosk was demolished. The bus stopped and we dived for cover behind a bomb barrier that shielded the front of 4 Shatz Street. We huddled there in terror. Here we were, a couple of twelve-year-old kids amazed and shaking. The fear was justified. More than a hundred were killed and countless others wounded in the attack. Mussolini's air force had bombed Tel Aviv, and I had nearly been a casualty of this distant war my father had followed so avidly over our radio!

When the immediate danger seemed to have passed, we looked with no success for a bus to get home. The city was in chaos. Finally, we persuaded a taxi driver to take us home, guaranteeing the fare by promising that my mother would pay when he delivered us. Mother was terribly worried because she heard that a bomb had been dropped on Dizengoff. She went down the street, stopped a friend, and said, "Leah went north up Dizengoff Street and I am very worried. Would you take me to my sister-in-law's house to see whether she arrived?" When she got there, I was nowhere to be found. So Mother went to the hospital frantically looking for me among the wounded and the dead. And she didn't find me there, either. When we were finally reunited back at our home, it was very emotional. However, the most indelible experience of the attack occurred later that same day, when we drove with my father to see the damage and passed by Tel Aviv's Hadassah Hospital. Cries and wails poured through the open hospital windows from the loved ones of the dead and injured. The sounds were horrifying and unforgettable.

Increasingly, uniforms strolled the streets of Tel Aviv. And more and more young men appeared in them, as they volunteered for His Majesty's army—and, later, the Jewish Brigade—as a counter to Hitler's onslaught. The world war had been raging for more than two years when an important change took place for me, as I moved on to secondary school. As I said, my parents were never members of the working classes, and my father was basically a businessman. Still they wanted me to have an education with liberal values and a broad cultural perspective. My parents were enthusiastic over the reports they heard about Toni Halle, headmistress of Tichon Hadash, or the New Secondary School. She also was of German origin, but belonged to B'rith Shalom, politically left of the left, and certainly left of my parents. Still they prized her humanistic beliefs. She was fiercely supportive of tolerance and free speech, values the school emphasized. I didn't want to enroll in Tichon Hadash; I was quite happy in my former school. But once there, I sensed how special Toni was. She herself taught art history and general history. Toni became an important mentor in my general education, due in large part to the openness and discipline of her thinking and her profound love for Greek and Roman history as well as later European art and culture. From her, we learned to love these subjects for ourselves.

The majority of the children at Tichon Hadash were from blue-collar, unionist, working-class families. The school's classrooms were always overcrowded, and vacancies were scarce. I was forever grateful for that four-year high-school experience. I considered it a privilege. It shaped in me a lot of what I became and remain today. The school conveyed a certain mood, hardly glamorous. The single-story building was modest, even stark. Students long since graduated had carved and scratched the desktops, creating the rooms' only ornaments. Not a single painting or plant. The schoolyard wasn't even paved. It was nothing but sand.

The first year I attended Tichon Hadash we could leave the

school and walk directly onto the promenade along the beach. That's where we spent the recess period. When the British and Australian military had increased their presence in Tel Aviv, Hayarkon Street became the center for the soldiers' and officers' clubs. At twelve o'clock, the clubs would open and start serving beer. That, of course, meant that the soldiers would often get drunk. One day, one of the soldiers opened our schoolroom door, barged in, and kissed the teacher right before our eyes. We stared in disbelief and then collapsed in giggles. From then on, the school doors facing Hayarkon Street were kept locked.

In 1941, while at summer camp, I remember a dashing British officer on the Haifa road giving me and a girlfriend a lift on an army lorry loaded with Indian soldiers. Although he was British, this captain was born and bred in India. Since he loved music and opera and was a stranger to Tel Aviv, I casually invited him to stop by and visit our home. Home hospitality to the forces was very in vogue, but I never expected to hear from him. Well, he sent a letter two weeks later asking if he could call. I was only thirteen at the time. "Leah, what kind of relationship have you established with a British officer?" my parents asked.

One Saturday afternoon, he appeared at our door. Captain Buck turned out to be a multilingual cultural whiz. My father and mother took a shine to him, and the captain even lost his heart to my sister, Aviva—who by no means lost hers to him. Later Captain Buck moved to the British Commando Unit and was assigned to work with the "German Platoon" of the Palmach—learning everything from German slang to German songs, gearing up for a mission behind enemy lines in the western desert.

Caught by the Germans and caged in solitary confinement, he wrote to us that he conscientiously studied Mandarin in his cell. When the war was over, his marriage to a prewar sweetheart was cut tragically short as his RAF plane crashed en route to a military location in Germany. I learned about the last chapter of his life from Yitzhak Ben-Aharon, a prominent Labor Party leader who was a close friend of Captain Buck in captivity in Greece during

World War II. In these times, the melodrama of reality often out-did any scripts from the back lots of Hollywood.

The growing presence of British troops on our soil reflected the expansion of the war into a truly global conflict. My father had managed to escape from Nazi Germany, but he had not succeeded in eluding the Nazi threat. Throughout the war, my father spent his nights anxiously twisting the dial of our radio to catch the latest news flashes. For most people, the war was remote and business went on as usual. I was young and essentially unaware of the scenario unfolding in Europe until the early forties, but Papa was very concerned. "Why do the Jews stay?" he would ask. "Why in the world do they stay in Germany or the Sudetenland? Why don't they try to escape? What are they waiting for?"

In 1942, Hitler's Afrika Korps, under Field Marshal Erwin Rommel, the "Desert Fox," was speeding toward Palestine. Rommel's forces threatened Egypt and the Suez Canal, Palestine and Syria. A friend of ours once heard Papa say, "They're coming. It's all over!"

She was an optimist and refused to believe it.

"Fima—stop it!" she retorted. "There's no way that forty years of Zionism were for nothing." In my heart, I was convinced she was right.

Like hundreds of other Tel Aviv children, I was evacuated to Jerusalem, considered a safe zone from Italian attacks because of the Catholic religious sites there. My time in Jerusalem was spent in Maaleh, a religious school—an eye-opener in hindsight, because I knew so little about Jewish religious life from my experience at home. Observant or not, however, we were all of a common people, and no one had to remind us of our identities in the eyes of the world in 1942, as the crematoria of the Holocaust raged.

World War II was to forever change the Jewish psyche. It changed mine. It changed Yitzhak's.

Claude Lanzmann, introducing a screening of his Holocaust film, *Shoah*, in Jerusalem, said: "When they went to the gas chambers, they were alone. We were not with them." And we were not.

The world had turned its back. It had averted its eyes. It refused to live with unthinkable horror.

The Holocaust touched my family personally. Indeed, how few Jews today are able to say their families escaped that sinister touch? We learned the details of our own loss only much later. Among those who perished in the Holocaust was my mother's father, Moshe Nachmanzon. He had lived in Italy since leaving Danzig in 1933, when our entire family ran away from Nazi Germany. On April 5, 1944, he was taken from the Fossoli concentration camp—where the Italian author Primo Levi also was detained and then transported—by one of those terrible trains. Moshe Nachmanzon arrived at Auschwitz on April 10 and was exterminated in a gas chamber the same day, when the soul of this seventy-eight-year-old man was returned to God.

He went to his death all alone, and we—his family—didn't even know. If only the vision of the Theodor Herzls and the Fima Schlossbergs had been shared by many others, what a boundless treasure of humanity could have been saved! Would we have been granted a Jewish state had it not been for the monstrosity of the Holocaust during World War II? That I do not know and very much doubt.

But this much is clear: Could there be any more compelling motivation to create a homeland and permanent refuge that would guarantee the safety of the world's Jews than this unspeakable tragedy?

CHAPTER
4

KING DAVID
AND THE PALMACH

I first became aware of Yitzhak when I was in the tenth grade. During the summer of 1943, he was twenty-one and I was fifteen. He caught my eye in an ice cream parlor on Tel Aviv's Allenby Street. To me, he looked just like King David himself. His hair was a rich auburn, and his eyes were somewhat gray, somewhat green, and incredibly intense. Most of all, he had the bearing of a Palmach—he would disappear for weeks at a time and then reappear. Although Palmach men made the hearts of schoolgirls beat faster, the lure lay far deeper than adolescent fantasy. These were the young underground guardians whose dreams and energy would create and defend a Jewish state.

The Palmach was a branch of the Haganah. The Haganah itself was created as a defense league for Jewish residents of Palestine by Jewish worker parties in 1920. The Haganah, in turn, spawned the Palmach as an elite force with Yitzhak Sadeh as its commander in 1941. The term *Palmach* is an acronym for Plugot Machaz—the Hebrew term for "strike forces." The purpose of the Palmach was primarily defensive, to protect the *yishuvim* (Jewish settlements) from the attacks of Arab marauders. My Yitzhak joined the Palmach in the year of its inception and saw his first military action as a member of that force in May 1941. Afterward, Yitzhak said that this mission—invading Syria to climb telephone poles and cut phone wires, assisting a British operation against Vichy forces—changed his beliefs for life. Issues of defense were to be of paramount importance.

Steadily the chance encounters between Yitzhak and me became planned ones. I recognized a uniqueness in him and began to understand what made him tick. That included learning more about his family.

Yitzhak's parents had come to know each other in the narrow lanes of the Old Jewish Quarter of Jerusalem during the Arab riots of 1920. His mother, Rosa Cohen, came to Jerusalem from her kibbutz in the Galilee after contracting malaria. His father, Nehemiah Rabin, was in the city as a member of the defense committee when the violence erupted. They both rallied to protect their fellow Jews.

Rosa, born and raised in Russia, was a person of exceptional qualities. While her father was a wealthy lumber merchant, she advocated working-class causes, although she never became a Communist or joined the Bund, the Jewish Workers' Zionist Group. She remained a very proud Jew all of her life. Fed up with the Bolsheviks, Rosa decided to leave Russia in 1919 and made her way to the Black Sea. From there, she intended to journey either to Sweden or the United States. Absolutely on impulse, she changed her destination and decided to sail to Palestine instead, arriving on the Russian ship *The Rosslen,* the first vessel to sail for Palestine from Russia after World War I. She started her life in Palestine on a kibbutz but didn't stay there. She was a brilliant accountant and held senior jobs in various prestigious companies over the years. She never joined a political party. It was only after she arrived in Palestine that she developed her commitment to a Jewish state. In 1921, as the first commander of the Haifa Haganah, Rosa combined her routine office work with the delivery of messages on horseback between Jewish towns, after the bloody Nebi Musa riots of the preceding year. She organized Jews, arming them with sharp-pointed stakes she bought, anticipating that anti-Jewish hostility might erupt. Later she stood guard together with her husband during the turmoil in 1936 in Tel Aviv, where they eventually settled.

Nehemiah was born in the Ukraine to a poor family and had fled the 1905 pogroms for Chicago, where he worked as a tailor in the garment shops and took night courses at the University of Chicago. After he joined the Jewish Tailors' Union, his commitment to Zionism grew. A British recruiting officer enlisted Nehemiah to come to Palestine as a member of the Jewish Legion, and Nehemiah never returned to the United States. That recruiter was none other than Yitzhak Ben-Zvi, Israel's second president.

To say the least, Rosa and Nehemiah had an intricate and complicated relationship. At the end of her regular workday, Rosa would do considerable volunteer work. She was deeply involved in the education of working-class children and later became a member of the Tel Aviv City Council, as a strong advocate for educational opportunity. She believed in a two-income household—one salary for the family, the other to help families in need. The number of families regularly and discreetly supported by the Rabins was considerable.

Yitzhak's mother demanded as much of the rest of the family as she did of herself. With no domestic help, Yitzhak and his younger sister, Rachel, would help keep house. Yitzhak never, I believe, got used to that. Later in our married life, he avoided giving me a hand in housework as much as he possibly could! Most of the time, I respected his attitude, considering how hardworking he always was. Why bother him with household chores he detested?

Yitzhak's father, however, was different and willingly took most household duties upon himself, including shopping and looking after the children's needs. A heart ailment plagued Rosa, and eventually her health began to deteriorate. It was a time before telephones had become widespread in our land, and Yitzhak never forgot how as a youngster he had to run frantically to find a doctor whenever she felt the onset of an attack. She died in 1937, when Yitzhak was only sixteen—her heart condition was compounded by cancer. It was the last time in his life Yitzhak ever cried, except—I am told—for a poignant incident that happened on the day he learned he was to receive the Nobel Peace Prize, which I will recount later.

Nehemiah had a difficult role to play in a marriage with such a tough, determined, and self-assured partner, during a time that held very different standards for men and women. But Yitzhak was very supportive of his father. Later in life, Yitzhak publicly praised his father's devotion and dedication in helping to raise the children and run the household.

Yitzhak was interviewed for the program "My Parents' Home" on Israeli radio after his triumphs in the Six-Day War and was asked to compare his life as a child with the lives of his own children. "Because of their public activities, your parents often left you and your sister alone at home, and you suffered for it," the interviewer observed, and asked how he felt being away so often from his own children.

"But my children have their mother at home with them," Yitzhak answered. I think he subconsciously played down his mother's dominant role during his early childhood as a way of honoring the importance of his still-living father. But Nehemiah reacted in an unexpected way. He felt Yitzhak didn't do his mother justice.

A sense of discipline, a contempt for any sort of waste, and a deep commitment to public service characterized Yitzhak's upbringing by Rosa and Nehemiah, and these were to remain key values of his for life.

Rosa and Nehemiah did have their disagreements. One of them was about educating young Yitzhak. Soldiers and farmers were the first heroes of the Jewish state in Palestine. Rosa wanted him to fulfill the Zionist dream—agriculture, turning the desert into fruitful land; Yitzhak's father wanted him to go to the most prestigious high school in Tel Aviv. Rosa prevailed. In fact, she helped establish the agricultural school Givat Hashlosha near Tel Aviv, where Yitzhak received his first two years of high school education. It was also where Yitzhak got his initial military training. His first duties were very basic—learning how to fire a rifle and some service in standing guard. In 1937, Yitzhak himself wished to attend

Kadoorie Agricultural School, an elite institution in the Lower Galilee established by the British Mandate, but not a school that taught English. Kadoorie meshed with Yitzhak's own plans. Yitzhak wanted most of all to become an irrigation engineer—that expertise would make Palestine the fertile country of Theodor Herzl's dreams. There was a price. He missed out on a good foundation in English, for example. However, Kadoorie was a great school in other ways and taught such values as honesty excellently. The instructors gave students tests but would not monitor them, trusting they would not copy from their fellow students or their own notes. Yitzhak's personal contacts at the school led him to the Palmach (most of Kadoorie's graduates became members), in itself an incredible education in leadership.

As a youngster, Yitzhak was regarded as special. His brilliance as a student was widely acclaimed. But even as a student and long before the days of the Palmach, he was involved in the military. Looking back today, one can see what a formative influence these early military experiences were for him. Kadoorie was the target of attacks from Arab guerrillas in 1937. Yitzhak trained under another Kadoorie graduate, Yigal Allon, who was later to become head of the Palmach and both a friend and role model for Yitzhak. In 1938, Yigal Allon recruited Yitzhak for an intensive training program at Kibbutz Ginnosar.

When I was first introduced to Yigal Allon several years later, it was like meeting a living god. We all adored him—his looks, his penetrating eyes and open features, the quality of his leadership, and his remarkable skill as a strategic thinker. He and Yitzhak collaborated in executing some of the most difficult military missions imaginable. Allon's subsequent advancement in the army was thwarted, primarily because he did not belong to David Ben-Gurion's Mapai Party, a forerunner of the Labor Party. Moshe Dayan—later chief of staff and then defense minister—was a favorite of Ben-Gurion. Despite his numerous achievements in the War of Independence, Allon was pushed aside to give preference to Dayan.

After the military, Allon went on to study at Oxford, where he deeply impressed leading intellectuals such as Professor Isaiah Berlin. Yigal Allon was enormously friendly with people and radiated accessibility. He seemed to earn trust almost effortlessly and had a natural instinct for praising others in the achievement of any success. On the personal side, Yigal Allon also had a weakness for fancy cars, stylish clothes, and a good meal among friends. Yitzhak and Yigal Allon developed a deep friendship that lasted until Allon's death on February 29, 1980. That foundation of friendship played a very important part in their lifelong relationship when Yigal Allon was appointed foreign minister by Yitzhak during his first term as prime minister.

Yitzhak graduated from Kadoorie in 1940 as a prizewinning student, and the next steps in his development came from real-world experience. The events of the time made it clear that the practical first priority for Jews living in Palestine was self-defense. So that's how Yitzhak focused himself. In later years, Yitzhak matched his intellectual gift with great discipline and vast experience. He had an enormous capacity for knowledge and never forgot a single detail of information. But Yitzhak's abilities reached far beyond just absorbing data. He had an impressive skill in organizing information, cross-referencing it, and discerning what was important.

The Palmach was the first large-scale setting for the development of Yitzhak's practical skills—especially the mastery of leadership and military strategy.

At the Palmach's beginning, the Jewish community in Palestine and the British had mutual interests. Even pre-dating the Palmach's inception, the British captain Orde Charles Wingate had established the SNS—Special Night Squads—in 1937, made up of *both* British soldiers and the Haganah, to combat Arab raids and carry out reconnaissance. When the Palmach was established in May 1941, the British initially favored its existence, seeing it as an additional source of resistance (albeit a Jewish one) against any attempted German or Italian invasion of the region during World War II and a vanguard reconnaissance and sabotage force in Syria ahead of an Allied invasion. The SNS was disbanded in 1939 and the British turned on the Haganah in the same year, arresting members for illegal possession of firearms. The Haganah's fortunes improved in 1940, with the threat of Hitler's blitzkrieg in Europe extending to Palestine. When the tide turned for the Allies in North Africa after Montgomery's decisive victory against Rommel at El Alamein in November 1942, the British turned their back on the Haganah. If the Axis powers were no longer a threat in Palestine, why should the British actively support the Haganah, which would ultimately go back to pressing for a Jewish state?

As early as mid-1942, opinion among Jews who lived in Palestine had been divided as to whether serving in the British army was the best way to support the Zionist cause. Most of the young Jewish men in Palestine opted for joining the British army directly, or later the Jewish Brigade within the British army. But leaders of the Haganah reasoned that this would leave no trained core of defenders to protect Jewish safety and well-being in Palestine. Gradually, the British and the Jews in Palestine developed different agendas. The Palmach became more of a challenge to British authority, especially when doubts arose as to whether Britain would make good on its promise of supporting a Jewish state. As the war resolved itself in North Africa, the Palmach was regarded first as a disagreeable nuisance in the eyes of the British and then as a threat. By 1945, the group was outlawed and participation in it declared illegal.

Modern legend has it that the Palmach existed by improvisation. When Moshe Dayan interviewed Yitzhak to join the Palmach in 1941, he asked Yitzhak if he could do five things: ride a motorcycle, drive a car, fire a machine gun, shoot a rifle, and toss a grenade. To the first three questions, Yitzhak's answer was no. However, he *had* fired a rifle and thrown a grenade. "You'll do," he said. That was good enough for Dayan. The Palmach and improvisation, yes—but not improvisation alone. Yitzhak always believed that improvisation was only an alternative when planning and physical resources were exhausted.

As the Palmach was driven underground, living in a kibbutz became the Palmach's camouflage as well as a major source of financial support. By 1945, I had graduated from secondary school and joined the Palmach myself—much to the trepidation of my parents. The first kibbutz I was stationed at was Tel Yossef, near Ein Harod.

The earliest kibbutzim—at first the word designated only sizable agricultural collectives—began in 1910 at Degania. The kibbutzim were the offshoots of smaller communes and really blossomed under the third *aliyah* of Jewish immigration to Israel, an influx that followed World War I. (The preceding two such waves were 1882 to 1891 and 1905 to 1914.)

Agriculture was the first economic priority if the fledgling state of Israel was ever to come into being, therefore the viability of the kibbutzim was essential. Putting us close to the land, as Yitzhak often recalled later, also familiarized us with the terrain that any resistance movement would need to know in a war of liberation. The tilling of land and the endless hikes of the youth groups not only were healthy, hard work, they also provided priceless tactical knowledge. A major emphasis during our training period was walking through the hills, valleys, and roads of Palestine—getting to know the country just through walking, looking, and remembering.

Yitzhak walked literally every inch of the land, from every vantage point—so well did he know our country! He could tell you how much weight the soil could support, the rockiness of the roads, the concealed positions where snipers might take aim. He also knew the nighttime temperatures in exposed desert areas and how rainfall could affect traction and visibility.

In Ein Harod, where I was assigned, we Palmach lived in tents while members of the kibbutz lived in houses. Sometimes we were invited to siesta in those houses, because during the summer days the tents were intolerably hot. Palmach members in the kibbutz wore no uniforms, no insignia, or any other means of identification. The British could routinely inspect a kibbutz, but they could not distinguish which of us were members of the Palmach.

Women in the kibbutzim strived to prove themselves the equal of men in day-to-day work. Life was tough for us but we didn't mind it much. The corn-husk mattresses prickled like a bed of thorns. The single good dress most of us had was hung on the pole that supported the tent. Reveille sounded at six A.M. While the men ran six kilometers in the morning, we women got off easy with a mere three. We mastered firearms and staged simulated commando attacks. The shower at night, after hours-long training marches, was often as cold as ice. Each of us had one little orange crate on the hard clay floor in which to store our belongings. Privacy was nearly nonexistent, and heaven help you if you didn't get on well with your tent mates.

All Palmach—men and women—worked on the kibbutz for twenty days each month; ten days were then granted us for training. We ate in the kibbutz dining hall and received a limited amount of clothes. For the men, even biweekly haircuts were rationed. Because the same people couldn't be expected to specialize in tending chicken, cattle, or crops routinely, day after day, we had to rotate our duties. I would work in the fields, picking grapefruit and oranges. Sometimes I would be sent to work in one of the child-care centers. One of my early jobs in the kibbutz—and one I held with some regularity—was tending the tea samovar in the dining hall. It became a regular rendezvous point for Yitzhak to appear at on Friday nights and for us to steal some hours together.

The kibbutz was both an excellent disguise and a practical solution to the economic challenge. There was no state to whom we could turn for financing an underground army. Integrated into the kibbutz, the Palmach was truly self-supporting. The kibbutz also helped define and defend Israel's later boundaries—as did, for instance, Manalra, a kibbutz on the Lebanese border, where Yitzhak's sister, Rachel, was a founding member in 1943.

Learning every inch of terrain was drilled into us Palmach as a number-one priority. Reconnaissance squads of six were usually camouflaged by adding one girl to make them look like hiking parties. One day our platoon commander, Oded Messer, put us on a three-day patrol of Arab territory in the Gilboa Mountains overlooking the Valley of Israel. On Gilboa, we spotted some Arabs and they saw us. Things got bad fast. The Arabs had run back to their village and spread the news that some Jews were nosing around Gilboa. A crowd of them came running after us swinging clubs. Our squad leader shouted orders for us to run to Arabuna— a nearby village with a more moderate reputation. We just made it, with me trailing behind the boys, but when we got there, those Arabs demanded that we open up our backpacks, suspecting that we were carrying weapons. We didn't have any, but we weren't going to put up with a search and told them to call the police if they wanted. To our surprise, they didn't back down and called the British police.

The police were furious they had to come so far, and when they opened our packs, they squirted the toothpaste out of the tubes and spilled the jam out of the jars, searching for weapons and ammunition. Then they rousted us to the PMF (Police Mobile Forces) station, where we were interrogated one by one. We were scared stiff! When I was summoned to the commander, I flashed a smile and tried to be as engaging as I could, sweetly saying we really *were* on our way to Tirat Zvi. My identity card saved me.

"I met a man in Netanya by the name of Schlossberg . . . ," my examiner said as he looked at it.

"That's my father!" I responded.

"A good, honest man, your father."

"You see, sir, my father's honest," I said, "and so are I and my friends." He decided to let us go; I never told my father how close I came to going to prison.

Mostly what I remember of the Palmach are the unforgettable human relationships forged among its ranks.

There was Zohara. Zohara—a girl with raven black hair and amber eyes—had been a first-rate student. We graduated together from the same high school and joined the Palmach at the same time. In the Palmach, she exuded energy and stamina through her strong, supple build. Once, in a heart-to-heart conversation, she said to me she envied my relationship with Yitzhak because she herself hadn't yet found her true love. But soon she did. It was a fellow named Shmuel Kaufman. She and Shmuel were to be married as soon as both of them ended their service in the Palmach.

Just before they were packed and ready to leave, Shmuel's commander asked him to supervise one more lesson on the grenade training range. She went back to the tent and waited for Shmuel. It was the eve of Shabbat—his white shirt was ready for him on his bed—and they were to go to dinner in the kibbutz dining hall together. She waited long after darkness had fallen, her anxiety mounting, when she decided to go to the dining hall by herself. There, a somber-faced ma'az (regional security commander) came toward her and said, "Zohara, I have to tell you something. . . ." He then explained how a recruit next to Shmuel had pulled the pin on a grenade but didn't throw it.

She wouldn't believe Shmuel was dead until she saw his body. For the first time in her life, she was confronted with a situation that was beyond her control and she had a terrible time coping with this tragedy. Zohara began to write Shmuel beautiful but heartbreaking daily letters asking how he could have left her alone. Both reflexes were nearly instant in me some fifty years later, when I lost Yitzhak.

Zohara was still young. She went to the States to study. After the United Nations voted to establish a Jewish state in November 1947, she enrolled in an air pilot course in California and upon finishing the course was recruited to return to Israel. At the course, she met and became very involved with Amnon Berman, whom we all knew from our Palmach unit in Ein Harod and who had also been a close friend of Shmuel. (The Berman family still owns one of the biggest bakeries in Israel.) Marriage was again on the horizon. But in the advance on Lod and Ramla, Amnon was shot down in his airplane and perished over Kibbutz Gezer. Six weeks later Zohara herself was killed in a small plane crash over the Valley of the Cross in Jerusalem.

What a dire sequence of tragedies, and yet it was so representative of a time when young people sacrificed their lives day after day. A whole generation was challenged, and so many paid with their lives so that the Jewish state would survive.

Palestine was so small that loss of life was an inescapable and constant reality. When you visited the various Palmach tent camps within the kibbutzim and talked with people, the topic of conversation inevitably turned to who had been hit the night before. When you unfolded the front page of the morning paper, headlines greeted you with the most recent casualties. These were young people we had gone to school with, who had packed groceries in the corner store, had attained the best score on the chemistry exam, or simply lived in the neighborhood.

I remember the songs.

We in the Palmach would usually sing together around the campfire on Friday evenings—gathering apart from others in the kibbutz. It was our way of bonding in a world where we couldn't reveal our identity. Many Friday nights the songs were plaintive and there was often weeping and expressions of deep grief for the constant stream of friends and lovers lost. In 1946, after the "Night of the Bridges," when the Palmach detonated bridges into Palestine from neighboring countries, fourteen Palmachniks were killed. We actually discussed whether singing was appropriate the following Friday night. We decided to sing nonetheless. Life had to go on. It was one way of keeping sanity and strength.

In the Palmach, I saw Yitzhak mature. Every appointment was a source of great joy for him. But no one thought about a career or advancement. He was really more concerned about the hardship, the sleepless nights, the responsibilities than the recognition. He wasn't following in anyone's footsteps. There were no role models. Nothing we could have known or learned would have made a difference. How could you fight a war with such outmoded weapons—and so few of them? How could you resist all these organized forces bearing down on you at once? It's extraordinary that the Palmach and the Haganah did what they did and still concerned themselves with ethics.

The Palmach did their best to avoid British casualties. But the Palmach was not the sole military voice of the Jewish community in Palestine. The right-wing political and paramilitary opposition had a different outlook. They tried to inflict as much damage as possible and weren't concerned about the loss of life. Revisionist organizations such as Etzel and Lech'i (founded by Avraham Stern, who had an admiration for Mussolini and who masterminded murders and bank robberies) were determined to get the British where they could and kill them. They even attempted to engage Mussolini and Nazi elements in their campaign against the British. Two members of Lech'i even went so far as to assassinate Lord Moyne, the British minister-resident, in November 1944.

Nothing divided the British and the Jews of Palestine more than the British position on immigration. By 1945, the British virtually closed the shores of Palestine to Jewish immigrants. (Despite the atrocities of World War II, only 71,000 Jewish immigrants entered British-controlled Palestine.) Furthermore, they made the unconscionable decision not to admit refugees from the Holocaust. The British set up camps in Cyprus to house would-be immigrants to Palestine, who were seized when they attempted to land on our shores and were then deported.

In October 1945, Yitzhak participated in one of his most daring missions in defense of these immigrants' rights. It was a raid on Atlit, a small town on the Mediterranean, south of Haifa. Two hundred immigrants, "illegals" according to the British, were detained in this coastal town's camp. The British planned to deport them. About 250 Palmach troops would be deployed to liberate the refugees and then to transport them to a nearby kibbutz and disperse them through the underground.

Yitzhak and I were sitting on the tiny children's chairs in a kibbutz schoolroom, and I could tell he was very tense. Then he confided the plan to me as he munched on some chocolate. Nahum Sarig would command the operation and Yitzhak was to be his deputy. This was Yitzhak's first big operation. He didn't say it, but I could tell he was worried that he might even get killed. Our meeting that night before he left was gripping, romantic, and dramatic. The warrior came to say farewell to his girlfriend. Yitzhak felt passionately about this operation because these people had survived the Holocaust, only to find themselves interred once again, this time by the British authorities. The rescue was to be launched in darkness. The insiders in the camp had snipped the barbed-wire fencing and snapped the firing pins in the rifles of the Arab auxiliaries so that the weapons would click harmlessly when the Palmach insurgents appeared.

The challenge was first to speed the survivors into getaway trucks. "The immigrants refused to be separated from their bundles," Yitzhak told me later, "the only possessions they had left." Then the group had to be guided over Mount Carmel with the Palmach carrying scores of them, especially the children, over that mountain on their backs. Yitzhak himself carried a small boy who relieved himself on Yitzhak's back during the escape—the child was so afraid. When the British tried to raid the kibbutz that was the relay point, thousands of Jews from Haifa descended on the kibbutz, creating human blockades and absorbing the survivors so that the British could no longer tell who was who. The raid was a resounding success as the British simply threw up their hands in frustration.

I learned the Atlit operation was a triumph the following day as I waited on tables in the dining hall. The kibbutz security officer came up to me and shook my hand, complimenting Yitzhak on the success of the raid. Not only was I relieved that Yitzhak was safe and the raid succeeded, I felt so happy because the officer recognized that Yitzhak and I belonged together.

These years of 1945 and 1946 saw ever-growing tension and bitterness toward the British Mandate authorities over immigration and the urgent, though still distant promise of a Jewish state. As I mentioned, one night—June 16, 1946—the Palmach exploded all the bridges between Palestine and the neighboring countries. (My friend Zohara was wounded and temporarily blinded in that attack, but later recovered full use of her eyes.) Another night the Palmach mined the stations of the PMF (Police Mobile Forces), focusing on destroying the structures. Yitzhak had a role in preparing for this raid. Riding on his motorcycle, disguised as an electrical inspector, Yitzhak entered the PMF station in Jenin to do reconnaissance on the site in preparation for the raid. Having fulfilled his mission and while returning on his motorcycle to report to his commander, an oncoming cement truck made a sharp turn and Yitzhak plowed into the lorry. He was unable to brake in time (from the day he got the bike he drove like a demon), and was hurled from the motorcycle, fracturing his leg badly. He ended up in the hospital and later spent many months in his father's apartment in Tel Aviv, disabled by a broken leg that refused to mend quickly.

As British-Jewish tensions mounted, both Palmach and Haganah members became the target of British raids and imprisonment. Yitzhak was among them. It culminated in what was called "Black Saturday," June 29, 1946; and indeed until November 4, 1995, it was the blackest Saturday I ever knew.

On that day, I was in a training session in a kibbutz called Beit Keshet at the foot of Mount Tabor. Friday night, I attended a wedding. The next morning I sensed something was going to happen. I told the commander I wasn't feeling well and asked him to let me go back to Ein Harod, where we were stationed. After a short ride in a small truck, we were stopped by the British. A CID (British Intelligence Unit) operating in a makeshift office in a cornfield checked our IDs and arrested a fellow who was traveling with us as a member of the Palmach. We were told a curfew was in effect and were sent back to Beit Keshet. One of the men in our truck said he just had to get to his home in Kfar Yehezkel (not that far from Ein Harod) and he was going to walk there, so I decided to walk with him. It was about thirteen miles. From an elevation, we could see British armored vehicles racing from one little village to another, ringing the villages in barbed wire and searching each area.

I stopped in Kfar Yehezkel for a shower and some rest. When I finally reached Ein Harod at about seven in the evening, I came in through one of the back entrances and met a friend named Neria who said, *"Where have you been?!"* Two hundred seventy men, she told me, had been arrested that day in Ein Harod alone. Three thousand were rounded up throughout the country in a massive action against the Palmach and the Haganah. Many of the senior people such as Moshe Sneh, Yigal Allon, and Yitzhak Sadeh, were forewarned through intelligence and avoided arrest.

Because Yitzhak was convalescing at home, the top echelon of the Palmach forgot to alert him! Both he and his father, Nehemiah, were arrested by the British, because they could not believe that Yitzhak, at twenty-four, was a leader of great importance to the Palmach; they arrested his father, too, thinking Nehemiah was the person they were after. I learned a day or two later that they had been arrested. His father hadn't even time to insert his dentures before the British hauled him off. Fortunately, Nehemiah was detained for only two weeks. But Yitzhak was imprisoned for months, until late fall 1946. He did not write me, but I sent him a few letters as well as a sweater I knit for him. During this time, Yitzhak wrote his father a touchingly matter-of-fact letter from the detention camp on the Egyptian border:

Rafah Detention Camp
October 6, 1946

Shalom, Father,

I received your letter and the parcel that you sent. I don't really have any news. Life here has entered the rut of routine. . . . I haven't yet been to Gaza for the X ray, but I hope that it will be arranged soon. Despite the growing coldness here, the fracture is not painful. On the other hand, my joints—particularly my ankle—are still weak and painful, but they tell me that since there is no possibility for intensive care here I will suffer from the ankle all winter. But don't worry. The hardship is not that great, and it doesn't hamper the little walking that I need to do here.

I do ask that you send me another pair of long blue pants, size 40/80, they are the best there is for this place. Also a couple of shirts, but dark and simple (certainly not white or anything like that) and my pen—it's not pleasant to have to keep asking other people. If you can, the rabbi comes here every Friday, and he leaves from the Labor Union Executive Council building. He knows me and will deliver.

I don't completely understand the nature of your illness. *

---

*Today, unfortunately, none of us remembers what Nehemiah's illness was.

I inquired here of the experts, and they say that if you take care, and are properly protected, it should clear up in a short while. In any case, keep me informed about your health. . . .

I got some greetings from you in letters of people who saw you. They say that you are too excited. I did write that you are familiar with the conditions here, and I really don't understand what you have to worry about. My time here is simply the best study time that I have had recently. . . . In short, I will come home a professor.

Shalom,
Yitzhak

I worried because Yitzhak's leg seemed to be mending so slowly, and he was genuinely afraid he might be crippled for life. The British said they wouldn't release him even if he broke *both* his legs. At Ein Harod, I spent the evenings with other women of the kibbutz. After Black Saturday, it became a kibbutz almost entirely without men! Overnight we women were given all kinds of grueling jobs. I, for instance, was assigned to feed fish in the pond, saddled with very heavy pails. Those of us whose husbands or boyfriends had been detained called ourselves "the Merry Wives of Windsor" and cracked jokes and teased one another to gain some relief from the anxiety and waiting. Yitzhak and the fellow prisoners in his detention hut even plotted an escape, but it became clear that he couldn't navigate well enough on his feet to carry it out. The men wouldn't leave him behind, even when he insisted, so they abandoned the plan. Eventually they were released from the detention camp in November 1946, having spent four and a half months of their lives as "prisoners of war."

Yitzhak arrived back home walking with a cane because of his broken leg. Later he walked absolutely normally and it never affected his physical activities—not even parachute jumping. (His broken leg was one-half inch shorter than the other, which caused problems whenever he bought a suit. I can't tell you the number of times the tailor shortened the wrong leg!)

It was mere months between the time that Yitzhak was back on his feet and the beginning of the toughest era in our struggle for independence. The statehood that we had fought for so agonizingly was now about to come upon us quickly. Still, we lacked the support and the resources to stand on our own. We were not a state—though surrounded by Arab states: Egypt, Syria, Jordan, and Lebanon. All of them self-sufficient, with their own military. All of them ready to supply arms and expertise to foes of Israel within our own borders. There was no parity.

On November 29, 1947, in Flushing Meadows, New York, the United Nations backed the establishment of the state of Israel by an unforgettably dramatic vote and defined the demarcation lines that formed Israel's boundaries. The Arab reaction to the as yet unimplemented decree was swift and lethal. Just a day later, on November 30, a dinner guest at my parents' home mentioned he would be taking a taxi from Tel Aviv to Jerusalem and was slain en route by an Arab as he passed through Ramla—a thrown rock hit him in the head. Controlling the road between Tel Aviv and Jerusalem became one of the strategic focal points for the Palmach and Haganah forces.

As Arab attacks increased, more and more people traveled in armor-plated buses or in convoys of cars between such points as Tel Aviv and Jerusalem. Palmach members were generally on the buses or dispersed among the rows of cars. However, the British Mandate authorities would not allow Jews to carry arms despite the obvious attacks on the roads. The practical need for weapons created a strategic role for girls, who hid the arms on the more intimate parts of their bodies. The tactic worked because the British were too gentlemanly to body-search women. The scarce Palmach weapons and ammunition were stored in carefully concealed hiding places.

In April 1948, Yitzhak was named commander of the Palmach's Harel Brigade. (Harel means "Mount of God" in Hebrew.) Yitzhak was not yet a general—that he did not become until 1954, as chief of training in IDF headquarters—but he was in charge of roughly 1,600 people as Harel Brigade commander in 1948. Up until that time, the Palmach was a single force. Later it was further divided into three brigades—Yfftach, Harel, and Negev, with Yitzhak commanding Harel. Yitzhak was given the assignment to complete "Operation Nachshon," the Haganah's biggest deployment to date, dedicated to securing the road between Jerusalem and Tel Aviv by rooting out Arab bases along the way. The operation successfully opened up the road. It was now the job of the Palmach to keep it open, which required ingenuity and contributions from unexpected sorts of people. During this period, for example, Yitzhak shocked me when he remarked one day: "Do you know with whom I have developed a very wonderful working relationship? Hari Yoffe!"

"You and Hari Yoffe?" I remembered Hari Yoffe as a debonair young man in Tel Aviv, always dressed to the nines and sporting a green felt hat with a feather. The Yoffe family owned the Ford dealership in Palestine. No one more epitomized the bourgeois playboy of Tel Aviv society than Hari Yoffe. Later, he joined the British army and became a major in a transportation unit. Who could have imagined the day would come that these two men from such different backgrounds would find a wonderful commonality of purpose? But they did. And the respect was truly mutual. Hari regarded Yitzhak—the product of a sturdy, sober working-class family—as a great guy. Hari was instrumental in organizing convoys for the Palmach.

Hari and people like him were exposed to the same risks as anyone else. One day, later in this campaign, Hari was on his way to meet Yitzhak at Harel headquarters. He and his deputy Bronek Shemer, who was the driver, were involved in a car accident. Hari's thigh was badly fractured as a result. Taken to a hospital in Jerusalem, he lay in agony in his bed. There wasn't any penicillin to be had in this besieged city, and gangrene set in. Still Hari was adamant and refused to let the doctors amputate his leg. For the rest of his life—until his death in 1974—he suffered from horrible pains in his leg.

Yitzhak and Hari's relationship was an early example of how Yitzhak could work with people of all different backgrounds when a common goal was at stake. This knack was what later made him so successful as a diplomat in Washington, having had only the experience of a soldier beforehand. It was also what enabled him to command such respect and admiration from heads of state in such countries as diverse as Japan, Morocco, and Italy during his second term as prime minister. The level and extent of the diversity may have grown enormously over the years, but the roots lie in the early years—in the urgent need to solve practical problems in the War of Independence.

As Yitzhak organized attacks in the area surrounding Jerusalem, it was a miracle he didn't suffer an injury like Hari Yoffe's or worse. Yitzhak was in constant danger, his life threatened as he shuttled between the command post and his units. As intensely as I had worried about him when he was in prison, this situation was now far more threatening. Snipers swarmed everywhere. The fire was constant and casualties occurred almost daily.

After eighteen months of teachers' training school, I reenlisted in November 1947, when the UN announcement was made and it was clear we were going to war. I worked at Palmach headquarters in Tel Aviv—known as "the Council" in pre-independence times—and Yitzhak was commanding the Harel Brigade. My job was to help publish a monthly newspaper with articles about the Palmach, the background of the war, and our neighboring Arab countries. The paper included a monthly list of casualties, and my main responsibility was to visit the homes of the fallen to get photos for publication as well as some personal background on the soldiers. The exposure to family grief was constant, but my most poignant memory was of a young man named Pessach, who was a technical aide in my office. A Holocaust survivor, he was totally without family, arriving as part of the "children of Tehran" who came to Palestine via Iran. When the *Altalena* battle occurred, which I'll describe shortly, he died of a bullet wound to the head, after lying in a coma for seven days. When we buried him, I wondered if it was better to leave behind a family in grief or to leave no one behind.

Palmach combat was bitter, and there were daily casualties, but often we learned about them only many hours or even a day later.

At this time, I was living with my parents, and Palmach headquarters was pretty close to our home. When I arrived at work in the morning, I would anxiously seek reassurance that nothing had happened to Yitzhak the day before . . . but I would, of course, never ask. So I walked through the offices and looked into people's eyes. God forbid that something should have happened to him, I would have seen it in their eyes. I would conduct this "eye parade" every morning, fearing for his survival more than in all of our years together. In those days, no news was most definitely good news.

On that Saturday night, November 4, 1995, in Ichilov Hospital, I once again used the "eye parade," to gauge how much hope existed for Yitzhak after the shooting. . . .

A recollection about the Road to Jerusalem campaign was triggered after Yitzhak's death. The mayor of Jerusalem, Ehud Olmert, conferred an honorary, posthumous citizenship of Jerusalem on Yitzhak late in 1995, and I was asked to deliver a speech on the occasion. I studied Yitzhak's memoirs and identified a pattern to Yitzhak's strategic thinking that I believe is very important. It stretched far beyond this particular operation: Yitzhak always advocated, if at all possible, avoiding head-on battles and tried to find alternative avenues to achieve an objective. So it was for the Road to Jerusalem.

On the road between Tel Aviv and Jerusalem, there is a very important location called Latrun, the site of a monastery and a police station that had become an Arab stronghold. At that time, this position was the main control point on the way to Jerusalem. Without possession of the Latrun position, you couldn't guarantee safe transit to Jerusalem.

Deliberations over the Road to Jerusalem led to Yitzhak's first important encounter with David Ben-Gurion. Ben-Gurion's wispy white hair and grandfatherly manner are what come across in all the pictures in the history books. However, Yitzhak knew a different person than the legend. Yitzhak's relationship with Ben-Gurion was complicated. First, he regarded this Polish-born Jew with enormous respect. From his father's stories and recollections,

Yitzhak also shared Ben-Gurion's enthusiasm for America, al-though unlike Ben-Gurion, he had not yet lived there. But there were also barriers. Like Yigal Allon, Yitzhak did not belong to Ben-Gurion's Mapai party and also, like Allon, Yitzhak lacked the British military training that Ben-Gurion prized in a commander.

It was far from easy to classify or explain Ben-Gurion's person-ality. His curiosity was immense, and he delved into Greek philos-ophy, Buddhism, and a host of other systems of thought. When in New York and London, he was constantly buying large quantities of books and had a compelling need to be regarded as a profound intellectual. Plagued by nagging back problems, Ben-Gurion fol-lowed an exacting exercise regimen, and his wife, Paula, watched over his strict diet and carefully planned hours of rest.

To budge Ben-Gurion from a course of action to which he was committed could be a difficult matter indeed. David Ben-Gurion insisted on opening a roadway to Jerusalem, but he was deter-mined that it be forged through the most *direct* route. The young, inexperienced, and ill-equipped Israeli forces—with miserably weak armaments—tried to attack the Arab stronghold at Latrun three times from two directions and failed. The loss of life was enor-mous. Ben-Gurion grew increasingly frustrated and Yigal Allon, then commander of the Palmach, became the target of his anger. Ben-Gurion once hotly suggested in a conversation with Yitzhak— to Yitzhak's great amazement—that he would like to put a bullet into Yigal Allon's head. Ben-Gurion felt Allon was incapable of re-solving the situation and opening the road.

Yitzhak's view was "Don't go charging head-on into a wall," and he said this directly to Ben-Gurion, which made him furious because he could not accept that the problem wasn't to be solved frontally.

A small group of officers in the Harel Brigade proposed a solu-tion whereby an alternative road would be created. They called it the Burma Road—really a bypass perhaps ten to twelve kilometers long stretching from a point west of Latrun to Bab El-Wad on the east. I'll never forget the day that the first dust-caked, bullet-riddled jeep arrived from Jerusalem and the look of achievement on the face of its occupants—Amos Chorev, who went on to become a general in the Israeli army, and Gavriel Rappoport, who later became a commander in the Palmach. From then on, the Israeli forces worked on that road, developing and fortifying it.

In what has come to be called the Battle over the Roads, a struggle that began in late 1947 and ended in June 1948, Yitzhak's most daring moment may have come in April, when on a single day hundreds of vehicles were convoyed to Jerusalem under his command. I was at the Palmach headquarters when they left Hulda, a kibbutz not far from Latrun, where all the cars assembled. Someone from the departure point had come to tell me that Yitzhak said good-bye—they were pulling out. Three hundred armored vehicles in the convoy, and Yitzhak was in an open jeep at the very end. That convoy was an important success but a costly one. At Shaar Hagai, it came under heavy attack. Twenty-two were killed and more were wounded.

People say that surpassing the obstacle of Latrun was a pivotal episode in Yitzhak's life and career. That's true, but it's easy to misunderstand why. It isn't the conspicuous bravery and courage that distinguish this achievement—although they surely were present. It was the conviction to define and persist in following a practical answer to a chronic problem. Yitzhak always believed he was deeply influenced by the result of those battles on the way to Jerusalem. He was only twenty-six, and hundreds of teenagers met their death under his command. It changed him forever.

The Burma Road was Yitzhak's first acclaimed feat as a strategist. It was certainly an illustration of his persistence and his gift for finding fruitful alternatives. Throughout his career as a soldier and as a statesman, Yitzhak was skilled at identifying paths of least resistance, that exacted the least loss of life. He deemed life a sacred trust and did whatever he could to prevent its loss.

Israel became an independent state on May 14, 1948, and the United States recognized our sovereignty the same day. When David Ben-Gurion made the announcement on the radio, Yitzhak was in a room full of exhausted troops in Ma'ale Hachamisha—a kibbutz near Jerusalem. Somebody yelled out to turn off the noise on the radio. They were so tired they didn't even know what they were hearing. Surprisingly the USSR, whose relations with Israel were to prove so ambivalent and difficult over the years, gave Israel formal recognition on May 16. Also, Israel benefited importantly in the War of Independence from Czech rifles that the Russians permitted Prague to send in April 1948, before our statehood was conferred.

Up until mid-May 1948, we were dealing with uprisings and turmoil inside the country. After the declaration of statehood, we had to contend with Arab forces invading from all directions. The first invasion of the new state of Israel took place on May 15 as the Lebanese, Syrian, Iraqi, and Egyptian armies all launched offensives. The attacks combined artillery, armored invasion, and ground forces. The Israeli situation seemed desperate. We were pitting cannons designed in the late nineteenth century against advancing Syrian tanks! National and personal survival drove everyone's agenda.

I saw very little of Yitzhak during this time. I occasionally wrote him short notes. We never telephoned. There was no way to do so. But we had known each other for three years, and the ties were very strong. Yitzhak was at war. And I waited. He would be gone for weeks, then, all of a sudden, he would appear. During my early days with the Palmach he found me tending the tea samovar. Later, when he would "appear," he looked for me at my parents' home or at Palmach headquarters, where I would be drafting copy for the next edition of our newspaper. All of us were working long hours and living day by day.

The War of Independence was a struggle for survival in which we sought to establish civil peace with those Arabs remaining in the new territorial state of Israel while resisting aggression from hostile Arab neighbors. On the eve of the War of Independence, Yitzhak constantly expressed the frustration that we were so poorly equipped for a major war, with no aircraft, no ships, no tanks. The number of rifles was scarcely more than ten thousand and the cache of mortars was less than eight hundred. Later, in a large operation in the Negev Desert in the southernmost part of Israel, only two tanks were left available—one with operational treads but a cannon that couldn't fire . . . and the other with a functioning cannon whose engine kept conking out. Yitzhak loved to tell this story. With typical Israeli improvisation, the two were chained together to create a single piece of machinery. One moved, the other shot!

The young state of Israel (which had yet to hold its first elections; those would come in January 1949) was the target not only of Arabs: it also found itself besieged by Jews from within. The effort to acquire arms provided camouflage for a bizarre attempt at a coup d'état. On June 22, 1948, a transport ship named the *Altalena,* loaded with French arms and a force of five hundred, sailed for Tel Aviv from France. While it was contended that the arms and recruits were for the Israeli independence effort, there was little doubt this contingent organized by Revisionists was bent on seizing power from the provisional government.

The *Altalena* confrontation occurred in June 1948, during the first truce in the War of Independence. That morning Yitzhak suggested taking me on a tour of Harel battlefield sites. For strategic reasons, the Palmach headquarters was positioned in a hotel on the Tel Aviv beach. Before we left, he stopped at Palmach headquarters to see if there were any dispatches he should know about. The Palmach's commander, Yigal Allon, had been summoned to the Haganah command, so Yitzhak, through sheer coincidence, found himself the senior officer in the facility. He had no real background on the *Altalena* situation. The night before, the *Altalena* had docked directly across from Palmach headquarters. After a heated exchange over megaphones with the ship, Yitzhak saw that a confrontation was brewing and took charge, immediately ordering non-combatants (myself included) off the premises. A powerful gun battle followed. Twelve of the force from the *Altalena* were killed while trying to land on the beach. Ironically, one of those who died in the combat was Avraham Stavsky—one of the suspects in the assassination of Arlosoroff. Later that night, the

Altalena was set afire by the field gun barrages from on shore on David Ben-Gurion's orders. Those on board swam to the beach. The government forces took control of the ship and seized the arms for the provisional government.

The War of Independence went forward haltingly with two cease-fires, the first in June and the second in August. Between the two came "Operation Danny," which liberated Lod and Ramla from Arab control. Through it all, the milestones of daily life went forward, too. We used the second cease-fire to get married. Yitzhak had been staying with me on his infrequent visits, so we figured that it was time to make our relationship official. In his memoirs, Yitzhak described our wedding as a "personal reorganization" in his life.

The ceremony took place in back of Beit Shalom Hall, located on Tel Aviv's North Dizengoff Street on August 23, 1948. My poor mother suffered so in the ghastly heat that day! Our close family and friends attended. Yitzhak and his army colleagues such as Yigal Allon wore their uniforms. I wore a white dress, white sandals, and white cotton stockings. Just for the wedding, I had ordered myself Greek sandals. They had crossover thongs that tied halfway up the calf. My aunt Nettie objected that the rabbi wouldn't officiate if I didn't wear stockings. So, just before the ceremony, I strapped the sandals on over white socks. Silk and nylon stockings were taboo. (When I first wore nylon stockings during the 1950s, Yitzhak thought they were awful.)

Yitzhak was shy about the official religious ceremony under the *chupa*, and actually told his friends it was to take place later than it was scheduled. Yitzhak would have preferred to keep the ceremony private. But things didn't work out quite the way he planned. The rabbi himself showed up late, so all his friends were there, on time. Yitzhak proclaimed, "This is absolutely the last time I'm getting married." He never changed his mind. A hoped-for honeymoon in Naharia was postponed for six months, because Yitzhak was urgently summoned to a meeting concerning the upcoming operation to liberate the south. Sometimes we shared several hours together on Friday evenings or early on Shabbat morning, but time together during the War of Independence was scarce. When the honeymoon in Naharia finally took place, the conditions were gloomy. Yitzhak had a searing toothache and the winter weather was rainy and miserable—but we made the best of it.

Perhaps one of the most joyous celebrations of 1948 took place on a star-filled night among the pressed sand walls of ancient Beersheba in the Negev Desert, right after Israeli forces liberated that city, when Leonard Bernstein was both soloist and conductor in a concert that included Gershwin's *An American in Paris*. I was still a soldier myself and we were all in uniform. The orchestra had made its way to Beersheba to be with our troops and to commemorate our young state's military skill in defending the UN-authorized borders of Israel. That concert illustrates what had become the focal point of our lives. Our nation started from scratch, and that meant a pivotal role for the military. Seventy percent of Israel's GNP was spent on defense, and so it was for many years to come.

The War of Independence coincided with a new torrent of immigration and a period of severe economic austerity. A glimpse of the consumer economy during this time is revealing. We were a community of 600,000, with no real infrastructure. We had citrus fruits in the winter as well as cauliflower, potatoes, and cabbage. Grapes, watermelons, and bananas grew in the summer along with cucumbers and tomatoes. There was neither modern agriculture nor modern refrigeration. The kibbutzim were innovators in irrigation, and combines harvested the grain, but the rest of the farming was largely primitive and relied on backbreaking manual labor. Scarce fresh produce, such as tomatoes, bananas, and eggs, were given first to the children. In those days, hardly a mother in Israel believed her child could grow and survive without a daily egg or a banana! When a child was sick and needed an apple, it was a luxurious request, because apples came from California. Apricots or pears just did not exist for us.

We all learned to hate the odor of those fish fillets that became a chief source of protein. Queues became commonplace and, with them, a wait of hours for a meager pound of tomatoes. When Yitzhak returned from a peace negotiation in Rhodes in 1949 with a coveted tin of butter, my mother was astounded. The whole experience of scarcity left me anguishing over throwing away a single slice of bread, even today.

Liberty brought with it other kinds of traumatic change. Another era—the time of the Palmach—was approaching its end. Between 1941 and 1948, the Palmach grew in sophistication, and Yitzhak had risen with its evolution. In October 1947, he was named the Palmach's deputy operations officer. With statehood in 1948 came the official founding of the Israel Defense Forces. David Ben-Gurion called together a meeting of top Palmach officers in October 1948. He praised them for their enormous contribution and then explained the realities of modern statehood, that no nation could have both an official army and an unofficial fighting force. The announcement that the Palmach was to be formally disbanded was made a month later, with its units being gradually absorbed into the new Israel Defense Force.

In January 1949, Yitzhak was sent on his first diplomatic mission as a member of the Israeli team negotiating an armistice agreement with Egypt on the island of Rhodes. Yigael Yadin, chief of operations of the IDF, led the Israeli delegation, of which Yitzhak was a somewhat reluctant participant, because he felt Israel had halted its offensive against Egyptian forces far too early, denying Israel a decisive victory in the Sinai. When the agreement was hammered out, Yitzhak felt that Israel had made far too many compromises, especially in leaving Egyptian forces in the Gaza Strip, and refused to put his signature to the document—a symbolic gesture that did not invalidate the agreement in any way, but made Yitzhak's position clear.

The trip to Rhodes was Yitzhak's first time abroad . . . and the first time he wore a tie! The tie had been knotted for him by a friend in Israel, and when Yitzhak removed it upon arrival in Rhodes, he was careful to leave the knot intact. A valet came and pressed the tie and returned it unmade on the day the talks were to begin. Yitzhak was in a panic—he even considered missing the first session. Eventually, Yigael Yadin came to his room and retied the knot for Yitzhak, saving the day.

That autumn, Yitzhak, was appointed a full colonel and assumed responsibility for the IDF's battalion commander course training.

Several months after the Palmach's dissolution was announced, its commanders organized a reunion—somewhat a show of frustration. If they'd had their way, the Palmach would have stayed intact as a separate, integrated fighting force, perhaps like the United States Marines, but that wasn't in the cards. I'm sure that Yitzhak regretted seeing the Palmach dissolved, but the arguments that it was now inefficient and somewhat of an anachronism were also, I'm certain, too compelling for Yitzhak to dismiss. The reunion event was to start on Friday night and end with a Saturday parade in Tel Aviv. Seeing this as a test of loyalty, the IDF command issued a directive prohibiting any IDF member from attending. Yitzhak regarded the bond with his Palmach comrades as too deep, and was determined to attend, even if this meant breaching a direct order.

Hardly a coincidence, David Ben-Gurion called Yitzhak for a briefing in his home the very Friday afternoon of the reunion. After the briefing, they discussed the reunion. Yitzhak said to Ben-Gurion that he didn't think it was fair to regard participation in the parade as a breach of loyalty. The discussion went on past sundown and Ben-Gurion surprised Yitzhak by asking him to stay for dinner. His motive was clear if unspoken—he was going to prevent Yitzhak from attending the event. Yitzhak declined the invitation, and hurried home to change out of his uniform and attend the rally. He participated in the reunion and the parade the next day. All IDF officers who took part were called to the chief of staff on Sunday morning to explain themselves, and I was afraid Yitzhak's army career was at an end; but he came away with only a sound reprimand. At a social visit years later, the events surrounding the reunion came up. Ben-Gurion contended he didn't even know Yitzhak had been reprimanded for his participation and claimed it was unjust if he had been! Perhaps a case of selective memory?

∞

On the thirtieth of November, 1995, the veterans of the Palmach came to your grave. They came with their white locks, their creased faces, their stooped backs.

They are here, but you are not. You are there . . . I cannot take my eyes away from the grave. Nor can I forget that from now till eternity you are here, and that we are without you until we too are part of that eternity.

They talk about you, sing to you, caress the memories of what you were, but you are no more.

Graves, cemeteries.

So many times I was by your side when we buried friends and fallen soldiers. But now I am here alone, without you, at the burial site of our leaders and I am trying to comprehend. It has been almost four weeks—yet I understand nothing.

Such a sad memorial service. Hayim Hefer, Haim Guri, Amnon Lipkin-Shahak, and Shimon Peres each spoke from their hearts. Kind, warm, reassuring, and sad. They sang the songs of the Palmach and its anthem. They sang "Hatikvah." I cried all the time, I just could not stop myself.

Here were the friends with whom you took your first steps as a warrior, determined to defend the Jewish community and secure the state. You fought with them during the bloody War of Independence. You lost the best of your friends together. "Only those who lost their best friend could understand us," go the words of a Palmach song. With the Palmach, you understood how youngsters fall in battle. Through the Palmach, you gained the determination to build a powerful military that would protect the youth of the future.

On this clear, cold day in Jerusalem, the massive cypress trees bent under the forceful wind and the strings of my soul tore. One more minute by the grave, covered with carnations and roses, and we moved on. Your struggle is over. Your friends of long ago bid you farewell.

∞

Looking back at the Palmach, the War of Independence, and the creation of the IDF, Yitzhak's father was doubtless proud of his son's rapidly growing number of achievements. My father felt that I would never have to worry about my future because he was certain Yitzhak would excel in anything he chose to do. My mother had high esteem for Yitzhak and his sensitivity to others.

Unfortunately, neither of my parents lived to see Yitzhak in his glorious hours after the victory of 1967.

After we married, I suggested to Yitzhak that we live with my parents in their apartment on the corner of Rothschild Boulevard and Cremier Street. We stayed there until 1952. During that time, in September/October 1949, my mother had developed pancreatic cancer, a cruel and painful disease. She died in December. When my mother passed away, we had no choice but to stay on with my father. Her death changed my role in the family significantly. Losing my mother was a terrible and devastating shock for my father. Until that time, I knew nothing about cooking anything more complicated than fried eggs for breakfast; I lived in a fantasyland with my parents, believing that no unexpected tragedy would ever befall them. I didn't want to believe she really died. And in my naiveté I imagined that my father wouldn't miss my mother so terribly if I could handle all the services she had provided. Of course, that was far from the case.

Adding to the stress, I was pregnant with Dalia at the time. She was born in March 1950 in Tel Aviv. Dalia was an enormous baby, and I had a very hard time and ended up quite sick after the birth. I still smile today when I think back to the journey to the hospital. When I realized that the time was close, I said to Yitzhak, "You know what? I will walk to the hospital." Surprisingly, he let me. I remember setting out and meeting someone on the street who asked how I was. "Just on the way to the hospital," I explained.

"No doubt about it. You're going to have twins," he said with a broad smile. And I continued my slow and careful procession down the sidewalk.

And where was Yitzhak? Inching down the street right behind me in his car, with a look of determination on his face, his eyes checking every footstep I made, as intense as if he were in that open jeep trailing the three-hundred vehicle convoy to Jerusalem.

Birth and death. Maturity and so much change.

In the space of less than two years, Israel's independence had been declared, a war had been fought and won, and six thousand young Israelis—among them our finest—had lost their lives. One percent of our young country's population had perished!

Also in less than two years, I had completed my schooling, ended my service in the armed forces, married, bore a child, and was preparing for a new life as the wife of a rapidly advancing military officer during a brief interlude of peace.

HERO ON
MOUNT SCOPUS

After years of hostility with the British, our next experiences were in England itself. When the War of Independence was over, the nation realized how short its military leadership was on formal training. Encircled by hostile neighbors, it was clear that excellence in defense and security matters would be pivotal to our survival for a long time to come. The most promising commanders were given opportunities to study in places such as England, France, and the United States. Yitzhak had a choice between attending staff college at Camberley in Britain or the American senior officer training program at Fort Leavenworth in Kansas.

Yitzhak decided he would go to Camberley Command and Staff College in England, located in Surrey, thirty miles outside of London. The course was for one year, spanning from 1953 to 1954. Camberley was founded in 1801, and it began training staff officers of the Commonwealth as well as other nations' officers in 1945. Dalia and I accompanied Yitzhak to England. Our first weeks were spent in London. Although the intimidatingly large city and the cold, damp weather kept me close to our lodgings, I can remember Yitzhak taking a map and exploring London inch by inch, as if reconnoitering new territory.

At Camberley, we rented a flat in an old manor house that had been subdivided into a number of living units. Each room had its own fireplace, and the house overlooked a large garden—in which one could observe the cycle of the seasons, a new phenomenon for us after our years in Israel. Most of Yitzhak's evenings were consumed with a considerable amount of homework. We both became familiar with England's customs. Elizabeth II's coronation took place in June 1953, and I remember donning gloves and a hat to partake of the strawberries and cream at the annual garden party reception at Buckingham Palace. The Israeli embassy received a group of invitations and we had been invited. I remember the mound of strawberries Yitzhak piled on his plate (who had seen strawberries!) as the band struck up "God Save the Queen." Having no place to set down his plate, Yitzhak spotted an admiral holding his plate in one hand and smartly saluting with the other. He emulated his pose.

Yitzhak showed remarkable humility in attending the college. Although he had considerably more battlefield experience and was in fact a full colonel, he was assigned the rank of lieutenant colonel so that he wouldn't outrank his peers. Most of his colleagues in the college debated strategy in purely theoretical terms, while Yitzhak had actually "been there." Camberley Command and Staff College gave us the chance to meet people from a vast array of nationalities. We befriended the Indians Colonel B. P. Singh and his wife, Kavita, although Yitzhak never completely enjoyed dinners at their home, for one reason: Indian food was much too spicy for his taste. I loved the food and Kavita very much. Spending considerable time with her, I learned a good deal about India.

One afternoon Kavita had a little tea party. Another Indian woman attended and her four-year-old son fell into the icy garden fish pond. They were both panic-stricken when the caretaker yelled, "Mrs. Singh—the boy has fallen into the pond!" Since I was the only one who had a daughter, my presence of mind was probably the clearest and I ran the fastest. When I pulled him to safety, people celebrated me as a heroine, but I did little more than grab his leg and yank him out.

Also at Camberley was the good-natured Italian Colonel Ruffino who was forever mocking the British for their unadventurous taste in food and clothing. Our daughters were the same age, so our families became friendly. Yitzhak also befriended an Iraqi Colonel Faik—a Kurd—and both agreed that peace was the only long-term solution to the troubles of the Middle East.

A Jordanian officer, Colonel Fawaz Maher—a Circassian—wouldn't even talk with us at the time, and yet that acquaintance was to grow into one of great warmth in years to come. The dashing Jordanian drove a flashy sports car and was friend to King Hussein, who was an eighteen-year-old student attending the Royal Military Academy at the neighboring village of Sandhurst. Colonel Maher and his Turkish wife had a daughter who was about one year old, and they were expecting their second child. News traveled around the staff college that when Mrs. Maher gave birth to a second daughter, the colonel wouldn't even visit her at the hospital, he so deeply wanted a son. He held her responsible.

Seeing her at Woolworth's on High Street, I said to myself, Leah Rabin, here's a woman whose husband wouldn't even visit her at the hospital on the birth of their child. You are now going over to congratulate her no matter what her husband may think. Mrs. Maher was anguished over her situation. I said to her that it was wonderful that she had a second daughter and she would surely have a son later. Then Maher shipped his wife and children off to Jordan. At the school's farewell party for the foreign students, the Iraqi Faik approached Yitzhak and asked permission to talk with me. Yitzhak said that in our society you don't need permission to speak to wives. Faik was carrying a message from Mrs. Maher. Colonel Maher didn't convey it himself, but asked Faik to pass it on to me: "Faik, you talk to the Israelis, so tell Mrs. Rabin that she has regards from my wife."

And so our relationship with Maher ended for about forty years. In the papers, we would occasionally read about Maher's steady advancement. He became vice chief of staff of the Jordanian army and then chief of staff even before Yitzhak did in Israel. He was then appointed ambassador to Taiwan, the Soviet Union, and Turkey. After that news we completely lost track of him.

In October 1994, one week before the final peace agreement with

Jordan was signed in the Arava Desert, on the Israeli-Jordanian border, my husband was sitting with King Hussein in the Hashemiyah Palace in Amman. The two were having a tête-à-tête dinner to finalize the treaty details. Yitzhak told His Majesty the story of Maher at Camberley. He said to the King, "I know that he was your friend. Whatever became of him?"

"He still *is* my friend," said the king with a broad smile.

Half an hour later, Maher was standing in the doorway. Yitzhak rose immediately and they embraced each other. It was a very emotional meeting. Yitzhak told me that evening, I wouldn't recognize Maher: "He's chubby, bald, and aged. Nothing like he looked before."

After the peace agreement with Jordan, when Yitzhak, our children, and I went to Petra, an ancient Nabatean city hewn out of rose red rock, a long receiving line of officers and ministers greeted us. Yitzhak nodded toward one of the gentlemen in the file of dignitaries and quietly said to me, "There is Maher."

He had been quite sick and now walked with a cane. But when he approached us, we hugged as though we had always been close friends. Later, at the reception in the hotel, I excused myself and said I had to look for Mr. Maher—I wanted to find out what had happened since the birth of the second daughter. I found him sitting alone on the terrace and said, "OK, now, shoot."

"After our second child, my wife had two *more* daughters," he explained. "Then I said to my wife, 'My dear, if the fifth time it is another daughter, you will be fired. That very week I'll take another wife.'"

"Mr. Maher," I said, "you are a modern man. You must know that you are in charge of—"

"No, no, no," he interrupted me, "it's not true, it's *her* responsibility." I know for sure that he would never have thrown her out, they loved each other so much. In any event, their fifth and last child was a son.

We then left the hotel to visit the sites, and he and I chatted again in a reception tent that had been set up. "Oh, I remember you," I reminisced with him, "you were *so* handsome—with those blond locks and blue eyes."

"And I was so naughty," he added. He invited us to visit him and his family in Amman.

What a wonderful reunion—two people who had never spoken before. Powerful, high walls had separated us, and they tumbled like cards the moment the climate for change came about. Forty-two years later, I found myself continuing a dialogue that never had words, and we met as the best of friends.

But that is still not the end of the Maher story.

Later, on a visit to Ukraine in 1995, we heard in Kiev that Maher had suffered a stroke. His Majesty King Hussein sent Maher to Jerusalem's Hadassah Hospital—a Jewish hospital—in his own helicopter. We returned on Thursday of that week and I visited the hospital with two girlfriends. We were there also to say hello to the wife of Egypt's ambassador to Israel because she had just undergone surgery.

As I entered Maher's room, I found his wife and the fabled fifth child, Maher's son. The son, Ali, was thirty-five. Mrs. Maher fell into my arms, crying. She had hardly changed. And Maher cried, too. After the stroke, he was very shaky, but so moved that I came to visit. Then they introduced me to Ali, who was every bit as handsome as his father had been.

Ali, this wonderful young Jordanian, is head of the cultural center of Amman. Very interested in modern art, he had attended architecture school in Moscow. He is a very modern and exceedingly gentle young man. Ali joined me as we visited the wife of the Egyptian ambassador, who is Syrian by origin. Her husband, Ambassador Bassiouni, was with her. There we were, together in a hospital room in Jerusalem on the eve of Shabbat: a Syrian, an Egyptian, a Jordanian, and myself with two other Jewish friends. Ten years ago this event would have been unthinkable. Now it was a living example of a new reality—peace in the Middle East.

Sunday morning I went back to the hospital and fetched Ali— bringing him to the Israel Museum in Jerusalem. I left him in the good hands of the director. From there, they escorted him to the new and extraordinary Supreme Court building, which impressed him greatly. Then, every other day, Charlie, my driver, brought a food basket up to the hospital, knowing how terrible the food is even in the best of hospitals. Up he went, with a basket, like Little Red Riding Hood, throughout the Mahers' stay.

Maher wrote me a letter after the assassination. Then Ali came with his young wife to visit me, and what an adorable couple they are. It is amazing how we are on the same wavelength. Between Ali and his wife and me there is no cultural gap whatsoever. There are no barriers. With these walls falling, and with the will to see things through, a totally new entity of coexistence can be created in the Middle East.

And this entire saga began at Camberley.

In 1993, Yitzhak and I revisited Camberley. The exterior of the manor house where we had lodged had been redone and lost much of its charm. The distinguished college commander had retired long ago with several successors following him. The current commander seemed so very young but was probably as old or older than the one we knew. It was we who had aged forty years! The college had made a special effort to bring together alumni and classmates for Yitzhak's visit. Yitzhak delivered a speech to the students of the staff college, and this time they were *all* there—including representatives from Muslim countries—to listen to him.

What a dramatic change from the days of being a "native" student, to use the terminology of the British Empire. I remember Yitzhak telling me about classroom encounters. An instructor would ask him for his views about a hypothetical battle scenario between armored units. After Yitzhak gave his views, the instructor would then ask disdainfully, "Most interesting, I say. And, by the way, just how many divisions does the Israeli armored corps *have,* Lieutenant-Colonel Rabin?" The commander of the school had actually served in Palestine, and they knew Yitzhak had been in the Palmach. I'm sure that they regarded Yitzhak as something of a model terrorist from that upstart little Jewish community that drove the British out of Palestine. His poor English didn't help, and the British have always been enamored with the charisma of Arab leaders, witness T. E. Lawrence ("Lawrence of Arabia") and his remarkable relationship with the leaders of the Arab revolt during the First World War.

The Israeli founding fathers' preference for senior officers with British training and military experience was undeniably a factor in Yitzhak's seeking the Camberley experience, but I don't think he came away from Camberley with much British "polish"—though he learned quite a bit about large army formations and methods of strategic planning and thinking. Also our experience of the cultural wealth of London was considerable.

After Camberley, Yitzhak had applied for a two-year course at the London School of Economics and was accepted. His intention was not so much to study economics per se as it was to increase his experience abroad and to prepare himself for a career in public service should he ever leave the military. But Moshe Dayan, who had become chief of staff, tempted Yitzhak to return to Israel to head up training for the IDF, with a commitment that he would be promoted to general.

The first task in the training assignment was to create a staff college for the Israeli army. This is where the Camberley experience bore significant fruit. The most important things that Yitzhak may have learned at Camberley were an appreciation for the finer analytical side of strategy, the British method of deploying tanks on a battlefield, and most of all, a system for training officers. This was totally new for Israel. Our officers had learned on the battlefield. When Yitzhak returned to Israel, he and his team had discussions evening after evening, late into the night, on how the curriculum and structure of the college would be designed.

When we came back to Israel, we returned to a home in Zahala, a northeastern suburb of Tel Aviv that we had moved to shortly before the stint at Camberley. Our house at Zahala was a modest single-level home with three bedrooms, but it was all ours. For two decades, while Yitzhak was in the army, we lived almost continuously in Zahala. During a business trip to the United States, my father had arranged to ship back a number of appliances for our home. So we had more than the normal share of conveniences: a washing machine and kitchen appliances such as a mixer, a blender, and a toaster. But even with these, our home had its shortcomings. Early each morning in winter I had to light kerosene stoves in each of the rooms at dawn so that they would be warm enough for the family when they got up. The insulation in the structure was primitive; we roasted in summer and froze in winter.

Zahala was in the sticks, and our home was on the fringe of the housing development. As you might expect, that meant field mice—lots of them. Even after years of "roughing it" in the kibbutz, *I still abhor mice!* One day, I saw a mouse scampering across the floor of the house, and it threw me into a total panic. My first instinct was to call Yitzhak at headquarters; finally I reached him. "Yitzhak, please come home now—right now," I implored, and my heart was really racing. "We have . . . *mice!*" He was sympathetic but explained that he was on his way to the base at Sarafand, and there was no way he could help me out. Then I called my father at his trading company, Haspaka, whose inventory of agricultural products included pesticides. "Papa," I panted into the phone, "bring your poisons and save me! We have a mouse!" He did . . . laying out saucers of poisoned beer and nailing the mouse in no time. My command post, I understood, was the home, and I would have to deal with any problems that cropped up in it, by any means necessary.

While his career continued to advance, Yitzhak felt the promotions he got in the military were fully deserved and usually long overdue—delayed because he was not a member of Ben-Gurion's Mapai faction. When Yitzhak had been promoted to general in 1954, I sat next to Moshe Dayan at the celebration party. Dayan said to me, "Your husband is very lucky to have a Mapai-nik like me as chief of staff. What other chief of staff would have dared to give Yitzhak the rank of general and to tell other Mapai candidates to sit and wait." Dayan thought that he had done something very courageous in making Yitzhak a general, and by the norms of those days he had indeed.

Yitzhak would always downplay the risks he was exposed to. In 1955 he and Dayan had decided all generals should take a parachute jumping course after they learned that every American officer mastered either parachute jumping or diving as proof of both fitness and courage. He kept the parachute training a secret from me because I was pregnant with Yuval at the time, and he didn't want me worrying. Yitzhak graduated unscathed, but Dayan injured his hand and couldn't complete the course.

Yitzhak became commander of Israel's northern forces in 1956—our son, Yuval, was one year old—and was in that post during the Sinai campaign of that year, after Egypt had seized the Suez Canal. So the war was far away from us. From 1956 to 1958, the children and I briefly moved away from Zahala to Haifa to be closer to Yitzhak.

In 1956, Ben-Gurion was both prime minister and minister of defense. Dayan was chief of staff. The year before, Egypt's president Nasser sponsored Palestinian *fedayeen* guerrilla attacks in southern Israel that killed about four hundred Israelis. In fall 1956, the harassment continued as he closed the Straits of Tiran and the Suez Canal to Israel. In conjunction with French and British airpower, Israel mounted the Sinai campaign between October 29 and November 5. Israel seized the Sinai, and the straits were reopened, but the UN compelled Israel to withdraw from the Sinai and return it to Egypt, which it did by the spring of 1957.

When the campaign started, Yitzhak spent the entire week at his command headquarters. No one knew how hostilities would develop and if other Arab nations would become involved. Israel's military resources were dedicated to the south, so surveillance of the situation in the north was very important. My sister Aviva's husband, Avraham Yoffe, commanded the Ninth Brigade, which moved south to the Straits of Tiran. During the war, Aviva and their children stayed with us. We blacked out the windows and prepared for the possibility of all-out war. Aviva was convinced during most of the campaign that Avraham had been killed, which happily proved untrue.

Israel had pulled out of the Sinai when the War of Independence was over. Yitzhak believed that was a mistake, and Nasser's decision to close the straits demonstrated how right Yitzhak was. At this moment in Israel's history, the south was really the action point for senior officers seeking advancement, because Israel's principal source of friction was with Egypt. Yitzhak was not a part of the Mapai clique that tended to receive the choice assignments, but he took the limitation that was imposed on him in stride. Haim Laskov, who directed the attack on Rafah, the central battle of the campaign, went on to become chief of staff when Dayan left the military in 1958.

More than he might have expected, Yitzhak absorbed important background in the Northern Command that benefited his awareness later as both minister of defense and prime minister, when the focus of Israeli military attention shifted from the south to the north and the east, where the borders increasingly became a place of conflict between Israeli forces and Arab guerrillas. During his assignment in the north, Yitzhak developed a great grasp of border engagements (the flow of incidents was continuous), the management of demilitarized zones, and the strategic significance of the Golan Heights. Yitzhak was learning military command decision making detail after detail, from deploying armored tractors to plow the plains beneath the Golan Heights to preventing the Syrian army from harming our fishing boats in the Sea of Galilee.

After General Laskov's appointment as chief of staff, Yitzhak wanted to go abroad again and study public administration at Harvard. His goal was not so much to develop a particular expertise as it was to broaden his understanding of international affairs should he ever leave the army. He was accepted at Harvard, but a strange twist of fate intervened. In April 1959, a simulated mobilization of the Israeli armed forces took place. It was not an actual alert but many people believed it to be one when the test messages were broadcast on Israeli radio in a number of languages, including Hebrew, French, Spanish, and English—because of the number of immigrants in the IDF. People were sent scrambling in response to this false alarm. The incident became known as the "Night of the Geese." Ben-Gurion, in his role as minister of defense, removed the chief of operations and the head of military intelligence. Yitzhak became the new chief of operations, and that was the end of his plans to study at Harvard.

As chief of operations, Yitzhak's skills in two particular areas were called upon: first, his grasp of the relationship between the military and intelligence sectors and, second, his expertise in armaments. The Soviet Union played an ever-growing role in the Middle East, providing both technology and advisers. The Soviets were then flooding the Middle East with military might at a pace with which Israel and its traditional European allies—especially the French—could not possibly keep up. Yitzhak was impressed with the military technology in the United States, especially in "early-warning" radar installations. He used one situation in early 1960, when Israel was late in responding to a potential Egyptian attack, as proof that Israel needed stronger early-warning systems, such as those manufactured by the United States. Yitzhak also was a very strong believer that weapons selection should be handled by the military people who used them, and not by civilian staff—which sometimes put him at odds with the deputy defense minister, Shimon Peres. Peres had been a member of the Mapai Party. Ben-Gurion appointed him first director-general of the Defense Ministry and later as deputy minister of defense. Peres had been sent on defense missions abroad, especially to procure arms. Both Yitzhak and Peres were influential in Israeli defense policy, but each saw the issues from a different vantage point: Peres from the staff standpoint and Yitzhak as a battlefield commander.

After we returned to Zahala in 1958, I taught English in the Neve Magen School. I didn't have a car, so I rode to work with another teacher. Getting back home, I had the choice between taking two buses or walking through open fields and fragrant orange groves—a nice walk but forty minutes long. This went on for two years, but the experience of teaching isn't a notable memory of mine. The pay was meager, the commute was long, and the opportunity to have a serious impact on the students was not available. It was a breather, a chance to spend time out of the house, and I wanted to put to work the skills I had acquired, but the trade-offs were many. Yitzhak never saw much sense in the idea. I came to agree with him and gave it up. I never truly had a career of my own, but I feel no regret about that. My responsibility was raising our children. I have called it our "division of labor." While the children were very young, Yitzhak would help me out, feeding them when I asked, though I can tell you he never changed a diaper. He cut the grass with a manual lawn mower and enjoyed gardening.

The children were blossoming. Dalia was so perceptive and intelligent. She excelled in her academic studies, and my father—who had built his own home nearby—had a special fondness for her. Yuval was totally devoted to his father. On Fridays, fathers would start to come home from work by two P.M., maybe four. When it was five or six or seven and Yitzhak hadn't returned, Yuval would go outside and wait for his father. I remember him coming back into the house and saying, "All the fathers have returned but my father isn't here yet."

In raising children, Yitzhak and I didn't discuss our convictions much. Formal beliefs mattered little to our method. That approach was based on our own values, which were assimilated more by example and through our way of life. Our children experienced what we believed in and understood why we believed in it on a very concrete level. They saw their father serving his country, and they grew up inspired by his dedication. They never saw him looking for material rewards for what he was doing. Family budgets were strapped at certain times, but there was never a wish amongst us that he make more money in a career out of the army or government. Dalia and Yuval understood Yitzhak was a public servant. That is what he loved and what he desired to do most.

Both knew—it never had to be discussed—that being their father's children would never endow them with privilege. They always understood that they should never abuse their father's position, take advantage of it, or feel entitled to special favors. Yitzhak was a very powerful living example of real-world humility and respect.

We always ate breakfast together, assembling over a properly set table. Lunches and dinners with Yitzhak were rare, except for the eve of Shabbat, which was strictly observed. My father-in-law shared that meal with us, too. On Shabbat for lunch we were either at home or often on a picnic, but always together. There was no other way to stay in touch with each other's lives. As a rule, Yitzhak drove the children to school in his military-issued car. It was a near-daily routine. The trip wasn't long but it gave them a chance to be together for a while longer. I insisted upon the practice of family breakfast, and it continued after the children moved out and it was just the two of us. Even when Yitzhak had to get up at six in the morning, I was always there with him at the breakfast table.

Dalia and Yuval, when they were youngsters, would squabble in the car as kids do. That would make Yitzhak angry. "Would you stop it?!" he would say.* Sometimes, you could tell that Yitzhak had an imaginary Do Not Disturb sign hanging above his head. Still, he was there for the children when they were growing up, especially on weekends, when we would join friends and picnic on the beach or on the hillsides of Jerusalem. Yitzhak never made the children feel that they were expected to live up to a certain standard. He was happy when they succeeded, not so happy when they occasionally missed the mark, but completely encouraging of their record of achievements. He gave them the feeling he was there for them, right or wrong. He always had confidence in them and wasn't reluctant to express it.

The children grew up in military housing. They matured in an environment that had an absolute and clear sense of direction: ser-

---

*The car also was the battleground for Yitzhak and me for those spats that darken even the happiest marriages. In later years, on weekends, I would often drive our private car. A security agent would sit in the passenger seat. Yitzhak would sit in the back, as a security car with two other agents trailed behind. After a light turned green, if I hesitated for a fraction of a second on the pickup, a great grumble would erupt from the backseat: "Why don't you go?!" I would clutch the steering wheel in a rage and answer back, "Why can't you shut up and relax?" Without a doubt he was the worst backseat driver I have ever known.

vice to the people of Israel, the founding of the state of Israel, the building and development of the Israeli army—all the urgent needs that had to be satisfied.

The *ma'abarot* were temporary housing facilities for the influx of immigrants. New immigrants lived in very primitive conditions, and it could take a couple of years before they were transferred to their own small apartments or homes, often state provided. Our children grew up within sight of a *ma'abara*. They witnessed a standard of living very different from their own. I remember our daughter, Dalia, going to this area in the afternoon and playing with the children and instructing them in Hebrew. Even as young children, Dalia and Yuval realized that there were commitments to be honored and the need to lend a hand to others.

∞ My father suffered his first heart attack, a severe one, in 1941, when he was just forty-seven. His recovery was slow and only partial. In fact, he was debilitated by heart problems for the rest of his life, though he wouldn't change his lifestyle and routine—working, traveling, and smoking the way he always had. His philosophy was, "I want to enjoy the years left for me to live, and if my pleasure in smoking advances the end—so what!" Eighteen years later, in 1959, he could no longer elude destiny. With his second wife, Hilda, he set off for Europe as he did each summer. He had booked return passage from Zürich on El Al on September 1, with Hilda remaining in Europe for several more days.

Before driving to Lod Airport from Zahala, I phoned to check that the plane would arrive on schedule, but learned that it had already landed. "Please tell a passenger named Schlossberg that his family is on the way to the airport," I said to the El Al representative. "He has a heart condition and I'm afraid that he'll be anxious if he's not met." There was a silence on the line. Then the El Al operator nervously urged us to come quickly.

Just ten minutes after the plane was airborne from Zürich, my father grew short of breath and asked the cabin attendant for an oxygen mask. His waxen face alarmed her, but he tried to calm the young woman down. "Don't panic. People don't die that easily," he said. A moment later he was gone forever. It was a horrible shock to find out he had arrived dead. Losing my father marked the end of what used to be home. No more parents. No more home.

∞ Between 1949 and 1964, Yitzhak's career seemed to be a series of small steps up the ladder in the military chain of command. Every step demanded total dedication and energy, and Yitzhak was ever ready to invest it. He, at the same time, fostered strong ties with representatives of other armies, traveling extensively to Italy and France and maintaining a constant exchange of information. He also journeyed to East Africa and the Congo and took a long trip to the Far East, visiting with military authorities and heads of state from Burma, South Korea, Thailand, Japan, and Singapore.

Major General Zvi Tsur was appointed chief of staff in 1960, and Yitzhak felt he had been passed over again. While they were contemporaries in age, Yitzhak was senior in command experience. But once again, Yitzhak recognized Tsur's advantage as a member of Mapai. Ben-Gurion told Yitzhak he knew he might feel slighted over the Tsur appointment and reminded Yitzhak he *had* violated an order (referring to the attendance of the 1949 Palmach reunion). No doubt in Yitzhak's mind, Ben-Gurion was using the incident as a justification for blocking his career at that moment. Yitzhak wasn't pleased, but what could he do about it? Nonetheless, Ben-Gurion promised Yitzhak that he would be the next person to hold that post—which meant in about three to four years—and saw that Yitzhak was named deputy chief of staff on January 24, 1961.

David Ben-Gurion's pledge became reality, even though Ben-Gurion was no longer prime minister. Yitzhak received his appointment to chief of staff on January 1, 1964, when Levi Eshkol was prime minister. Eshkol was a very appropriate choice to succeed Ben-Gurion. He was an excellent administrator and planner and was extraordinarily successful in assembling the master design for immigration to Israel. Eshkol also chose to retain the defense portfolio as Ben-Gurion had done, but his interest was more in the budgetary and administrative dimensions of defense, rather than in strategy and operations. In this respect, Yitzhak was his perfect counterpart.

Steadily, the Israeli armed forces showed Yitzhak's imprint as deputy chief of staff, and it became only stronger with his promotion. Yitzhak insisted that training be conducted against Russian weapons and tanks and that maneuvers anticipate Russian military doctrine because Israel's adversary in a future war would be supplied with Eastern Bloc weapons and trained by Eastern "military advisers." He also prepared Israel for the eventuality of a multi-front war. Until that time, Israel "lacked strategic depth," as he put it. A major emphasis for Yitzhak was strengthening Israeli airpower so that it could rapidly overcome an adversary's air force: If a foe's air force could be quickly demolished, then it lost the umbrella of protection for its ground forces. The next priority for Yitzhak was to develop a cadre of fast-moving tanks and armored units that could take advantage of the enemy's lack of air cover and advance positions quickly. In 1956, Israel had the power of British and French air support. Now the country needed the capability to provide its own air shield.

Administratively, Yitzhak catapulted the Israeli army ahead in training, organizational planning, logistics, and computerization. He revolutionized the way decisions were made by officers to ensure they conformed to a clearly defined national defense doctrine. Yitzhak was ever pragmatic. When he sent Ya'acov Heifetz, then director of the defense budget, to the United States to study computer systems, he told him "Go to the United States to study the principles, and to Canada to study the implementation." The United States was on the cutting edge of the technology, but the scale of operations and financial wherewithal of Israel was much closer to that of the States' northern neighbor. Ya'acov came back with the recommendation *not* to computerize the military payroll system— as nearly every Third World nation was then trying to do as an "emblem of advanced civilization"—since most of the rank-and-file military were conscripts serving in border territories and a complicated pay system would just interfere with their need for ready cash.

In another demonstration of pragmatism, when several hundred highest-quality Russian tanks were seized in combat, Yitzhak created a unit that was specifically trained to operate this newfound tank arsenal. He also centralized services such as logistics and ordinance so that they would come under the direct control and supervision of the IDF headquarters, rather than existing as the separate fiefdoms they had been. Through these measures, enhanced and expanded weaponry (especially airpower) and relentlessly detailed operating disciplines, Israel had developed a military force that was every bit the "coiled spring" Yitzhak so often evoked, well equipped with U.S., French, and British weapons.

∞ In the spring of 1967, the Egyptian-Israeli border was held stable by a peacekeeping force from the United Nations. The border had been quiet for a decade. In the north, Syria was backing guerrilla assaults on Israel with air cover. On a single day in April, Israel shot down six Syrian jets in retaliation. The United Arab Republic, which included Egypt, Syria, and Yemen, had been dissolved in 1961, but Syria and Egypt still had a military alliance. Through a misinterpretation of an Israeli press briefing, Egypt became convinced that Israel was about to attack Syria and used its conclusions to provoke anti-Israeli sentiments among other Arab states, which began to put troops at Egypt's disposal.

On May 15, 1967, as Israel celebrated its nineteenth Independence Day, Egyptian president Abdel Gamal Nasser declared a state of emergency and began a deployment of five hundred Egyptian tanks in the Sinai. This was not the only warning that war might be imminent. On television (we could pick up Egyptian television on a neighbor's set), Nasser was screaming day after day, "Death to the Jews! We'll throw them into the sea!"

That we were on the eve of a major confrontation became more apparent as the days wore on. Eight days later, at three forty-five on the morning of May 23, Nasser closed the Strait of Tiran, which isolated Eilat, Israel's port on the Red Sea. It was as good as a declaration of war. I remember Yitzhak literally running out the door as he put his trousers on at four A.M., after the telephone call that informed him of Nasser's blockade.

Yitzhak had such confidence in the IDF that he was prepared to wage all-out war against the neighboring Arab states. Yitzhak believed Israel could win the war but expected heavy casualties and advocated a preemptive attack or an anticipatory counteroffensive because Israel could not absorb the costs of a drawn-out war. Although Levi Eshkol had succeeded David Ben-Gurion as prime minister, Ben-Gurion was nevertheless very vocal in his skepticism about this idea and he remained an important and respected authority in people's minds—Yitzhak's included. Ben-Gurion was regarded as the political grandfather of the state of Israel, but he was not current in his knowledge of the Israeli military or the strategic situation in the Middle East, therefore he persisted in advocating the need for British and French air cover.

In a meeting on May 22, he challenged Yitzhak with the words, "How dare you pit the IDF alone against the entire Arab world?" In 1956, Ben-Gurion pointed out, the Israeli campaign had been mounted only after receiving British and French support. Yitzhak responded that unless Israel was willing to go to war to defend its right to navigate on its own, the "deterrent capacity of the IDF will be proven worthless."

Ben-Gurion wasn't alone in voicing his disapproval. Interior Minister Moshe Haim Shapira also attacked Yitzhak for his boldness the following day, May 23, suggesting that the Eshkol-Rabin combination was trying to be more "daring" than the duo of Ben-Gurion and Dayan. Shapira was convinced that "Israel's existence will be endangered if we go to war." It was not as though Shapira were seconding Ben-Gurion's views in support of the party line. Shapira was a member of the National Religious Party, so these were two independent viewpoints coming to the same ominous conclusion.

In his memoirs, Yitzhak admits that never in his life had he "come so close to feeling so depressed." By May 23, 1967, Yitzhak was fatigued to the point of exhaustion and smoking like hell. Ben-

Gurion's and Shapira's comments were powerful assaults on his confidence and convictions. "Suppose he's right?" he thought aloud, referring specifically to Ben-Gurion's skepticism, pacing up and down the hallway of our home. That morning he had left the house at four A.M. and returned at six P.M. He had hoped for backing and a vote of confidence from Ben-Gurion. Instead, Ben-Gurion left him wallowing in self-doubt. It suggested shortcomings both in the chief of staff and Eshkol as defense minister. Another factor that I'm sure weighed on Yitzhak was the considerable loss of life he anticipated in such a war. While he thought that the conflict was inevitable, he also was projecting thousands of casualties. Knowing his sensitivity for human life, I am sure he acutely felt that crushing burden. In retrospect, I can only speculate on these factors, because he didn't articulate them all. He was obviously exhausted and deeply troubled, but troubled in the sense of an individual who had to confront a mammoth and complex problem on his own and very quickly.

After his obvious display of stress and exhaustion, Yitzhak announced he was headed to Beersheba, the headquarters of the Southern Command. Helicopters weren't commonplace then, and his trip would have meant a two-hour drive. At that point, I intervened. I looked at him and said, "You're not going to the Southern Command. You're not going anywhere. Instead, you're going to sleep. You're exhausted and upset. Relax now. You need a break."

I wanted his physician, Dr. Gilon, to come over and examine him and maybe prescribe something that would enable him to sleep. Before Yitzhak agreed to the doctor's visit, he insisted on calling Ezer Weizman (now the president of Israel), who was then his deputy, asking him to come over to the house. I think that Yitzhak wanted a sounding board who was fully familiar with the military situation. The two spoke privately. Although he did not tell Weizman about the confrontations with Ben-Gurion and Shapira, Yitzhak did ask Weizman if he, Yitzhak, was responsible for the predicament that Israel now faced and if Weizman felt that Yitzhak should resign. Weizman, Yitzhak reported afterward, was highly encouraging and counseled him not to resign.

Yitzhak told Weizman that these were fragile times but that he was going to sleep anyway. Yitzhak's sense of responsibility obligated him to tell someone that he might be sleeping for a good many hours in such a volatile time. He had to create a contact point in the chain of command. Weizman later spread the news that Yitzhak was having a nervous breakdown and that he'd offered Weizman "the keys to the car"—in other words, he invited him to take command. I seriously doubt that he did. Besides, Yitzhak knew that he couldn't make such a unilateral decision. A chief of staff does not appoint his own successor. What would have motivated Weizman to have given a different version of events? It's no secret that when Yitzhak left the post of chief of staff, he did not recommend Weizman to replace him Weizman's bitterness about Yitzhak seems to stem from this time.

Dr. Gilon arrived, diagnosed "a severe case of exhaustion," and gave Yitzhak an injection to help him sleep. Yitzhak slept that night and rested half of the next day. He got up, put on his uniform, and went back to work as usual on the twenty-fifth. I've never seen a nervous breakdown. I don't know what one looks like, but I *do* know that nobody recovers from a nervous breakdown in a day and a half. As his wife, I knew letting him go on as he had meant something of a serious risk. On the other hand, I was absolutely convinced that a good, solid sleep would restore both his stamina and his perspective. Why wasn't anything more drastic done? Because nothing more drastic was needed. What was at stake was not a mental collapse, but a simple case of exhaustion and probably nicotine poisoning coupled with unbelievable stress. The clearest proof of all is that Yitzhak went on to achieve something in the next several days that was never equaled before or since in the history of the state.

On May 25 King Hussein authorized Iraqi troops to move into Jordan and to be deployed along the Israeli frontier. On May 30 Hussein signed a mutual defense pact with Egypt. Iraq joined the pact on June 3. By the end of May Arab forces numbered 547,000 soldiers. Yitzhak, seeing what stood on the horizon, made a series of morale-boosting visits to Israeli troops during the last days of May.

Moshe Dayan (who coincidentally was Ezer Weizman's brother-in-law) was brought into an expanded cabinet as defense minister on June 3 because doubt existed that Prime Minister Levi Eshkol could command sufficient popular trust in a major conflict.

Eshkol had stammered—seemingly unnerved—in a radio speech on May 29, giving the general impression he was rattled by the mounting tension. On June 1 Levi Eshkol was forced to form a National Unity government. Dayan's joining the cabinet had the effect of enhancing the people's morale. Dayan had formerly been chief of staff and was seen as a valiant hero of the War of Independence and a daring general in the 1956 campaign. With his eye patch and rugged face, he was a symbol of strength and personal courage. The public—especially women—cheered Dayan's appointment. Though Yitzhak had some reservations about it, he knew having Dayan as defense minister would result in an enormous boost to the nation's morale and improve their receptiveness to the inevitable conflict they faced.

Eshkol conceded diplomacy had failed, and both Yitzhak and Dayan pressed their case for immediate military action. Yitzhak advocated a "mailed fist" approach—thrusting with rapid and decisive movements into every territory. In the early hours of June 4, the cabinet voted for war. As we went to bed on the night of the fourth, Yitzhak revealed nothing more than a gesture with his eyes, that made it clear that war was imminent.

I can remember the wailing of the sirens at eight o'clock on the morning of Monday, June 5, 1967. The children had gone to school as on any other morning—just as all the other children did. That morning, Yitzhak was on the tarmac, giving our pilots encouragement before they soared off for their mission in Egypt. The Israeli air force attack began at 7:10 A.M. They struck simultaneously at Egypt's key air bases across the vast country. In 170 minutes, Israel's pilots had demolished Egypt's best-equipped air bases, bombed runways, and destroyed 300 out of 340 of its combat planes. Twenty more Egyptian planes were shot down in dogfights that morning. Three hours after he left the house that day, he telephoned me to report, "So far so good. The Egyptian air force is totally destroyed." I bought vegetables from Naji the greengrocer and cooked lunch for Yuval and Dalia just as I would have on any other day. I have termed moments like these my unalterable commitment to the momentum of everyday life.

With the Egyptian air force annihilated, Yitzhak deployed tanks into the Sinai. Then he launched a successful defense in the north against the Syrian air and tank initiative and three offensives against Gaza and the Sinai at eight-fifteen. The air force was then unleashed against Jordan, Syria, and Iraq with similar success. Yitzhak knew the power of intelligence, and Israel had gathered much of it from agents in Arab countries on troop movements and strengths, which benefited the overall strategy of the war.

Even schoolchildren went into action in the weeks before the war began. Scout troops in Zahala had dug foxholes. Dalia would change into khakis after school and put her foot to the shovel to help dig the trenches that crisscrossed the military living quarters in Zahala. We used our foxhole on the very first evening of the war, when shells whizzed overhead. Yuval wanted to do the foxhole one better. He kept saying, "I want to be where my father is." That was in the headquarters war room in Tel Aviv—underground, reinforced, and known as "the Pit"—the most secure place in all Israel. Shelling that evening landed in areas near our home and even reached Masaryk Square in Tel Aviv. When we were able to go back inside the house, I phoned Yitzhak to tell him his family had just been under a shelling attack. He said, "Yes, I know. By tomorrow morning it will be okay." And it was.

Yitzhak spent the first days of the war in the Pit. For information on the war's progress we relied on the radio. Chaim Herzog, later Israel's president, was an excellent radio commentator, reporting on the actions and advances of the IDF and analyzing them. He was an important source of information for so many Israelis—ourselves included.

Yitzhak launched an attack to take control of the heights

around Jerusalem, which succeeded by the morning of June 6. By Wednesday, June 7, day three of the war, the Egyptian forces were totally defeated, and Jerusalem had been taken and reunited as Israeli paratroopers reached the Western Wall, the only remaining wall of Solomon's Temple. All over the world, you could see the pictures of Moshe Dayan, Uzi Narkiss, and Yitzhak passing through the Lion's Gate into the Old City. On the radio, the minute after this monumental event, you could hear a paratrooper yell, "The Temple Mount is in our hands!" The soldiers were literally crying, weeping with joy and disbelief over the airwaves. Yitzhak later described his visit to the Western Wall as the "peak of my life" and the "fulfillment of a dream." The same day Sharmel Sheikh and the Strait of Tiran were ours. On Thursday, the Suez Canal was in our hands.

When the war began, King Hussein had been advised through diplomatic channels not to intervene, but he entered the war based on false information from Egypt of stunning Egyptian victories on day one. He thought the Arabs had a chance to unify Jerusalem as a Muslim city and concentrated on trying to take Jerusalem and on shelling Tel Aviv. Those shells that whistled over our foxhole were Jordanian shells. But Jordan lost control of half of Jerusalem, which had been in their hands since 1948, and the West Bank (the capture of which was complete by June 7). The Jordanian army suffered 15,000 fatalities and saw its entire air force turned into wreckage. The victories of June 6 and 7 surprised even Yitzhak. Seven Egyptian divisions numbering 100,000 men had been crushed in four days. A cease-fire with Egypt was announced the night of the seventh and Hussein accepted a cease-fire soon after.

I was visiting wounded soldiers when the historic breakthrough in Jerusalem occurred. Yitzhak's driver came to the hospital with a note saying, "At six o'clock there is going to be a press conference with Yitzhak and Dayan. Come by all means." During the two days of the Battle for Jerusalem, a neighbor came over a few times asking, "Are we really advancing to the Wall?" I assured her it was true. As I was on the way to the press conference, I saw people gathered on the street corners, talking in disbelief. To quote a Jewish prayer, *hayinu kecholmin,* "we were as though dreaming." I went to the press conference. It was to be the first of only two times that I saw him during the war—I hadn't seen him since Monday. My pride was enormous. His eyes were bloodshot at the press conference from lack of sleep, but he was clearly confident and in command. We spoke only a few words, and I did not see him until the next evening.

Later I saw newsreel footage of an event that took place within two days of the Wall's capture. A group of convalescing soldiers in bathrobes and pajamas, their heads wrapped in bandages and their arms in slings, drove up to the Wall in a bus from Hadassah Hospital, waving their arms and crutches out of the open windows. These lightly wounded casualties had participated in the battle. They were on their way to the Wall, and Yitzhak was there to greet them. When they discovered him, they *swarmed* over him, hugging him, tugging at him, jumping on him in joy. And poor Yitzhak stood there yanking his officer's hat down over his ears, trying to stay in one piece . . . but with a quiet, proud smile on his face.

June 7 also brought a tragic error. One of our naval vessels torpedoed an American ship, the *Liberty,* from the U.S. Sixth Fleet, which was monitoring radio transmissions between headquarters on land, believing the ship was actually Egyptian. The death toll was thirty-two. The Americans had been told to steer clear of the coastline during the hostilities but the message never reached the *Liberty* due to a breakdown within the American communications structure. When the Israeli command learned it was not Egyptian, they suspected it might have been Soviet. Had it been, such a provocation could actually have triggered a third world war. "One can talk with friends and render explanations and apologies," Yitzhak wrote in his memoirs. But I know he felt considerable grief and regret over the incident even as there were victories to celebrate.

Thursday night, after the fourth day of the war, Yitzhak came home. And he wasn't smiling. He was glum partly because of the casualties we had incurred and the *Liberty* tragedy. But something else of strategic importance was tearing at him. Moshe Dayan would not authorize an advance on the Golan Heights, because he feared a conflict with Syria, which was then backed by the Russians. Yitzhak knew that failure to control the Golan Heights would fuel the same pattern of border attacks that had gone on for years, and he pressed Dayan on this issue. Syria was not prepared for war and did not rush into an attack as Jordan did but was firing artillery shells into the northern Galilee. Yitzhak could not respond without Dayan's authorization.

At seven A.M. on Friday, June 9, Dayan reconsidered. Instead of following the chain of command and contacting Yitzhak as chief of staff, Dayan called Brigadier General David Elazar directly with orders to take the Heights. Yitzhak's belief that this was the right course of action far outweighed the slight. He flew north by helicopter and took command. He visited the troops on the Golan June 9 and personally oversaw Elazar's battle plan. The operation was completed in twenty-seven hours on June 10, with 2,500 Syrian fatalities and a loss of over 200 of our boys.

The war was a catastrophic event for Syria: in just over one day they had 2,500 killed, 5,000 wounded, and a third of their tanks and half their artillery destroyed. The cease-fire went into effect at six-thirty P.M. on June 10.

But nothing matched the glory of unifying Jerusalem again. Israel had been a state for nearly twenty years but without a united Jerusalem, it was a state without its heart. There is a nostalgic Jewish prayer in the *Haggadah,* read at the conclusion of the Passover seder that expresses the hope "next year in Jerusalem." For nearly two thousand years a reclaimed Jerusalem was a holy mission. Suddenly Jerusalem united was a reality. This was a great triumph, but it was also a profound shock. Everything had happened so suddenly, so unexpectedly. And shock—good or bad—can bring about emotional paralysis or even depression.

The Six-Day War.* The Israeli army was pitted against Arab nations on three simultaneous fronts. Yitzhak had been the com-

*Yitzhak gave the war its name in a magazine interview on July 5, 1967.

mander of the Israeli army for four years. He had planned for any eventuality on all those fronts. He had groomed a tiger ready to pounce in retaliation if provoked. He had prevailed. But even after this achievement, Yitzhak wasn't a happy man.

Yitzhak's enormous sensitivity to loss of life was flamed once more. As well executed as the war was, Israel still had to reckon with eight hundred fatalities. The nation's leadership had feared many more. Announcement of the fatalities was withheld until the war was over. Then they were all announced on one day.

Our children probably appreciated that Yitzhak was an exceptionally gifted man at the time of the Six-Day War. His achievement was overwhelming. But I'm sure it was not just a matter of aptitude. Perhaps it was then that the children realized that all the hard work their father had done day and night was what had been required. And now they felt somewhat rewarded.

That Saturday when the war was over, I came home and found Dalia—who was then seventeen—lying on her bed, crying. "Mother, there's no justice. Not at school, not anywhere," she said. What did she mean? "Everyone says Dayan won the war, not my father. . . ."

"Dalia, plenty of people will say that," I said. "Don't cry. Success, the saying goes, has many fathers. History will show what role your father played in this war." Then I told her that the people who lost loved ones would be told the next day, and that they truly will have a reason to weep. I don't think that Dayan's glory troubled Yitzhak too much. There was a great deal to share. Yitzhak had considerable confidence that history has a way of sorting these realities out . . . and indeed it has.

The Sunday after the war concluded was a terrible day. Yitzhak, as chief of staff, oversaw the communication to eight hundred bereaved homes. On June 11, everyone in Zahala and all over Israel who had a child or a husband in the war dreaded the arrival of taxis at their doorstep with representatives from the Ministry of Defense.

The general staff had wisely decided there would be a thirty-day period of mourning before any victory celebrations took place. During this time, a friend of mine came back from the United States with a gift of a cocktail dress for me. At first I even forgot to pick it up. When I did and tried it on, I wondered if the time would ever come again to wear such a sleek and stylish gown. It seemed so remote during those bleak days of mourning.

From the day the war ended, people in Israel communicated their appreciation to my husband in all kinds of ways. Yitzhak always had a sweet tooth and was constantly eating nut-filled chocolate bars during staff meetings in "the Pit." He received a veritable mountain of chocolate bars after the victory! Endless letters, so many flowers, there was so much admiration and love bestowed on him.

The Israeli armed forces do not confer medals or decorations except for valor in combat, but Yitzhak was honored for his achievement in the Six-Day War in a way that far surpassed any decoration previously bestowed in recognition of military accomplishment. The Hebrew University conferred on him an honorary doctorate of philosophy in a ceremony on Mount Scopus on June 28, 1967. Twenty years earlier, just before the War of Independence, I was sitting on Mount Scopus with friends watching a ballet matinee performed by the Rina Nikova Company, peering east through the columns behind the stage over the hills of Judea down to the Dead Sea. As I turned around during the performance, my gaze went west, where the setting sun casts a unique shade of pink on the hills of Jerusalem.

For twenty years I had not seen Mount Scopus. For two decades this land had been accessible to Israelis only through special UN convoys, and few ever went. Gathered around us were friends of the Hebrew University from all over the world, assembled together after the war to celebrate this dramatic homecoming. Suddenly we were here again, and I was tense—the night before, Yitzhak had privately sized up the speech he was going to deliver this way: It doesn't flow right. He predicted the speech was going to be mediocre.

But when he started in, something took flight. I looked around me. This time what caught my attention was not the hills of Judea.

It was not the magical pink glow to the west. It was the tears well-
ing up in people's eyes and unabashedly streaming down their
faces, because they were so moved and entranced by his words.
Thirty years later, our dear friend Norman Bernstein observed,
"Yitzhak—so unassuming, even seemingly passive—could gener-
ate a dramatic intensity when he spoke on certain occasions that
was nothing short of laserlike." Surely, this was one of those moments. Broadcast on national radio, Yitzhak's acceptance speech
stirred the entire country.

David Ben-Gurion, who heard the speech on the radio, wrote a
beautiful letter praising Yitzhak:

> *Dear Yitzhak,*
>
> *While on my way in the car, I heard your speech at the
> University following your honorary doctor acceptance. You
> were right to express your pride in the commanders and sol-
> diers of the Israel Defense Forces. But I was proud of your
> speech. I understand why they applauded you so much more
> than any of the others. To this day, I have never heard you
> make a speech. This was more than a successful speech. It
> was your privilege to be chief of staff during the greatest
> hours of our glorious army. And you truly deserve it.*
>
> *Yours,*
> *David Ben-Gurion*

What was the heart of this talk that moved so many so deeply?
These brief excerpts describe the values and achievements of an Israel that had not yet reached the twentieth anniversary of its existence:

> *War is intrinsically harsh and cruel, and blood and tears
> are its companions. But this war which we have just waged
> brought forth rare and magnificent instances of courage and
> heroism, and at the same time moving expressions of broth-
> erhood, comradeship, and even of spiritual greatness.*
>
> *Anyone who has not seen a tank crew continue its attack*

though its commander has been killed and its track badly damaged . . . who has not witnessed the concern and the extraordinary efforts made by the entire air force to rescue a pilot who has bailed out in enemy territory, cannot know the meaning of devotion among comrades in arms. . . .

The entire nation was exalted and many wept when they heard of the capture of the Old City. Our Sabra youth, and most certainly our soldiers, do not tend to be sentimental and they shrink from any public show of feeling. But the strain of battle, the anxiety which preceded it, and the sense of salvation and of direct confrontation with Jewish history itself cracked the shell of hardness and shyness and released wellsprings of emotion and stirrings of the spirit. The paratroopers who conquered the Wailing Wall leaned on its stones and wept—in its symbolism an act so rare as to be almost unparalleled in human history. Rhetorical phrases and clichés are not common in our army, but this scene on the Temple Mount, powerful enough to break through their habits of reticence, revealed as though by a flash of lightning truths that were deeply hidden.

And there is more to be told. The joy of triumph had seized the entire nation. Nevertheless, a strange phenomenon can be observed among our soldiers. Their joy is incomplete, and their exultation is marred by sorrow and shock. There are even some who abstain from celebration entirely. The men in the front lines saw with their own eyes not only the glory of victory, but also the price of victory—their comrades fallen beside them soaked in blood. I know too that the terrible price paid by our enemies also touched the hearts of many of our men. It may be that the Jewish people have never learned and never accustomed themselves to feel the triumph of conquest and victory, with the result that these are accepted with mixed feelings. . . .

We have always demanded the cream of our youth for the Israel Defense Forces. We coined the slogan Hatovim latayis *[the Best for the Air Force] and this became a household phrase. It referred not only to technical and manual skills. What it meant was that if our airmen were to be capable of defeating the forces of four enemy countries within a few short hours, they had to be imbued with moral values and human values. . . .*

All this springs from the spirit and leads back to the spirit. Our warriors prevailed not by their weapons but by their sense of mission, by the consciousness of the rightness of their cause, by a deep love for their country and an understanding of the difficult task laid upon them: to ensure the existence of our people in their homeland, to protect, even at the price of their lives, the right of the Jewish people to live in their own state, free, independent, and in peace.

SABRA STATESMAN

O ur first joint visit to the United States (Yitzhak had been there before) took place in November 1963, just before Yitzhak was appointed chief of staff of the IDF. In preparation for that appointment, Yitzhak embarked on a high-level orientation trip to America. I can appreciate now how momentous it was to have visited the United States at that precise time. We went to New York and Washington, and Yitzhak traveled to several other cities, mainly military centers and installations—all so exciting and awesome and the source of many important new ideas.

I remember Yitzhak making an offhand comment to me on our way home to Israel: "You know, when I finish my term as chief of staff, I'll be ready to replace Abe Harman." Harman was Israel's ambassador in Washington at the time. Yitzhak's premonition later materialized.

Our 1963 trip to the United States lasted three weeks. I was astonished at the size and the excitement of New York. This was a fast-moving lifestyle, unlike anything I had known in Europe or Israel. Dalia and Yuval, along with a number of officers, met us at Lod Airport in Tel Aviv upon our return. We were told that President Kennedy had been shot—his condition was as yet unclear. We had never met the Kennedys, but we could sense how the promise of John Kennedy's future had stirred Americans and imagined how devastating it would be if something serious had happened to him. Just as we walked in the door of our home, I picked up the phone to hear shocking news: John F. Kennedy was dead. To have just returned from the United States and for Yitzhak to have been in Dallas just hours before—albeit as mere coincidence; Fort Bliss was a stop on his military briefing tour—was disorienting. Yitzhak was about to become chief of staff and had just completed an intensive study of state-of-the-art defense and security practices from the most powerful nation in the world, and suddenly we learned that this country's chief executive was slain by a lone gunman.

Since the 1963 visit, Yitzhak's belief in America's importance to Israel's defense grew steadily. When Yitzhak first proposed to Prime Minister Levi Eshkol that he wanted to leave the military and become ambassador to the United States, Eshkol said, "Hold on to me or I'll fall out of my chair." He simply couldn't imagine that Yitzhak would want to become an ambassador with all the cocktail parties and receptions and society small talk that came with the job.

The reality was that Yitzhak was ready for something new. In 1967, he was forty-five years old and had served as chief of staff for four years. He was at the end of the military road. The Israeli chief of staff never advances to minister of defense, certainly not immediately. Roughly a third of all generals went on to careers in government, and Yitzhak was far more interested in public service than in business.

Certainly the post in America was Israel's most important diplomatic assignment abroad. But Yitzhak was chief of staff and had the powerful credential of the Six-Day War. He also had an intense interest in the United States and the conviction that relations with the Americans would be essential for Israel's future security. Abe Harman had been ambassador to the United States for nine years and he too was ready for a change.

The only official approval Yitzhak needed was from the prime minister. Not even the approval of the foreign minister was necessary, though it was helpful. Foreign Minister Abba Eban, Abe Harman's predecessor as ambassador to the United States, didn't think much of Yitzhak or his intellectual capacity, and I'm sure he groaned over Yitzhak's English. Abe Harman, after all, came from South Africa and his English was perfect. Eban himself, another South African, studied in England and had taught at Cambridge. How is this Sabra, Rabin, I'm sure he thought, with his limited diplomatic experience and his rough-hewn English, going to represent us well in the United States? The biggest competitor for the job was Yakov Herzog, Eshkol's political aide. But Yitzhak's drive, his commitment to work with diverse people, and his convictions compensated for his lack of polish in Eshkol's mind, and Yitzhak got the appointment.

We knew what we were headed toward. Now we had to settle what we were leaving behind. Yuval would go with us. Dalia would not. She was graduating from high school and would be entering the army. This would not be an easy time to leave her, but we anticipated there would be reasonably frequent travel by us to Israel and occasional trips by her to the United States. I was excited by the thought of getting to know the country better.

The day Yitzhak left the chief of staff position, he was the happiest man in the world. I remember him coming home after his official farewell from the army, literally jumping up into the air, saying, "At long last, I no longer have responsibility for human life." He may well have felt that he was the best-qualified person to discharge that responsibility, and he accepted it as part of his body-and-soul dedication to serve his country. Nonetheless, it was a profound weight. Going to America would enable him to serve his country in a most meaningful—and distinctively innovative— way, by trying to take the Israeli-American relationship to a whole new level.

At this time Israel was still strongly oriented toward France as both our leading backer and weapons supplier. When Yitzhak became the ambassador to the United States, Israel had been buying almost all its airplanes from France. Prime Minister Eshkol and Yitzhak questioned this situation and believed that no European country would ever put itself at risk to support Israel in a conflict.

Most of all, Yitzhak wanted the ambassadorial post in Washington because he realized that Israel could be helped best by developing contacts and building a relationship with the United States, which was, in his opinion, the only hope for eventual peace in the Middle East. Yitzhak had particularly strong convictions about this, and his appreciation of America's role may have been a factor favoring Yitzhak's appointment to the United States. One of Yitzhak's great achievements was in helping secure the sale of highly advanced and strategically important Phantom jets to Israel during his first year as ambassador.

Nineteen sixty-seven was a great turning point in Israeli-American relations. Before the war, a trip to Israel was considered by Americans to be a risky, Third World experience. The "adventurous" Americans who went would complain how unsatisfactory the hotels and restaurants were. Between 1948 and 1967, we always had the sense that American Jews looked down on us. In their manner, many seemed to say, "We're pouring money into this country, and you're not doing very well." Israelis, on the other hand, felt the Americans were disrespectful: "They sign the checks and then come and patronize us. They feel obliged to lecture us on how to run our country better than we do."

No doubt, there was misunderstanding on both sides, and a rift had developed. All this changed abruptly after the Six-Day War. Suddenly there was all the respect in the world for tiny Israel and what it had accomplished. Overnight a golden era emerged between the American Diaspora and Israel—centered on events such as the unification of Jerusalem—with an enormous outpouring of emotion and gratitude. Tourism surged. Also a new wave of American immigration—a new *aliyah* for both young people and old people—began.

When we came to Washington in February 1968, we were welcomed with enormous anticipation, warmth, and admiration. Yitzhak was the first Israeli-born ambassador to Washington and the hero of the Six-Day War. Everyone wanted to see us and to shake our hands—especially his.

The ambassador's home in Washington was quite a departure

from our officers' quarters in Zahala. First of all, the scale of the residence was vast—the dining room could seat over fifty people! An ambassador's home is a tool. For the Israeli ambassador in America this is especially so—because Israel's destiny is very reliant on the goodwill of political leaders, the media, and public interest groups. That requires constant visits and entertaining. It was in Washington that I first put into practice several rules for entertaining, such as taking great care in seating arrangements—a matter of diplomacy all in itself, as it requires that protocol and hierarchy considerations mesh with placing together people who would be interested in talking with each other—and avoiding serving the same menu to guests who were making a return visit. Because Israel is an immigrant culture, our cuisine in fact is a mixture of Middle Eastern, Mediterranean, and European cooking, so that offered many opportunities for diversity.

The first round of diplomatic visits for an incoming ambassador is rigorous, with about 120 diplomatic representations in Washington. Most countries did not have diplomatic relations with Israel, so that limited the number of visits required. Therefore, our calls focused on the countries that held a special interest or meaning.

While the courtesy visits and dinners are usually assumed to be superficial affairs, important signals can be communicated through these events. The Women's International Club, an organization made up mainly of spouses to diplomatic corps members in Washington, provides an opportunity to learn about other countries, including their homes, art, and cuisines. On one occasion in 1970, a holiday reception took place in the home of a Nebraska congressman. Yitzhak was out of town and I attended alone. Ambassador Andrew Mossbacher, chief of protocol in the Department of State, was there. Mossbacher casually came over and started a conversation with an unusual inquiry: "Mrs. Rabin, you are invited frequently to the home of Joseph Sisco [the deputy secretary of state]. How's their food?"

"Fine. Why do you ask?" I replied.

"Because I'm invited to a stag dinner tonight in honor of King

Hussein." It was clear, Mossbacher was trying to let me—and therefore Yitzhak—know that he would be meeting with the king.

Two months earlier, in September 1970—"Black September"—the Jordanian army had clashed with PLO guerrillas in Jordan. Many PLO leaders (but not Arafat) advocated the overthrow of the king and the establishment of a Palestinian state inside Jordan. King Hussein decided to strike back decisively. Meanwhile Syria threatened to send tanks into Jordan, and the United States was concerned that the king's Hashemite government would fall.

The United States wanted to rally support for the king. Israel was the conduit to send a preemptive warning to Syria to keep their tanks out of Jordan, but eventually Jordan did this all by itself. I told Mossbacher, "Please tell King Hussein that you and I met at a cocktail party and I asked you to give him my regards, and to say that we Israelis very much admire his courage and determination in his struggle with the PLO." Perhaps it wouldn't do any good, but it certainly could do no harm.

Very early the next morning, Mossbacher phoned to say, in his deep voice, "Mrs. Rabin, we all have our problems. Perhaps King Hussein has more than we do. You made the man happy last night. He was so excited that, when I escorted him to his car, he repeated, 'Please don't forget to give the Rabins my heartfelt thanks and best wishes.'"

Our stay in the United States was our first opportunity to live among a Jewish Diaspora community. We experienced firsthand the variations between Orthodox, Conservative, and Reformed Jews. We attended a Conservative synagogue chiefly because that had been the choice of the embassy and the ambassadors before us. We didn't really attend synagogue services in Israel on a regular basis. In Washington, attendance became a matter of protocol. Yitzhak may have suffered a little, but it was something that he had to do, at least for the High Holidays and such special occasions as bar mitzvahs.

Yuval's thirteenth birthday came just three months after our arrival, but we decided to postpone his bar mitzvah until fall, during

Succot, the Feast of Tabernacles. Yuval began studying his *haftarah*, his reading of that week's portion of the Bible, in a special synagogue class at Adas Israel in Washington. When the time came, Yuval mastered his reading beautifully. One hundred fifty people attended the ceremony. Dalia left shortly after to go back home and begin her military service. Saying good-bye to her was devastating. Yuval couldn't stop crying. It was so hard being apart.

Our rabbi at Adas Israel—Stanley Rabinowitz, who has since retired—remains a close friend of our family to this day. He delivered truly brilliant sermons that were a compelling intellectual and Jewish experience. He used to publish them after the High Holidays, and I collected them faithfully. Rabbi Rabinowitz gave a sermon in 1976, which I have often recalled since Yitzhak's death. In it, he said:

> *In the Jewish ghettos of Europe, a world gone by, mourners, both friends and family, would draw near the wooden coffin as it was carried to its repository. And as they gently touched the starkness of the raw lumber, they whispered . . . reverentially, "Forgive me, please forgive me."*
>
> *There was therapy in the pathetic and simple plea, but we are more sophisticated.*
>
> *How do we live with our mistakes? . . . First, we must be brutally honest in our introspection. In our searching of soul we may recall the cross words that may have slipped from our lips. Or the times we lost our temper about matters that now appear so trivial.*
>
> *To attain true repentance we must first be ready to recall the times we were guilty of defective speech. Candor is the finest form of atonement.*

How many Israelis should have touched Yitzhak's coffin to apologize for the inflamed rhetoric and hostility that created the climate that brought about his death? How many now—left and right, unspoken and outspoken—feel remorse for Yitzhak's death?

∞ We were miserable being away from home on the holidays, but we could not avoid it. Sometimes we were with both our children, but now that Dalia was in the IDF, our chances to be together were limited.

The largest Jewish community in the United States is of course in New York. People often say that every second person you meet in New York is Jewish and you always seem to be meeting the second person. You sense Yom Kippur on the streets of New York, but it was business as usual in Washington, a most peculiar sensation for an Israeli. Going to services on the eve of Yom Kippur while seeing buses roll down the streets and stores jammed with shoppers was disconcerting. On Yom Kippur in Israel, daily life is totally suspended.

Each year anew I missed being home. However, on the evening of Yom Kippur, the square in front of the Washington synagogue glowed with powerful floodlights for the Kol Nidre service, and masses of Jewish people would assemble for prayers and the rabbi's sermon. The feeling of Jewish identity demonstrated through these services enabled me to ignore the bustle on the way home, and left me feeling internally strengthened. The experience also helped us recognize the power of the Jewish religion as a unifying and cohesive force for the Diaspora.

∞ The Jewish community was an important focus of ours in Washington, but so was the city's cultural life. Washington is a city rich in architecture and a feast in floral color during springtime with its fiery azaleas, the pink-and-white flowers of its dogwood trees, and the immense beauty of its cherry blossoms. Yitzhak had become an avid amateur photographer in the years before our Washington assignment, taking photos of foreign cities, which he would share with us back home. That interest remained lively during our Washington years, and the cherry blossoms became a favorite photographic theme for him.

Washington really lacked world-class facilities for the performing arts until the Kennedy Center was built, with its integrated concert hall, opera house, and theater. As finishing work was done on the Kennedy Center, foreign embassies were invited to offer their thoughts on embellishments. It was suggested that Israel decorate one of the guest reception rooms, and we selected a room next to the concert hall on the second tier. As Yitzhak put it, this "baby" was mine.

Our dear American friends Norman and Diane Bernstein and I visited the uncompleted center in hard hats to inspect the site. Yitzhak didn't want to involve the Israeli government in funding; he felt it should be an American project. He also thought it would serve several important purposes if the funds were raised in the Washington community. After all, Washingtonians would be using the room, and their contributions would make them part of an Israeli legacy in Washington. So I called five or six friends, all of whom were from the Washington area, and invited them to our home. Joseph Meyerhoff of Baltimore was marvelous. "What's the big deal?" he said. "Each of us will give ten thousand dollars and we'll call it a day." Indeed, the $100,000 target was nearly reached in a single afternoon, as others were quickly involved in the fund-raising venture.

The project was a labor of love, all around. The narrow, long, high-ceilinged room reminded the architect Rafi Blumenfeld of the Sistine Chapel, so he had the ceiling painted with illustrations by the artist Shraga Weil to make it seem lower. As a central theme for the room, Rafi chose musical events described in the Bible. On the richly painted ceiling of blue, white, scarlet, and gold, Miriam sings her song; Joshua's troops bring down Jericho's walls with their shofars; and David—the centerpiece—plays his harp.

One of the four walls was carved out of hazelnut by the sculptor Nehemia Azaz and portrays musical instruments from the Bible surrounding a copper plate engraved with verses from Psalm 152. The other walls are coated with painted wool cloth. Shortly after the opening, the director of the center seized someone he thought was vandalizing the wall art. It turned out to be Yehezkel Kimhi, who was just signing his drawings!

When the room was officially opened, Yitzhak invited Senator Ted Kennedy to deliver the acceptance address. In a moving speech, the senator said, "We are used to thinking of the State of Israel in concepts of our support and assistance to the young country that fights for its existence. And here we have this wonderful room as a symbol of what Israel grants us in tradition, culture, and nobility." The papers trumpeted the "Israeli Victory at Kennedy Center," and the *Washington Post* art critic compared the room to a "holy shrine." This mission meant a lot to me, and Yitzhak was proud and happy when it was dedicated.

∞ We moved to America in turbulent times. Detroit had been engulfed in riots the preceding summer. About a month after our February arrival, Lyndon Johnson declared that he wouldn't seek reelection. The Vietnam War protests were mounting. On April 4, 1968, Dr. Martin Luther King was assassinated and the resulting riots in Washington led to a citywide curfew. Two months later Senator Robert Kennedy was murdered—just a few days after Yitzhak had met him. We saw looting and rioting. The racial conflicts were perhaps the most alarming for Yitzhak and me—all the accumulated hatred and discontent. I remember thinking all the time, "Here is this vast, strong nation we admired so much and look how seriously troubled they are."

The Vietnam War was particularly perplexing to our son, Yuval, coming from Israel just after the Six-Day War. He said, "I don't understand what they're talking about. What peace? Peace where? Peace for whom? What does this word *peace* mean?" Yuval's questions had substance. The United States was in South Vietnam to defend it. The war with the North Vietnamese was escalating. But . . . peace? Were Americans truly using the right term? That the Americans didn't want to be involved in the war was one thing. But the moment the Americans withdrew, would that mean peace for Vietnam?

The Vietnam War was a situation quickly worsening, and it presented the president with a terrible dilemma: if America pulled out, then all the blood already spilled would have been in vain. Yitzhak felt that America should achieve something for itself and for South Vietnam before withdrawal. He agreed with Kissinger's and Nixon's concern that pulling out would be a declaration of failure. Yitzhak believed in diminishing the damage done in a situation that has become unexpectedly menacing. He believed this was Kissinger's and Nixon's goal as well.

Yitzhak first met Richard Nixon in the summer of 1966 in Israel. The U.S. ambassador to Israel at that time was Wally Barbour. His chargé d'affaires invited guests to a dinner for Mr. Nixon, and we were among them. Since it was August and a great many people were on vacation, putting together a guest list was not easy. However, the chargé d'affaires assembled a group of about ten or twelve. During the dinner, Nixon sat at one end of the table and Yitzhak sat diagonally across from him. The dialogue focused on the role America could and could not, should and should not play in Southeast Asia. We were all impressed with Nixon's skill at expressing his ideas.

Then Yitzhak asked Nixon about his plans for the next day. He extended him the hospitality of the IDF, offering a small plane or a helicopter and a guide, and the opportunity to visit the northern part of the country. Of course, Nixon accepted. He was accompanied by the head of Israeli intelligence, General Aharon Yariv (who, by the way, is the uncle of Itamar Rabinovich, the Israeli ambassador in Washington during Yitzhak's second term as prime minister). When Nixon became president two years later, he would recall these days of "being our guest" with sincerity and appreciation.

In January 1968, Yitzhak knew he was headed for Washington, but had not yet begun his new assignment. While he was still in Israel, he met with Henry Kissinger, then a distinguished American professor from Harvard who was born in Germany. The professor was lecturing in Israel. The two were first introduced in 1966, when Kissinger lectured at Israel's National Defense College. In the 1968 meeting, Yitzhak was so overwhelmed with Kissinger's vision and insight that he wasn't even sure how long the meeting lasted, but it was surely on the order of two to three hours. In his memoirs, Yitzhak recalls Kissinger's concern that Vietnam was sapping America's resolve and making the nation more isolationist. Meanwhile, the Soviet Union was exploiting United States uncertainty and enjoying America's costly engagement in Vietnam. What if Israel found itself in a similar protracted conflict? How long would the United States support its ally? The conversation with Kissinger was a powerful eye-opener for Yitzhak just before he assumed Israel's most significant ambassadorial post; I'm sure it helped Yitzhak define his objectives and priorities. Neither of them knew at the time that Yitzhak had just finished a conversation with the next national security adviser of the United States!

The admiration didn't just flow one way. Nixon and Kissinger grew to respect Yitzhak's judgment, too. That included his views on the military situation in Vietnam. When Kissinger asked for an assessment on how North Vietnam would conduct a particular major offensive, Yitzhak would give his strategic analysis as to what the North Vietnamese might do. Kissinger had asked many experienced leaders in Washington for their advice and opinions. Once the offensive finally took place, Kissinger remarked with some admiration that the only general who correctly diagnosed the North Vietnamese battle plan was the Israeli ambassador to the United States. I believe President Nixon and Secretary of State Kissinger were the most influential international figures with whom Yitzhak consulted regularly over the years.

Golda Meir had assumed the prime ministership in February 1969 after Levi Eshkol died in office of a heart attack. Golda was the first female prime minister of Israel and enjoyed great popularity at home and abroad as the leader of the country at one of its most triumphant moments. Twenty months after Yitzhak's tour of duty as ambassador had begun, Golda alerted him that he might be invited back to Israel to join the cabinet as minister of education. I was becoming more receptive to returning to Israel to be close to Dalia. Yitzhak was more ambivalent. A cabinet post had a certain allure, but he was not sure that education was the right portfolio for him, plus he felt that he had not yet fully exploited his ambassadorial assignment. There was still so much left to accomplish on his agenda. He summed up his feelings in a letter to Dalia in late 1969, days before a visit she made to the United States:

WASHINGTON, NOVEMBER 30, 1969

Shalom, Dalika,

I will use the opportunity of Arale's* return to Israel to send you this letter. I apologize for not writing more often. This has been one of the more serious faults I have had since childhood. For some reason I have never been able to overcome it. It seems that in my age it is very difficult to change old habits, as bad as they may be. In any case, mother is the talented one in this area and so she is the one who maintains contact between us and other parts of the family separated by the immense ocean. I really and truly am looking forward to your arrival soon and I am certain that a month together will benefit us all.

As you know, I have no great news. Mother is quite tense because of the uncertainty of where we will live. Yuval is also very nervous. He is dying to return home. Since he is much more introverted in expressing his thoughts and emotions, his feelings are less apparent. As for me, I am not indifferent to what the future holds, but for some reason I am quite calm. Maybe the main reason for being this way is that I am not at all excited about the possibility of becoming the minister of education. Nevertheless, if the prime minister decides that she wants me to return to take up the position, I will do so. I told her as much when we spoke. However, having said all that, it is not a field that I feel most comfortable with. . . . I am not at all scared of the job, and I most certainly would return to Israel for it, but I would not be too saddened if I were to remain in my present position.

My only sorrow would be that we would not all be together in Israel. I feel that our stay here causes you and Yuval great discomfort and maybe even more. I hope that

*Israel's head of military intelligence.

• 1 3 1 •

*even if I do not return to Israel now, and this possibility is
quite realistic, we will find ways to decrease the damage the
separation causes our family. I am convinced that your visit
here will be very beneficial to all of us, although a somewhat
limited compensation for our unfulfilled hopes.*

*Nothing much is happening here. There is a lot of work
to do and so far the job is very interesting. Israel is unfortunately becoming more and more dependent on the United
States. We have no closer ally than the United States. Taking
into account the negative response of the British concerning
the sale of weapons to Israel, as well as the French em-
bargo—we are almost completely dependent on the United
States for the supply of weapons outside Israel.*

*Lately, as the result of the gloomy economic forecast, we
demand and hope for American financial aid. This is, of
course, on top of the support we already receive from the
American Jews. The Jews here are well aware of our problem, and in spite of the worsening economic situation here,
donations to the UJA and the Bonds have increased. An increase of 25 to 30 percent from last year is being hoped for.
There is even a chance that donations next year will reach
the level of 1967. In short, there is a lot to achieve in areas
that are crucial to Israel, during the difficult times that lie
ahead.*

*Dalika, if you should encounter any difficulties in arrang-
ing the forthcoming trip, do not hesitate to call us and I will
do anything possible so that you will indeed arrive by December 10, 1969.*

*Many kisses,
Abba*

After all the buildup, Yitzhak learned someone else had been
appointed minister of education. He accepted it easily because he
felt he still had lessons to learn, and because the appointee was far
more of a comrade than a rival: Yigal Allon!

As ambassador to the United States, Yitzhak strengthened our bonds with the Americans. During the Nixon administration, the relationship between our two countries reached a level of strategic importance previously unknown. Yitzhak made every attempt to educate American leadership that countries—even small ones like Israel—must negotiate their relationships with others on a bilateral basis. He felt that one can never ignore or bypass the Americans, but the Americans needed to let us resolve our challenges in the Middle East on our own—to stay away when things go right, but to be there for us when we ran into the occasional tough situation. Nixon and Kissinger understood this very well, though they sometimes had a difficult time accepting it.

In Washington, Yitzhak made a series of important contacts—especially on Capitol Hill and with the press. Two Democratic senators who were great friends of Israel, and whom Yitzhak truly respected, were Hubert Humphrey and Henry "Scoop" Jackson—the latter was a natural because of his expertise in security issues. Yitzhak had a strong working relationship with Deputy Secretary of State Joseph Sisco, whom he found to be very supportive. The brothers Rostow were an imposing Washington duo—Eugene served as undersecretary of state and as Lyndon Johnson's national security adviser. His economist brother, Walt, had been an influential adviser to both Kennedy and Johnson. Among the press, we got to know Katherine Graham, Joseph and Stewart Alsop, Rollie Evans, William Safire, Max Frankel, and Barbara Walters. Becoming acquainted with other members of the international diplomatic community was harder. Yitzhak never ascribed much importance to these relations with other foreign ambassadors. He had his hands full dealing with the various U.S. authorities and the Jewish communities. Though the Soviet Union didn't have diplomatic relations with Israel, the Soviet ambassador to the United States, Anatoly Dobrynin, and Yitzhak were friendly, and I got along well with the ambassador's wife when we met at diplomatic functions.

We also formed an unusual friendship with Rolf Pauls and his wife. Pauls had been Germany's first ambassador to Israel and had done an exceptional job of gaining acceptance for postwar Germany within Israel. He was brilliant, very detail oriented, and a charming dance partner. (The Paulses loved to dance, and many parties they threw were dance parties.) After we came to Washington, he was appointed Germany's ambassador to the United States, and we were able to get to know them better, having had Israel as common background and because the Paulses had so enjoyed their assignment in Israel.

During the 1972 Munich Olympics in September, I was visiting Zahala while Yitzhak was on a trip to Seattle. It was a Saturday night, two days before Rosh Hashanah. I was in the home of friends, raising a glass and eating an apple with honey in the tradition of the Jewish holiday. But it was not a happy gathering. All of us were alarmed and anxious about the kidnapping of our Israeli athletes on German soil. Two of the athletes being held hostage had been killed. The tension was building. The Palestinian terrorists demanded the release of Arab prisoners in Israeli jails. After hearing a radio update that the nine remaining athletes were safe, we were somewhat relieved, said *"Mazel tov,"* and *"Shanah tova,"* and left for our respective homes. A friend called me up at seven o'clock in the morning and said, "You won't believe this. All the rest are dead." It was a shock to have gone to bed with the news that they had been rescued and to awaken to the nightmare that the terrorists had murdered them. Yitzhak phoned me. He was rushing to Washington to respond to the media. All day long, Israeli radio played the Funeral March movement from Beethoven's *Eroica* symphony. To this day, I associate that piece with this tragedy.

I returned as scheduled to the United States that week. We had been invited to Ambassador Pauls's home for dinner weeks before. I was hesitant about accepting the invitation, but Yitzhak felt it would be a serious diplomatic breach to decline. Yitzhak was not a man of provocation; he did not want to translate the tragedy to a personal level between us and the Paulses. They were about to leave Washington, and this was one of their farewell dinners. I was eventually pleased that we did go because the Paulses very openly expressed their sadness and regret over this tragedy especially in light of the friendship that Germany and Israel had forged—one that the ambassador played no small role in developing.

∞ It was becoming clear to Yitzhak that he would need to return to Israel to further advance his political career. His feelings about the imminent change are captured in two letters he wrote to me while I was on visits back home. At the time, Yitzhak had become the target of some controversy and criticism in the United States because he was an outspoken supporter of Richard Nixon's bid for reelection.

WASHINGTON
July 9, 1971

Shalom, Leah,

I write this letter in the office after Yuval and I ate our last lunch together before his return home. It all seems a bit strange: the family is beginning to retreat homeward. We have just finished packing (according to your instructions) and I have returned to the office. Yuval has gone for his last spin in your car before two years' driving break.

When we sat down to eat, he said: "It's strange to leave this house now and know that I won't return to it." All in all, it's a little sad, but what is there to do—we have to go home, to our real home. . . .

I was happy that you phoned. Pay no attention to the despicable reports in the papers!* They're all envious of my success and they'll try any kind of smear. . . . The bottom line—I'm happy about my part in U.S.-Israeli relations so far. I was never convinced that, even when there are differ-

---

*Yitzhak was criticized for several controversial positions in the press at the time. One was his support for Nixon. Another was his backing for deep bombing into Egypt in an effort to bring about an end to the War of Attrition. The latter particularly irked the Israeli foreign minister, Abba Eban. Yitzhak was even dubbed the "undiplomatic diplomat" in the American press and was proud of the moniker.

ences of opinion between friendly countries, like the U.S. and Israel, they should be reduced to the "witch-hunt" dimension.

True, we do have differences of opinion with the United States. And sometimes sharp differences. But at the same time there is no entity outside of Israel other than the United States that helps with aid and armaments in unprecedented scope and quality, and with unprecedented financing. Despite all the uproar that we cause, no other country in the world is closer in political views to Israel than the United States.

I have no doubt that we must fight, and fight hard, with America on the subject of arms, aid, and so forth, but there is no need to bring it public attention in a manner that presents the United States as the enemy of humankind. . . .

All these happenings trouble me more for their content than for the degree of my personal involvement. The newspaper attacks on me do not concern me at this stage. They have raised my status and prestige here to truly alarming dimensions. There have already been approaches in the name of the president and others to Golda to keep me here in this job out of consideration for United States–Israeli relations. Of course I did not initiate them, and I gather that she is annoyed, as are her close associates. I also have no desire to remain here beyond what we discussed between us. Nevertheless, the approaches by Nixon, Kissinger, [Attorney General John] Mitchell, and [Senator Henry] Jackson have not met with my dissatisfaction. . . .

I intend to phone you this coming Saturday night, at midnight your time. It will cost some money, but we'll talk and I'll hear about Yuval's arrival, etc., etc.

Many kisses,
Yitzhak

The second letter was on the occasion of our twenty-fourth wedding anniversary.

WASHINGTON
August 23, 1972

My dear wife,

The clock now shows one minute after midnight here, and the twenty-third of August has arrived in Washington. After I talked with you on the phone, I wrote a letter (I think a little too emotional) to Dalia. Her earlier letter touched my heart.

Dalia's letter, at the beginning of her new life,* caused me deep emotion because of her common sense, sensitivity, and fierce desire to make it easier for me, to seek words of encouragement. . . . It's difficult to write two emotional letters in one evening.

When I look back over our twenty-four years of marriage, I am sure that despite all the little irritating arguments, it would be difficult to find among the couples that I know a better pair than us. . . . I am certain that there was great luck in my life when I married you, and you know how much I value that. I don't always manage to express it in the accepted conventional forms of daily life. . . . We have been through so much together, in times so critical for all of us, that it seems as if the content of our lives could fill the lives of scores of families. I'm referring to the positive aspects and the depth of the experiences that we have had together.

It sometimes seems to me that each of the last two posts that I have held (chief of staff and ambassador) could serve as the peak of ambition and achievement for any man at the end of his career.

I know for sure that the transition stage will not be easy. . . . Your assumption that my first public appearances [in Israel] will set the tone is not accurate. Public appearances have only limited effect. What matters is the real situation, where you are, and how real is the power you hold in

---

*She had just gotten married in Tel Aviv. Yitzhak, of course, attended the ceremony.

your hands. From that point of view, I will be in a less than easy situation for quite a long while. I know this, however I also know that I have no choice but to do it. It's not an ideal situation. It is the reality that has been forced on me. And now I must function within that reality.

I'm closing now, for otherwise I will arrive in Salt Lake City exhausted.

I'm ending with many kisses to you and many kisses to Yuval.

Yitzhak

Yitzhak knew that his term as ambassador was ending, but he was not being forced to leave the position. He knew that he had to return to Israel and run for the Knesset if he were to translate his diplomatic experience into the foundation of a solid political career. This step was not without risk. He had once been enticed by a cabinet post only to have the offer vanish. If he entered the cabinet, he was not sure what the portfolio would be. While I was anxious to be back in Israel with the children, Yitzhak—as necessary as the return to Israel would be for his political future—faced many uncertainties, and his letter reflected them.

∞ Being the host to visiting Israeli dignitaries is among the most important roles any ambassador plays in Washington, and the two most important luminaries of the time were Moshe Dayan and Golda Meir. I remember a dinner we hosted for Dayan. He had taken a nap beforehand, and his daughter, Yael, didn't want to wake him. We had invited fifty people to arrive at eight. All were there except Dayan. When he strode in after eight-thirty, he casually said "shalom" and beckoned his military attaché to come into the next room with him for a conference. Treasury Secretary George Shultz was our most senior American guest and he had arrived punctually. Yitzhak had personally invited the secretary and had really twisted his arm on the importance of being there for Dayan's visit. Standing next to me with a big smile on his face, Shultz couldn't resist whispering, "You know, I have nothing against prima donnas—on the condition that they really know how to sing. I'm sure Dayan sings beautifully. . . ."

Golda Meir on the other hand was unwaveringly punctual. When we came to pick her up, we would always find her sitting poised and assured, a string of pearls around her neck, slowly drawing on her unfiltered Chesterfield. She made a total of three visits to Washington during her term as prime minister—in 1969, 1971, and 1973. We hosted her on all three trips.

Toward the very end of Yitzhak's period as ambassador, on March 1, 1973, she made her last official visit to Washington. It was Yitzhak's birthday, and President Nixon gave him a gift in front of Mrs. Meir. Yitzhak was about to campaign for the Knesset as part of Golda Meir's Labor Party. Later, the president paid tribute to Yitzhak at a dinner, again in her presence. "We're very sorry to see this brilliant ambassador leave Washington," Nixon said. "I hope you will use him well when he returns to your country. . . . And, if you don't, we would be very happy to give him a job here in Washington."

"That depends on how he behaves," Meir retorted. Obviously, she bristled at the public kudos that Yitzhak was receiving from the president. I bit my tongue, but personally found her remark embarrassing.

Yitzhak's relationship with Golda Meir was a complex one. Yitzhak admired her determination. Golda also had a very special relationship with the American community, as she had lived in Milwaukee and had a wonderful mastery of English. The fact that Golda was a strong-willed woman never bothered Yitzhak. Everyone who knew her competence saw her as transcending that issue, and after all Yitzhak's mother, Rosa Cohen, was cut from similar cloth.

Golda was not as selflessly dedicated as a Rosa Cohen . . . or, in the political echelon, as a Levi Eshkol. She wasn't as generously minded toward certain people. Golda used to come to Washington prepared to negotiate for what Yitzhak called a "shopping list" of arms purchases. He didn't know if she realized that it was all predetermined before she came. Golda surely did not favor Yitzhak as the hope for the future and never saw him as her successor, but then again, Golda had a hard time seeing anyone as her successor.

That March, Henry Kissinger returned from Paris after having negotiated a tentative agreement between North and South Vietnam. The journalist Joseph Alsop loved to entertain and he always had a weakness for inviting military figures. He was excited about the chance to host an event on the occasion of Yitzhak's departure and General Creighton Abrams's return to an assignment in Washington. General Abrams was William Westmoreland's successor in 1968 as the American commander in Vietnam and held the post until 1972, when he was appointed U.S. Army chief of staff.

As coffee was being served, I found myself sitting beside Henry Kissinger and began to talk with him. Yitzhak always had a great respect for hierarchy and never addressed him as Henry; he called him Dr. Kissinger, as did I. "Dr. Kissinger," I said, "we've been in the United States five years. We have suffered through the horrible nightmare of the Vietnam War, with all its agony and traumatic events. You are about to sign an agreement to resolve this conflict. Please do me the favor of signing the agreement before we leave Washington."

Three weeks later, the memorial for President Lyndon Johnson took place in the Capitol. Yitzhak attended the ceremony. I was listening to the eulogies on the radio, packing suitcases because we were soon to leave.

After the memorial, Yitzhak went to Dr. Kissinger's office for one of their regular meetings. Kissinger had returned the night before, after having finalized the Vietnam agreement. Yitzhak congratulated him, "Well, Dr. Kissinger, you finally made it." With his dry, understated sense of humor, Kissinger looked at Yitzhak and said, "Mr. Rabin, I was under orders from your wife."

∞ Shortly after coming back to Israel in April 1973, Haim Shur, who was then the editor of the daily newspaper *Al Hamishmar*, requested an interview with Yitzhak. We were back at our home in Zahala. While the taping was taking place in our living room, a phone call came through. The girl's voice on the other end said shakily, "I have to speak to Haim Shur. His son was killed last night in a raid on Beirut." (This seaborne commando attack was a reprisal against Black September leaders for the terrorist murders at the Munich Olympics.) The news stunned me, and I asked her what she wanted me to do. She asked to speak to Yitzhak. As I walked to the bedroom crying, Yitzhak picked up the phone and I heard him say, "Yes. I understand. Okay. Thank you. Good-bye."

When he went back to the living room, Yitzhak said to Haim Shur, "I think it would be better to stop the interview. Your son was wounded in the operation last night." Haim asked no questions, prepared for the worst as we all had come to be, and simply got up to leave. My tears had stopped, and I came out to say good-bye to Haim. Yitzhak offered to drive him to the newspaper office, but Haim said he would drive himself. He was very pale when he left.

Here it was again, the seemingly unstoppable cycle of death for our young. Later Haim Shur authored a book in memory of his son titled *Avida—Sound and Touch*. That book joined an all-too-long row of volumes in our library dedicated to Israel's sons who have fallen in battle.

During the 1970s, terrorism against both military and civilian targets became more pervasive. It was a topic that clearly played on Yitzhak's mind. His thinking crystallized as acts of terrorism became more sophisticated. Yitzhak saw all terrorist acts as tinged by the same fundamental, villainous evil-mindedness. However, all terrorist acts are not alike, nor is all terrorism the same. Golda Meir's position had been hard and fast: one doesn't negotiate with terrorists. Yitzhak always preferred military responses to terrorist situations. The raid on Entebbe, which will be described later, was the most sophisticated anti-terrorist operation Yitzhak ever oversaw, but not every incident permitted this kind of solution. Yitzhak's philosophy was simple: If a reliable military option existed, that was the preferred course of action. If not, one must negotiate, at least until other options suggested a more positive outcome.

But dealing with terrorism committed randomly by guerrilla

cells is vastly different from the kind of terrorism Israel faced in the late 1980s, when the whole occupied Arab population rose up en masse against Israeli military rule. Clearly, new ways had to be found to confront the uprising, and Yitzhak's attitude changed.

He frequently drew an analogy between the rise of localized terrorism in areas such as southern Lebanon and Gaza to the methods that underpinned the spread of world communism decades earlier: local campaigns linked to a global conspiracy. During the Intifada, or Palestinian uprising, of the 1980s, he recognized the increasing power of the media in influencing terrorist acts. In the face of this kind of terrorism, he would ask, "Who is the terrorist?" One certainly does not negotiate with children. He believed if you do, you will suffer for it. Suicidal terrorism, spawned by Muslim fundamentalism, has become a force of recent years. It is very different from the political terrorism of the seventies and eighties, and it requires different solutions. Terrorism has no one format. It also has no one answer.

∞ After the setbacks of the 1967 war, and with considerable Soviet assistance, Egypt and Syria were rebuilding and strengthening their armed forces. A "War of Attrition," more a series of border incidents, was waged by Egypt against Israel between 1968 and 1970, chiefly along the Sinai-Suez Border. This led to the construction of the Bar-Lev line, a series of bunkers in this region, which had the effect of shifting Israel's defense mentality toward fixed fortifications reminiscent of the French Maginot Line. Both Yitzhak and General Ariel Sharon, a battle-hardened 1967 war hero, were skeptical about this approach, believing that the Israeli army's strength resided in its mobility. Yitzhak was concerned that Israel could be lulled into complacency based on the Bar-Lev line, which could become a horrible trap and cost many lives. Defense Minister Moshe Dayan, on the other hand, boasted that Israel could repel any attack within thirty-six hours.

In 1973, Yuval was attending a naval officers' school in Haifa. On the eve of Yom Kippur, while visiting us for the holiday, he received an urgent call to report to his unit in Haifa. At the time, it was not a high-risk assignment for Yuval, so we weren't particularly concerned about his call-up, but our son-in-law, a tank commander in the Sinai, was put on alert in this high-risk location. Yitzhak *was* worried about what this meant, though he did not expect war to break out. During a phone call from the Labor Party leader Yisrael Galili the next morning, Saturday, October 3, Yitzhak learned differently. All-out war was on the horizon. Yitzhak was asked to meet with the defense minister and other former chiefs of staff at three that afternoon. On that morning, a cabinet meeting took place in which Chief of Staff David Elazar asked for approval to mobilize the army. Dayan opposed it as yet another false alarm—of which there had already been several. The compromise was to mobilize only two brigades that morning.

At two that afternoon, the silence of the High Holiday was shattered by the wail of sirens. Yitzhak was at home, preparing for the three o'clock meeting. We froze in shock at the sound of the sirens. Radio broadcasts started, violating the holiness of the day, and calling up the units by code. All of a sudden, people were running out of synagogues to their units and the entire country was on wheels. War had broken out! The warning signals came so late that no one knew we were about to be attacked. Dalia's husband had just received permission from his superiors for some elective surgery, so little did the military leadership anticipate the beginning of a war. He drove back to their home on Saturday. Not expecting any broadcasts, he didn't listen to the radio. Only when he appeared at the door did he learn that our nation was at war. He hitch-hiked to the Sinai but couldn't catch up with his unit, so he simply joined another.

This was a most frustrating time for Yitzhak, because when things really didn't look good, he was in no position to contribute in one way or another. "Dado" Elazar brought him along to the fronts and asked him for his thoughts, but Yitzhak knew the risks of second-guessing a chain of command from the outside. Finance Minister Pinhas Sapir asked Yitzhak to head an emergency loan initiative, and he agreed to do it, because of his diplomatic experience and his contacts. But his heart would have been in helping to steer the military strategy in a direct way, which he knew was not in the cards.

Namaat, the Labor Party's Women's Organization, organized transportation for families to be with their wounded loved sons, who were being cared for in remote hospitals, and I worked on their behalf. After the war was over, recognizing the disarray and weakness of the military at the time, Yuval asked to be relieved of his prestigious two-year course as a naval officer and joined the Armored Corps instead, where the losses had been greater. He just couldn't see the value of spending two years with copy books in the sunshine. We were very proud of him—all the more so because he was motivated to do it on his own, not because he was the son of a national war hero. We discussed his plans only briefly, and it was I who communicated Yuval's decision to Yitzhak, who was then abroad on his fund-raising mission.

Our nephew Yiftach, a son of Yitzhak's sister, Rachel, who served in an armored unit in the Sinai, was badly wounded when his tank was hit by a rocket. I can still remember how alarmed we were when we saw the extent of the blackened burns all over his body at Ichilov Hospital. The doctors immediately commented his condition wasn't as bad as it looked. However, he did suffer considerable damage to one hand and lost two fingers. The doctors were able to restore sensation and some movement and he can even drive with it today.

Instead of thirty-six hours, the Yom Kippur War lasted twenty-three days. Despite Israel's ability to make the best of a terrible situation, the ultimate cost in life was staggering. With 2,701 Israelis dead and 7,500 more wounded, with 300 prisoners of war, 100 planes and 800 tanks destroyed, this was the worst aftermath of a war in Israel's history. Could we have survived if the United States had not authorized an airlift of more than 500 flights of munitions and equipment? I will never forget going to the airport and seeing the Galaxy transports opening up as replacement tanks sped out of the aircraft—one after another. This $10 billion war nearly crippled the Israeli economy and sent inflation skyrocketing. We succeeded in defending Israel's territory but just barely.

The war had not only added young lives to Israel's cemeteries and maimed to veteran's hospitals in horrific proportions, it also emptied the coffers of the state. Most of all, this war struck deep at the roots of popular trust in the government—especially in the way casualties were handled. So many were killed in the first two days—on the Golan Heights, on the Suez Canal, and in the Sinai Desert—but because of the disarray, many weren't found and their deaths weren't registered for weeks and sometimes months. The missing, the unaccounted-for wounded and dead, left families bewildered and angry.

Across the street from our home in Zahala lived a neighbor named Francie Oberlander. Her son, Danny, was part of a unit deployed in the Golan Heights. She hadn't heard from him since the beginning of the war. As time wore on, other soldiers began calling their families, but he did not. She became more and more desperate. One day, she stopped by our house. Yitzhak was home, and she said, "I'm going out of my mind. Do you think you could help me?" Yitzhak was helpless. He couldn't do much for her in his position. In total frustration she screamed, "But it is not possible that the earth swallowed the boy—he cannot have disappeared!" I believe it was two or three weeks later that we learned he had been killed in a tank on the first or second day of the war. It had taken weeks for an official announcement. The systems were simply not in place to record and report casualties. For years, on Memorial Day, I would join Francie and many of our neighbors to visit Danny's grave.

Eyal, one of Dalia's classmates who fought in the war, had married a girlfriend of Dalia's. One night, Yitzhak and I came home after dinner with a journalist to find the two girls sitting in the kitchen. I already knew that her friend's husband had fallen in action. But the family hadn't been notified yet. I could say nothing. The inefficiency created grotesque human dilemmas and forced us into cruel and torturous emotional situations.

The whole episode indeed *did* cast Yitzhak's fate . . . but in a way he never expected, sitting on the sidelines as he was. One comment of Yitzhak's at that time stands out above all others: "In wars, personal fates are determined. In this war, my fate will be determined as well because I'm not there. Where will I be when this is all over?"

I reassured him more than once, "You will be the hero who was not there."

CHAPTER
7

THE FIRST
TIME AROUND

he 1973 war postponed the national elections, which were ultimately held in December. It would be misleading to say that Yitzhak enjoyed campaigning, but he was a dedicated and active campaigner, dutifully hitting the trail each evening for his party.

In 1973, when we'd just returned from the United States, Yitzhak wasn't in the army, he wasn't in the government—he was simply a candidate for the Knesset. He used to joke about being an ex-soldier and an ex-ambassador, and because it looked unlikely that he would get any desirable cabinet post, he added "ex–candidate for cabinet" to his list of credentials. But now it looked likely he was destined for a cabinet ministry, though not certain which one. The years in the United States had eased the transition to political life. When the ticket rankings* were established for the Knesset elections, Yitzhak asked for slot number 20, not too low, but not too high, either.

Labor won the elections, but their mandate was weakened, with their share of the vote falling from 46 to 39 percent. Yitzhak

*In Israel, each party puts forward an electoral list. Because elections determine proportional, and not geographic, representation, those highest on the list have the best guarantee of a seat in the Knesset.

became a member of the Knesset. For a brief moment, it seemed that he would possibly become minister of defense (a post he would have dearly loved) when Moshe Dayan balked at joining the new cabinet. Many expected Dayan to resign because of protests by war veterans that he had mishandled preparation for the Yom Kippur War. He was not enthused about returning to the cabinet, but ultimately took the defense portfolio, and Yitzhak was appointed minister of labor.

Yitzhak became more and more involved in all the issues concerning the Labor portfolio and began to enjoy the challenge in it. He wasn't enthused about the particular assignment but he used it in his typically efficient way to acquire a specialized grasp of an area about which he knew relatively little. From then on, he could tell you the composition of the arriving immigrants each month by their various occupations. He would grin at the steady influx of mining engineers from the Soviet Union with its abundance of coal mines . . . especially since Israel doesn't have a single coal mine! He knew that it would take time for these new arrivals to learn new skills.

Even though Labor won the election, the cabinet felt the pressure of public dissatisfaction. People were demonstrating in the streets against Moshe Dayan in particular. The dashing war hero who had been portrayed with such charisma in 1967 was now faulted for allowing the IDF to deteriorate and failing to respond to warning signals. Others contended that the Bar-Lev line had been a "trap" that created a false sense of security. Still others wondered if the intelligence effort was as keen as it could have been. While Yitzhak never analyzed the war with me in this way—and he had been away from the military for five years at this point—he had strong convictions that the responsibility was as great or greater on the political level as on the military.

A governmental investigatory team—the Agranat Commission (named for Israel's Supreme Court justice Shimon Agranat)—was appointed to determine if military neglect led to the damage done in the Yom Kippur War. Assessing governmental responsibility was not the province of the commission. It was structured this way by Dayan, so that he would not in any event take the blame, but the people tended to hold him accountable nonetheless. When the commission delivered its report, all the blame was placed on the military, and General Elazar had no choice but to resign. Yitzhak was outraged and asked that the report be returned to be rewritten. How could the investigating authorities hold the chief of staff alone responsible? Was this the kind of backing the Israeli government gave to its chief of staff? When Elazar walked out of the cabinet meeting, Yitzhak left with him and was the only cabinet minister to do so.

Golda Meir—to her credit—wouldn't let herself off the hook for ultimate responsibility in the disaster. In the face of public protest, she announced her intention to resign on April 11, 1974. The cabinet tumbled with her, including Yitzhak and Moshe Dayan. Golda's government had been in office just about a month, but there was no requirement to call for new elections. Labor still ruled. The question was who would be appointed the new prime minister.

Everyone expected the mantle to pass to Finance Minister Pinhas Sapir, the strongest man in the cabinet at the time, but he didn't seek the job. One evening, Yitzhak came home with startling news. "Strange," he said, "Sapir claims that I'm his candidate for prime minister." Both of us had trouble believing it. What could have motivated Pinhas Sapir to be a kingmaker rather than pursuing the prime ministership himself? Was it Yitzhak's leadership in the Six-Day War? Was it the fact that he was one of the few popular party leaders not tainted by the ignominy of the '73 war? Or was it that Yitzhak was so akin to Sapir in their understated, selfless, and patriotic style? We did not know. We only knew this: If Sapir's backing was sincere, the only apparent rival would be Shimon Peres, who had been close to Dayan and who immediately declared himself as the countercandidate to Yitzhak. While Yitzhak and Peres clearly saw each other as rivals, they agreed that whoever lost would hold the number-two position of defense minister.

Given that general elections were unnecessary, the vote of the

Knesset to accept the new government would be sufficient. All that had to happen was for the Labor Party to conduct an internal ballot in the Central Committee to decide who would replace Golda as party leader and prime minister. It was believed that one of the strongest factors working against Shimon Peres was his close ties to Moshe Dayan, and that could well have been true.

When Sapir's approval became public, it was still by no means sure Yitzhak would get the nod. He had a lot to do to gain the support of the party on his own merits. A small volunteer headquarters was established to give him a hand. Hundreds of people had to be approached, and that was never an easy matter for Yitzhak, who was naturally shy and reluctant to ask for favors. Everything had to be accomplished in weeks. Quick, quick, quick!

Ezer Weizman—then a member of the right-wing Likud Party—did his best to undercut Yitzhak's campaign for the prime ministership by circulating reports, first within the Labor Party and then to the press, that Yitzhak had suffered a breakdown just before the Six-Day War. Yitzhak described it as Weizman "dropping his bombshell." Three generals and Yitzhak's physician, Dr. Eliahu Gilon, came forward to refute Weizman's claim. A bigger hurdle to his election was the contention that Yitzhak was a political greenhorn: except for a month in office in the Knesset as labor minister, Yitzhak had no experience in the world of elected politics. But perhaps that was his greatest virtue. His credentials of honesty and selfless leadership were impeccable.

Two nights before the vote, I had a dream that I was sitting at a political convention next to a Knesset member named Nava Arad, who had joined the group supporting Yitzhak, but the results of the voting remained shadowy in the dream. Listening to the radio on Monday, April 22, 1974, among a group of friends, I heard the decision broadcast as soon as reporters learned the news: Yitzhak was the Labor Party choice to form the new government, based on the secret ballot vote of the Central Committee. The first person to call me and congratulate me was none other than our friend Nava! Yitzhak won by a majority of forty-four votes. Yitzhak was now certain to be elected the next prime minister of Israel by the Knesset. Suddenly, almost overnight, "the hero who was not there" was to become the leader of the nation. Yitzhak was puzzled and surprised—not unhappy, but cautious. I was elated and stunned all at once. There were telegrams, a telephone that never stopped ringing, endless flowers, but both of us were too realistic to let this euphoria get the better of us.

Yitzhak's election meant fast action on some political appointments. Yigal Allon was slated to replace Abba Eban as foreign minister and Shimon Peres was named the new defense minister. Peres had never served in the military, but he had been deputy defense minister. His appointment seemed necessary at the time to obtain a ruling coalition within the party. Yitzhak later said he regretted the Peres appointment, since Peres lacked combat experience in the IDF and made various policy suggestions with which Yitzhak disagreed.

Putting together a coalition was no picnic. Yitzhak presented his cabinet choices to the president of Israel on June 3, 1974. An eleven-hour debate in the Knesset—long even by Israeli standards—followed Yitzhak's speech outlining his government and his agenda. Once again, our American friends Norman and Diane Bernstein were by our side—flying over for the presentation of the government. After the long ordeal, Diane insisted on going to the Western Wall in the Old City of Jerusalem and implanted a rolled scroll of paper between the stones. According to legend, this is the most effective way to request divine intervention. Did it work? Do I know? I know only that Yitzhak's government was accepted, and he became Israel's sixth prime minister. He rolled up his sleeves and got to work.

There was no little concern about Yitzhak's lack of experience in party politics. He may have been an expert in defense matters and international affairs, but what about his grasp of domestic matters? One of his best tutors was the finance minister in the cabinet, Yehoshua Rabinowitz, the onetime mayor of Tel Aviv. Every Saturday morning he would faithfully appear at our home, wearing his top hat and holding his little notebook in his hand. I would say smilingly, "Yehoshua has come for morning prayers." Perhaps prayers were in order. The financial losses of the Yom Kippur War were as great as Israel's entire 1973 GNP in scale. Yitzhak believed that a finance minister needed the strong support and collaboration of the prime minister if he was to succeed in his job. They worked closely, hand in hand, and the results were indeed quite substantial.

Yitzhak instituted a series of austerity measures, including devaluing the currency and restricting imports and luxury spending. He did what he could to move jobs from the public to the private sector, investing in education and trying to create incentives for agricultural workers to relocate to the industrial sector. Yitzhak knew that healing the Israeli economy was a long-term proposition, but the public didn't understand this easily, and a number of strikes resulted. Even as he sought to stimulate growth, he worked at reducing the budget deficit in a dramatic tax reform, allocated money to social security in order to support the very poor, and tried to close social gaps, which became ever bigger and more disturbing. Israel had reached the point where wealthy companies had come into being in agriculture and industry, and its upper class was more pronounced than ever.

Despite his inexperience, Yitzhak was immensely concerned with the socioeconomic problems of the seventies: tax evasion, corruption, and the economic inequalities amongst the social classes. There also was the issue of summertime hours demanded by government office workers. Office workers wanted the workday to end at three P.M. Yitzhak bitterly commented, "Why do the services, sitting in air-conditioned offices, deserve summertime hours, while the men who stand near open boiling furnaces in the factories would never dream of this luxury?"

In his first term as prime minister, there were those (both inside and outside the government) who took advantage of Yitzhak's lack of domestic experience all the time. Not that there weren't achievements during those three and a half years of the first term. There were. Quite visibly, the cabinet was certainly revamped from the standpoint of age. They were nearly all Sabras; the era of the "founding fathers" had passed. Yitzhak was only fifty-two when he became prime minister—at the time, the youngest in Is-raeli history. Most other new cabinet members also were in their fifties. That was a big change for Israel, which had essentially been governed by those we called "the Giants."

∞ Our little nuclear family was changing greatly. Dalia had joined the army at the end of 1968 and had begun law school in 1971. She married in 1972 and her children were born in 1974 (Jona-than) and 1977 (Noa). Our son, Yuval, was still in the army in the mid-seventies on his second tour of duty.

In December 1973 we moved to an apartment on Harav Ashi Street in the Tel Aviv suburb of Neve Avivim, as Yitzhak was cam-paigning for the Knesset. We kept the apartment as our private res-idence in Tel Aviv after Yitzhak was elected. When he became prime minister on June 24, 1974, there were two options for the prime minister's residence in Jerusalem. Israeli governmental resi-dences are not quite the same thing as, say, 10 Downing Street or the White House. Of the available residences, Golda Meir's or Abba Eban's, we chose that of Abba Eban, who was leaving his post as foreign minister. This house was in much better condition and would cost less to renovate, but Eban's post-governmental home took months to prepare and we lived on a temporary basis at the King David Hotel, one of the world's great hotels and the site of much official entertaining we were to do.

After Yitzhak had been in office just a couple of weeks, Richard Nixon came to visit, during the peak of the Watergate scandal. He was the first American president ever to travel to Israel. Nixon was embattled, and he resigned less than two months later, in August 1974. Yitzhak was deeply concerned about losing a U.S. president who had been so supportive of Israeli interests. Nixon was cheered by welcoming crowds and feted at a state dinner. He may have been in trouble at home, but he'd earned a place in the hearts of Is-raelis for his support during the Yom Kippur War. Despite the breaking scandal, he made a strong appearance and gave an excel-lent speech at the Knesset dinner.

When Yitzhak made his first trip to the United States as prime minister in September 1974, Gerald Ford was in office as president. After our years in Washington, this visit was exciting and felt very much like a homecoming for us. I joined Yitzhak on the trip, and we stayed at Blair House, which was a memorable experience. There was a lady in charge of the house who had been there for many years and who kept it in the most perfect spic-and-span condition. Every piece of silver shone. The rooms were filled with the most fantastic antique pieces. Altogether, we were made to feel we had full run of the house and were free to entertain friends, whenever and however we wished. The feeling of Blair House changed a little over time when the hostess retired, though not much. We were to stay there many more times. On each visit, it always felt like coming back home.

Betty Ford guided me and Vivian Dinitz, the wife of Israeli ambassador Simcha Dinitz, through the White House, which we had seen before, but this time we were shown Richard Nixon's private study with its fireplace. A curiously strong smell of smoke enveloped the room. During the Watergate crisis, which had ended in the previous month, President Nixon locked himself away in this retreat with a fire blazing while running the air conditioning full blast. The odor was so strong it was as though a fire had been kindled there the night before.

It was also on this trip that Betty Ford asked Yitzhak to dance after a White House dinner. It was a first—Yitzhak managed to avoid dancing even as ambassador. He tried to dodge the invitation, pleading he didn't know how to dance and that he was afraid of stepping on her toes. But she persisted, and Yitzhak made a heroic effort although truthfully, he had *never* danced before. When I next glanced at Yitzhak over the shoulder of my dance partner, President Ford, Henry Kissinger had cut in to save the day, saying he needed to talk with Yitzhak. On the same visit, Nancy Kissinger hosted a dinner party for me on a yacht on the Potomac River. We had known Nancy a long time before they were married and we always liked her very much.

Our first state visit had serious diplomatic dimensions as well. Yitzhak, who had known Gerald Ford when he was House minority leader, discussed America's continuing support for Israel and how a clear long-term relationship for weapons deliveries could help Israel project its future training needs and overall military program. Yitzhak also emphasized that Israel sought a sure "piece of peace" for any "piece of land" it might surrender in negotiations with our neighbors. Fortunately for Yitzhak and for Israel, Henry Kissinger continued on as secretary of state during the Ford years, providing continuity in Middle East policy after Nixon's resignation and until Jimmy Carter's election.

Vivian Dinitz hosted a luncheon for me in the Israel room of the Kennedy Center. Chief Justice Warren Burger's wife attended the luncheon. I had been deeply impressed by a visit I had made to a center for autistic children in Ellicott City, Maryland; treatment of autism is a major charitable interest of mine in Israel. When I mentioned my tour with excitement, Mrs. Burger said, "You people. You're so intelligent! I just can't imagine that you could have any problems like that." I could scarcely believe my ears: to think that autism had anything to do with race or intelligence, but I guess I have learned over the years that any comment beginning with "You people . . ." is bound not to have a very informed conclusion.

I discovered a warm, sensitive, and unassuming person in Betty Ford, though she suffered terrible pain, which led to the chemical dependency problems that eventually became so public. Both Yitzhak and I liked the Fords a good deal—he was an honest and principled president, and Yitzhak and he developed a sound working relationship and good chemistry.

∞ In 1974, the annual rate of inflation rose to more than 50 percent. Only with sustained peace could the Israeli economy make a lasting recovery. Internationally, Yitzhak believed that peace with Egypt would be the backbone for any long-term peace agreement in the Middle East.

To make peace with Egypt, Yitzhak had to build a personal bridge to Anwar Sadat. Sadat's predecessor, Abdel Gamal Nasser, personified the ultimate villain for Israel, vowing to throw the

Jews in the sea. Yitzhak actually met Nasser during the War of Independence, when Nasser was an officer with an Egyptian unit that had surrendered to an IDF command in Iraq-Sudan, which included Yigal Allon and Yitzhak. When Yitzhak explained how the Israelis had managed to effectively drive the British out of Palestine, Nasser's reaction was not so wild and wooly as his later rhetoric. He commented admiringly to Yitzhak, "You know we are fighting the wrong enemy at the wrong place at the wrong time." Anwar Sadat had succeeded Nasser to the presidency of Egypt in 1970, when Nasser died suddenly of a heart attack. Sadat was widely seen as a submissive underling while Nasser was alive, but with Nasser gone, Sadat came into his own. He put the Egyptian economy into gear and began to tread an increasingly independent line from the position of the united Arab cause.

On the diplomatic level, together with Henry Kissinger and Foreign Minister Yigal Allon, Yitzhak struggled to achieve an interim agreement with Egypt in 1975 for limited territorial concessions in return for non-aggression guarantees. This agreement fell short of a formal peace treaty, but was to prove an important step on the road to peace between our two countries. Even then, public sentiment about the concessions required to make peace with the Arabs was mixed. There were demonstrators on the streets of Jerusalem and Tel Aviv chanting, "Go home, Kissinger!" and "Go home, Rabin!"

Yitzhak prized Kissinger's powers of observation. Dr. Kissinger was personally acquainted with people in the Arab world whom the Israeli leadership knew only by reputation. He aided us in understanding their character and motivations and helped us anticipate how they would react to certain gestures or proposals. When the Yom Kippur War concluded, for example, Kissinger was the one who understood that it would be unwise to defeat Anwar Sadat totally, thereby creating a humiliation that would later prove a barrier to negotiating peace. Kissinger's diplomatic sensitivity was profoundly misunderstood in Israel for trying to save Sadat's face by allowing him to salvage the Egyptian Third Army, which Israel had threatened to obliterate in the last hours of the Yom

Kippur War. Kissinger was considered a traitor by many Israelis. Yitzhak, of course, felt that Kissinger was a "virtuoso" at the negotiating table—at times a formidable one—and that time would prove his great contribution to Israel's defense and security.

No period of their collaboration to achieve peace in the Middle East ever surpassed the marathon of shuttle diplomacy during the spring of 1975. Henry Kissinger is of course Jewish. While he, I felt, always had the interests of Israel deep in his heart, he did his best to keep his personal feelings in check. He was an evenhanded mediator between Israel and the Arab nations—at times for us Israelis maddeningly so! In the end, that made him more credible to all parties. Sometimes the dialogue between him and Yitzhak became heated. And the relationship wasn't without its moments of cunning on both sides. For example, when it became a pattern for the U.S. diplomats to visit Israel for meetings in the afternoon after spending the morning in Cairo, Yitzhak and the other members of the Israeli team began sleeping late before meeting with the Americans. Well into the night they would still be alert, while the usually energetic Dr. Kissinger would grow weary and was ready to call it a day.

In March 1975, the negotiations had reached an impasse over the extent of Israel's withdrawal from the Sinai, and Kissinger was simply unable, he felt, to return to Cairo with a viable compromise. When Kissinger blamed Israel for that breakdown in progress—which largely hinged on defining terms about aggression and belligerency—Yitzhak challenged him and pinned the responsibility instead on "Egypt's intransigence." The situation was in a stalemate. Yitzhak and Dr. Kissinger met privately at the airport before the secretary of state departed. While their conversation was going on, I remember talking with the journalists Marvin Kalb and Marilyn Berger and I recall their hoping that Israel had not taken too hard a line that might provoke war. In his tête-à-tête with Dr. Kissinger, Yitzhak made an unusually emotional comment, I later learned. "I regard every IDF soldier as my responsibility—almost as if he were my son," he said. "You know that my own son is in command of a tank platoon on the front line in Sinai. My daughter's husband commands a tank battalion there. In the event of war, I know what their fate might be. But Israel is unable to accept this agreement on its present terms, and there is nothing I can do but bear that heavy burden of responsibility—the national as well as the personal." When Kissinger later spoke to the press before boarding his plane, his voice betrayed deep feelings, and tears welled in his eyes. Was it the strain? The threat of war? Was it a bruised ego? To this day, I don't know what brought about his emotional appearance, but perhaps it was in part Yitzhak's somber realism. And perhaps, too, Kissinger's deep disappointment: his good friend Yitzhak was now ready to fail him in a crucial moment.

In July 1975 a world conference recognizing the International Women's Year took place in Mexico City. The Israeli Foreign Office got wind that Anwar Sadat's wife, Jehan, would head the Egyptian delegation and I was then asked to lead the Israeli one. The opportunity to build bridges at such a conference couldn't be bypassed, since the chasm between advanced economies (including Israel's) and the Third World was growing. The backdrop of impoverished Mexico highlighted that gap. Zionism was written off as yet another evil force in international affairs, and the PLO—a far more radical and destructive terrorist organization than the PLO of today—was enjoying days of favor at the United Nations. Chairman Arafat was received as a statesman and hero when he got up to speak before the UN General Assembly in 1974, still wearing the holster for his Beretta. Despite their repulsive terrorist attacks, the PLO had become something of a cause célèbre among left-wing and liberal circles of the day. In the same month, the UN adopted two resolutions endorsing self-determination for the Palestinians and conferring observer status to the PLO at the UN.

As soon as I landed in Mexico, and throughout my stay, the media attempted to orchestrate a meeting between Mrs. Sadat and me. Each of us repeatedly gave the same replies. I said that I had every hope of meeting her. She said, "No! I cannot meet her. The Israelis are holding territories of ours, and a meeting between the two of us will not solve the problems that trouble our nations." I was impressed with her presence in the various conference meetings, and my security person said that at the plenary sessions she was continually looking over at me, but nothing of consequence happened between us during the sessions. As host of the American news program *Issues and Answers,* Peter Jennings tried to arrange an interview in which the two of us would share the spotlight in a single broadcast. Mrs. Sadat agreed to be interviewed only if she and I appeared in separately recorded segments. On the first day of the conference, she delivered her remarks. She left Mexico a day later. And so our meeting, which could have happened so easily, was postponed.

When I got up to deliver a speech during the Mexico City conference, a few days after Mrs. Sadat left, two-thirds of the delegates, including those from the Communist Bloc and the Arab world (among them the additional attendees from Egypt), left the hall. Remaining were the United States, the Western Europeans, and a smattering of other nations. Someone had alerted me that a walkout would occur just before the meeting convened. In anticipation, I scribbled a new introduction to my talk as I was being introduced. The walkout forged my resolve to speak, but I felt more sadness than anger. No way would I let the situation intimidate me into not talking. I turned to UN Secretary General Kurt Waldheim and said:

> *Mr. Secretary, we shall wait for the "exodus" to end. . . .*
> *I am aware of the existing differences of opinion between*
> *members and peoples, but the unwillingness even to listen to*
> *each other stands in conflict with all the exalted objectives of*
> *this conference. Such a pity that women are still today sub-*
> *ject to all sorts of political manipulations by men, and they*
> *have neither the power nor ability to separate this confer-*
> *ence from the political contradictions that exist in the*
> *United Nations.*

That drew enthusiastic applause. I went on.

I speak in the name of the women of a small country, who time after time have shed their tears over the loss of sons, brothers, and husbands, who have fallen in war in defense of their country. The price that we paid for our independence was high, and the sacrifice heavy. To the same degree, we are aware of the suffering of mothers across the borders.

The time has come for us to raise our voices together, and as women locked into the reality of day-to-day life and isolated by frontiers fortified with deadly weapons, to attempt to show more understanding for our distress. Peace is such a simple word, but in our region it is full of illusions. The true expression of peace must be not the creation of diplomats but the relations between peoples on a personal and human basis.

We are an ancient people. Our heritage is peace. Our roots are in the land from which first came the message "Love thy neighbor . . ." Peace and security are supreme objectives for Israel. War solves nothing, as has been proven over the last twenty-seven years. Our area thirsts for peace for the benefit of all the peoples living there. Our true enemies are poverty, illiteracy, disease, and inequality of opportunity. I appeal to this conference, help us, the women of Israel, to meet with our sisters from across the frontiers; help us translate our monologues into dialogues of understanding and conciliation. For this is apparently the purpose of this international conference: to destroy barriers, to foster welfare, to eliminate inequality, and to create a better world in which to bring up our children in happiness, peace, and security.

The standing ovation at the end of my comments—the kisses and the embraces of those who were determined to stay and hear my remarks—made up for the mass walkout, but a declaration issued by seventy-seven nonaligned nations at this conference still condemned Zionism as a hideous evil, ranking it "along with colonialism, neocolonialism, imperialism, foreign domination and occupation, apartheid, and racial discrimination." The whole experience left me depressed and caused me much pain. I was representing the Jewish state, and so much of the world was running away from the Jewish people as from the plague. The sense of isolation and animosity was severe. But some twenty years later, I can say that I wouldn't have changed a thing about the way that I spoke or conducted myself.

The international reputation enjoyed by Israel in this period sank even lower: In November 1975, the UN General Assembly passed Resolution 3379, which condemned Israel as "the racist regime of occupied Palestine." Zionism itself was dismissed as "a form of . . . racial discrimination." Yitzhak felt this was a horrible slap in the face: pro-Arab, pro–Third World, pro-Soviet, and anti-Israeli. One thing he felt it was not: a surprise!

Despite the cold wave of international hostility, the treaties of the interim agreement between Israel and Egypt were ultimately signed toward summer's end, on September 4, 1975. This understanding restored parts of the Sinai and its oil fields to Egypt and allowed the Suez Canal to be reopened. Israel agreed to withdraw an additional eighteen miles from the Sinai, abandoning the Mitla and Gidi mountain passes. Egypt occupied four miles of the territory. On the Israeli side, the benefits also were clear. U.S. arms sales to Israel, which had been interrupted, were once again flowing, and that meant especially important F-16 fighters. The interim peace agreement with Egypt in 1975 ultimately led to Sadat's historic trip to Jerusalem in 1977 and then the Camp David meetings late in 1978, and the signing of a peace treaty with Israel in March 1979. Yitzhak's groundbreaking work in realizing the Interim Accords demonstrated his continuing commitment to peace and his constant striving to build a structure upon which peace could be sustained.

∞ In 1975, one of the most memorable state visits we made was to Germany. It was the first trip of an incumbent Israeli prime minister to Germany since relations between Israel and West Germany were established. It was also my first return to Germany since our family had fled the country in 1933. Initially, my resistance to owning anything German-made was considerable, but Yitzhak never had these sentiments and held no reservations whatsoever. (On a trip to the United States in the 1950s, he came back with a Grundig hi-fi. I stared at him in amazement! He could have bought any brand, but he bought a German-made Grundig.) Years later, I was anxious about my return to Germany and emotionally did not quite know what to expect.

Helmut Schmidt was chancellor of Germany at the time, and I wrestled for a long time over an appropriate gift. Initially, I considered a beautiful Polish *hanukiah*—the candelabrum used on the festive Jewish holiday of Hanukkah—but decided against it since so many treasures of European Jewry had been either looted or destroyed in the war. Why bring back to Germany an important Jewish object such as that? The gift we finally selected was an Eilat stone, because the chancellor was a collector of geological specimens.

Bergen-Belsen was the first death camp I had ever visited, and it was frightening beyond words. The mass grave sites are tranquil grass-covered mounds today. They bear plaques with numbers in the magnitude of 5,000 or 20,000—estimates of the bodies in each section. As I gazed at this site, my thoughts focused on my father and how my family likely would have shared this destiny, had he not been so swift and decisive about moving to Palestine.

Berlin prompted reflections of a different sort. When we ascended the scaffolding overlooking the Brandenburg Gate and peered into East Berlin, my mind returned to Jerusalem before it was united and how we used to see the Jaffa and Damascus Gates from atop the Notre Dame convent. I'm sure that Berliners—and Germans generally—had similar feelings before the Wall tumbled in 1989.

We found a special edition newspaper in our hotel room. The German publisher Axel Springer had emblazoned the front page of *Die Welt* with a Hebrew headline: "Welcome, Yitzhak Rabin!"

From Berlin we went to Bonn. At full military honors in Bonn, the band played the same national anthem that had been Germany's during the Hitler era as Yitzhak and I stood watching and listening side by side. Then the strains of "Hatikvah" followed as the Israeli flag was honored. What would my parents have thought of all this? I thought to myself. As the chancellor's wife, Hannelore, and I walked through the gardens after the ceremony, she remarked, " 'Hatikvah!' I still remember the first time I heard your anthem. It was at the Bremerhaven shipyards when a Zim ship was launched. When the band played 'Hatikvah' we all cried."

Cultural touches abounded. Chancellor Schmidt is a player of classical piano and a skillful conversationalist. During the visit, Hannelore Schmidt presented me with nosegays of sweetpeas; I had told her of my fondness for that flower because my mother would arrange them on the table amid my birthday gifts. We stayed at the official guest residence, Schloss Gimnich, outside of Bonn, founded in the eleventh century and enlarged in each of the important artistic periods that followed, with lush and beautifully manicured gardens. The German government leased the castle from a young baron with whom a small group of us visited. During our conversation, he walked over to a cabinet and removed two stunning antique *Jewish* candelabra—replicas of those Titus had taken to Rome from Solomon's Temple in Jerusalem. He said, "Mrs. Rabin, I think that these two belong rather more to you than they do to me. You will make me very happy if you take them with you to Israel."

Germany was an excursion to a very different and provocative world—returning to the evidence of unspeakable tragedy but with the realization that while you do not forget, you must build a bridge of reconciliation. Yitzhak was well aware of the economic importance of German arms shipments and World War II restitution payments—payments made to Holocaust survivors and their families since the mid-1950s that had been vehemently opposed by the Herut party under Menachem Begin's leadership. Ben-Gurion resolved to accept these monies and Yitzhak had concurred with him. All these years later, he felt positively about the trip. The need to have Germany as an ally in the court of world opinion didn't escape him.

∞ One of the great challenges in Yitzhak's first term as prime minister took place far away from Israeli soil, on the tarmac of the airport in Entebbe, Uganda. On June 27, 1976, two German and two Palestinian hijackers captured and diverted an Air France jet headed to Paris from Tel Aviv, after the plane made a routine stopover in Athens. About a third of the 230 passengers were Israelis. At first, the situation was very confusing: What were the demands? Where would the plane end up? No one seemed to know. I heard the news at home over the radio. Yitzhak was in a regular Sunday cabinet meeting. We didn't really have a chance to talk about what was happening until he returned home that night.

The plane was refused landing in Sudan and touched down at Entebbe. Its further progress was stalled as the terrorists voiced their demands. They wanted fifty-three so-called freedom fighters being held in five different countries released—Israel, West Germany, Switzerland, Kenya, and France. It was a global ransom—so many Israelis were involved yet the prisoners to be released were being held in other countries. This was a dreaded situation for another reason: Uganda and Israel were not on friendly terms, and no one knew what the response would be if Israel attempted a rescue.

As this crisis descended on Yitzhak, a family milestone was about to take place. The ceremony marking Dalia's admission to the bar was to be held on the Tuesday of the hijacking crisis. We were of course invited to attend, but she was very conscious of the pressures on Yitzhak and said more than once, "*Abba,* you don't actually *have* to come!" Yitzhak insisted that he wanted to be there, and I believe he truly did. At the ceremony at Neveran Auditorium on the campus of Hebrew University, the speeches were endless, and impatience got the better of Yitzhak. He kept glancing at his wristwatch. After a while, I quietly reminded him that, since he had chosen to come, he needed to stay through to the end. At the time, I didn't know all the complex dilemmas buzzing in his head.

Public attention was riveted on the destiny of that plane. Efforts to reach a diplomatic solution were under way in Paris. I remember the words of Avishai Davidson as the discussion of alternatives wore on. His son, his daughter-in-law, and their two children were being held as hostages: "You agreed to every price demanded of you for the return of coffins after the Yom Kippur War," he said. "You released thousands of prisoners of war in order to get back the remains. Are you waiting now for them to be returned in coffins? Save them while they're still alive! Pay any price for the lives of our children!" There was passionate public debate over whether concessions were acceptable. Shimon Peres then took a strong position in the cabinet that a rescue should be attempted. Fine, Yitzhak said, but *where's the plan?* To advocate a rescue on principle is one thing. To have an operationally sound and tested plan is quite another. Yitzhak responded to terrorist acts on a case-by-case basis. For every military rescue operation that was attempted, many more were discarded because the plans to execute them were simply not adequately reliable or thorough.

Ultimately, a plan was devised and presented to Yitzhak. The rescue had to be cloaked in secrecy. Dubbed the "Hercules Plan," it called for Israeli planes to land in Uganda interspersed between normal landings and takeoffs. The plan was devised by military staff members working with the Mossad, the Israeli intelligence agency, and it was carefully rehearsed. Yitzhak was later convinced that a fundamental reason it worked was a credit to the precision of the intelligence information that had been gathered on the Entebbe site. "Every detail, every phase of the operation," Yitzhak later wrote in his memoirs, "was etched in my brain." He also says he was calm *before* the raid was executed; he believed it was the best possible option—though not without risks.

I learned of the plan at six P.M. on Saturday evening, July 3, after the planes had left Israel and two hours before Yitzhak left our home for the command center to oversee the mission. Yitzhak had described the raid to me himself: Intelligence established that the hostages were held in the terminal building. Four Hercules transports and a Boeing 707 command center—all Israeli planes— were en route to Entebbe airport. Unidentified by radar at the airport since it would land on the tail of a scheduled British cargo flight, the first Hercules would unload a Mercedes limousine and two Land Rovers that replicated Ugandan president Idi Amin's standard entourage convoy. The troops in the vehicle would proceed to the terminal, while the other transports landed, providing support forces and a withdrawal option. The terminal building was to be stormed and the liberated hostages escorted to a waiting plane.

The diplomatic initiative continued in Paris as a diversionary tactic. At seven o'clock Yitzhak was talking to the head of the negotiating team in Paris over the phone in a very detached, low-key way, actually *prolonging* the conversation with questions about details and nuances in order to avoid giving the slightest hint that the planes had already been launched. What nerves of steel the man had in a crisis! Striding out the door, he said to me, "Tomorrow morning, either Israel's shares will be sky-high, or I will be hanged in Kikar HaMedina."

The landing at Entebbe was flawless, the terminal was attacked, all six terrorist guards were killed, and the rescued hostages were sped back to Israel. The casualties numbered five: three hostages killed during the raid, a hospitalized hostage later murdered in Kampala, and a very brave unit commander—Yonatan Netanyahu (brother of the current prime minister). Yitzhak felt terrible about the losses, but the daring rescue mission was hailed worldwide as a stunning military accomplishment. The success of the raid rivaled news coverage of the celebration of the United States Bicentennial.

The raid on Entebbe was both a peak in Yitzhak's first administration and a high point before a difficult decline over which he had little control. Things started to go awry in December 1976, when Israel received the initial delivery of fighter jets from the United States. Because of airborne refueling and other complications, the jets arrived on a Friday afternoon, the eve of Shabbat. Since a ceremony in Israel to welcome the critical new technology was involved and many officials attended, one of the religious parties came forward with a no-confidence motion contending the

Sabbath had been violated. Because Yitzhak's coalition contained other religious parties, this seemingly trivial incident in the Knesset had an unforeseen ripple effect.

Ultimately Yitzhak and his entire cabinet, rejecting the constant pressure of the religious parties, decided to resign and call for new elections. "I'm tired of being squeezed and blackmailed by them on every occasion," he said to me. He was hoping to oust them from the coalition. Following the rules of parliamentary practice, Yitzhak was now heading a caretaker government. Elections originally scheduled for the fall of 1977 were advanced to May of that year. Many in Labor accused Yitzhak of having broken long-term ties with the National Religious Party, but the ultra-Orthodox had roadblocked many initiatives, including authorizing construction for a building that might house Reform services or a public pool where people could swim on the Sabbath.

Meanwhile, in March 1977, Yitzhak made his first trip to Washington to meet with President Carter, who had taken the oath of office just two months earlier. Jimmy Carter was the first American president with whom Yitzhak did not see eye to eye. Yitzhak believed a chief executive had to rely on his staff, as did Presidents Nixon and Ford. Yitzhak used to subject his staff's reports to intense scrutiny, but he was also accustomed to strong professionals in subordinate roles. President Carter was different. He always felt a need to climb into the details of an issue.

Yitzhak didn't believe Jimmy Carter delegated well. Also President Carter could be unpredictable. At the end of one long day of debates and a stag dinner at the White House, President Carter excused his guests and said, "Now the prime minister and I must have a private meeting upstairs." When they had settled down, President Carter said to Yitzhak, "Now, Mr. Prime Minister, tell me what you *really* think." Yitzhak was shocked.

"Mr. President, we had long talks today. I don't have two agendas or opinions. I have only one and you heard all about it today." Later, President Carter spoke at length about his religious beliefs and Yitzhak said his eyelids felt very, very heavy. It was late, he had arrived from Israel that morning, and he was exhausted. Before we left Washington, President Carter made an open declaration about the rights of the Palestinians to their homeland.

For several reasons, then, Yitzhak was having a difficult time with the U.S. administration. That situation wasn't helped by Yitzhak's having been such a vocal supporter of Richard Nixon in 1972. The essence of the matter was not that Nixon was a Republican and Carter was a Democrat—Yitzhak's relations with members of the Johnson administration were excellent, and later, with the Clinton team, superb. It had more to do with the policy-making style of the Carter White House.

Back home in Israel, being a caretaker prime minister exposed Yitzhak to attacks from both rivals and the media. Not only was he facing the tough rhetoric of his Likud opponent, Menachem Begin, but Shimon Peres announced he would openly seek to be Labor's prime ministerial candidate in opposition to Yitzhak. The two frequently clashed on policy issues, including the construction of Jewish settlements in the occupied West Bank, which Peres wanted massively increased and Yitzhak wanted to limit. Yitzhak attempted to negotiate a long-term understanding with Peres that would enlarge his platform for speaking out in exchange for withdrawing his candidacy. But nothing concrete resulted, and the two were now engaged in a second battle for the party leadership. A party convention of nearly three thousand was to choose the Labor candidate. On February 22, Yitzhak was able to beat back the Peres challenge and received the nod, but the margin was slim—only 1,445 to 1,404, with 16 abstaining.

The media began to hack away, driven by an array of tantalizing leads. There were financial scandals involving the Histadrut—the Central Labor Council—and questionable public investments in Britain. Facing public inquiry, the housing minister committed suicide. Yitzhak was not involved in any of these incidents, but generally the conviction that the Labor Party was corrupt acquired momentum and a life of its own. Ultimately, and almost predictably, the spotlight shifted to Yitzhak and me. He was criticized for honoraria he had accepted as a public speaker while serving in the United States, although the amounts were modest, and his predecessors had done the very same thing. Then came the revelations over our American bank accounts that thrust me onto center stage.

In March 1977, I was with Yitzhak in Washington on the day of his first meetings with President Carter. The following morning I wanted to close out a checking and savings account we'd maintained for everyday business while Yitzhak had been ambassador. Although Yitzhak was technically a co-signer on the accounts, he never actually used them. The combined accounts had scarcely $20,000 in them at their high points and $2,000 when they were closed. This closeout procedure was to require some time, and security people were impatiently waiting to shuttle me to a ceremony at the American University, where Yitzhak was to be given an honorary degree, so I let the checking account stand, moving whatever was left in the savings account to the checking account. I planned to settle the matter on our next visit to the States.

At the time, Israel had rigorous banking laws that prohibited a private citizen from maintaining a foreign bank account unless they were actually residing abroad. A newspaper reporter named Dan Margalit got wind of the bank accounts.* The sensationalized story about our bank accounts became public on March 15. Finance Minister Rabinowitz was not content with a fine. Attorney General Aharon Barak, presently head of the Israeli Supreme Court, insisted on a fine for Yitzhak and a court trial for me. The bank account matter was an oversight, an unintentional violation, and it would be hard to imagine another world leader—certainly no one of Yitzhak's integrity—being imperiled by such a technical breach. I stood trial on April 17 for illegally maintaining a bank account in a foreign country while not residing in that country. Although Dalia was not my legal counsel, she sat beside me. Yitzhak repeatedly asked if he could join me in the courtroom, but I insisted that he stay away. When I was in the courtroom, it was like an out-of-body experience. The judgment was far harsher

---

Television viewers will remember Margalit as the moderator of the Peres-Netanyahu debate televised immediately before the 1996 Israeli elections.

than anybody expected. The judge gave me a lecture that many found outrageously stern and the choice of paying a 250,000 Israeli-pound fine—approximately the price of a decent condominium in those days—or serving a year in jail. We paid the fine with the help of money borrowed from friends, whom we later repaid.

Hundreds of people sent supportive letters. Some even sent checks, which, of course, we returned. A Likud member of the Knesset wrote a touching letter about how the incident had no shame attached to it, which particularly moved Yitzhak, since it came from a member of the opposition. One dear fellow even offered to sit out my jail sentence for me!*

Was there justice done? Just a month after the news of our bank accounts was publicized, another prominent Israeli was exposed to have a foreign dollar account in six figures. He wasn't even tried! And the reason couldn't have been more transparent: he was not a political sitting duck.

The most drastic outcome of the bank account revelation, however, had already occurred shortly after the story broke and ten days before the trial took place.

On the evening of Thursday, April 7, all Israel had gone "hoop" crazy. A Cinderella contender whom few expected to reach the finals, the Tel Aviv basketball team, known as the Maccabi, was pitted against an Italian squad from Varese for the basketball championship of Europe. The matchup took place in Belgrade, Yugoslavia. All Israel was glued to their television screens for the game, and jubilation resounded in the streets when the Maccabi won the encounter by a single point. However, this was not to be the big news event of the evening. Not long after the final basket was scored, Yitzhak appeared in an interview on Israeli television.

Yitzhak had decided to announce his resignation.

Yitzhak's decision to resign was both more complex *and* less tortured than many think. First of all, it was totally unlike Nixon's decision to resign, and even Golda's, because no one was clamor-

---

*The law under which I was tried was ultimately repealed.

ing for Yitzhak to quit. Surely he didn't want to abandon his career, but this was not the first time that he had offered his resignation in a crisis. On May 25, 1967, the day after his bout of exhaustion before the Six-Day War, Yitzhak had marched into Levi Eshkol's office on his own initiative and said he had just had a problem with his health, that he felt well, but that the prime minister could have his resignation if he liked. Eshkol waved the idea off and told him to forget the matter. This time the issue wasn't so simple, but neither were the reasons for holding on to the job now as compelling as they were a decade earlier.

I don't know how Yitzhak reasoned, but in retrospect a pragmatist might analyze it this way: Labor was not doing very well. It had not rebuilt its popularity after the 1973 Yom Kippur fiasco. The recent scandals had further shaken the party. Yitzhak had just been endorsed as its candidate by a very slim margin. If the party lost the general elections, he would surely be tagged for the defeat, with the blame most likely pinned on the bank account brouhaha. He would be political history. On the other hand, if he extracted himself before the elections, he could be seen only as scrupulous beyond reproach, which he was. People might accuse him of being politically inexperienced, and he admitted as much. Resigning was a much better guarantee of an eventual political comeback than sticking it out.

Outside of drumming his fingers a good deal on the top of his desk, a habit he had when he was faced with a difficult decision, Yitzhak fundamentally kept his own counsel in this matter. It was often held against Yitzhak that he had no kitchen cabinet. He really did not have close friends that he would confide in. He was his own closest friend, and I was next in line. The most difficult situation he had ever faced previously was certainly right before the Six-Day War. He felt the need to consult with Ben-Gurion and then with Weizman. Where did it get him? Once bitten, twice shy. His attitude in 1977 was quite different. As he wrote in his memoirs, "A man is always truly alone at such times."

Yitzhak always had confidence in his own judgment, and in 1977 that faith was even stronger than it had been in 1967. I remember our son, Yuval, at about the age of nine, saying with authentic conviction and after obviously thinking about it for a long while, "My father is probably the wisest man in the whole country." It's quite possible that Yitzhak believed this, too, and he could well have been right.

While he didn't have a kitchen cabinet, he did have his official staff of advisers, and he had me. He didn't ask the children for advice; he probably felt they were still too young to appreciate the predicament. His position was unshakable. "Nothing will make me withdraw my resignation," he said to me and others before the broadcast. "It's unthinkable for a prime minister to hold office while legal proceedings are being conducted against his family." I told him that I supported his decision, and I think that is what he both wanted and needed to hear.

The public was shocked by the news. The entire televised interview took no more than a quarter of an hour. Dalia, Yuval, and some friends joined us at our home when we returned from the television studio. I remember handing out cups of coffee to our visitors, but the feeling of emotional exhaustion was overwhelming.

Toward me personally, Yitzhak was a classic gentleman from beginning to end of the bank affair. He never chastised me or questioned my judgment. He never asked me how I could have let something like this happen—even though managing the family finances was a duty that had fallen to me in our "division of labor." He never accused me of precipitating his fall from office. Most of all he was there for me—just as he would have been there to rescue a wounded IDF comrade on the battlefield. He felt that he had to step up and share the responsibility, even though it wasn't actually his. Naturally, I felt terrible about the whole episode. But Yitzhak had no patience for dwelling on the matter. We just went forward as two comrades, determined to face the future together.

If I contributed anything to the fine-tuning of Yitzhak's resignation decision, it was to help him not take the matter of honor to excess. He saw three factors as inseparably linked: resigning as prime minister, stepping aside as candidate for the prime minister position, and sharing responsibility with me for the bank account

problem. A much less certain matter was whether he should remain in the Knesset. While Yitzhak's legal counsel had encouraged
him to resign his seat in the Knesset as well as his post as prime
minister, I and other advisers felt that such a step was far too extreme. Fortunately we prevailed, and Yitzhak decided to remain in
the Knesset. When he left office, Yitzhak was given a tiny suite in
the Kiryah, the government office complex. He had one secretary
and a driver and would have had nowhere to put more staff were
he assigned them. Overnight he had moved from prime minister to
back-bencher, just about as quickly as he had catapulted out of political nowhere to the premiership three and a half years earlier.
What next? Yitzhak had no interest in a business career. All he
knew was public service, but he had just suffered a major setback
and neither of us knew where the road would lead now. Still, he
was not defeated in his attitude.

Throughout the bank account incident and Yitzhak's resignation, close friends stood by us with great commitment. Along the
way there also was support from unexpected sources.

At the Ministry of Defense reception on the Day of Independence, we bumped into Meir and Yona Amit, who host an annual
Independence Day singing party at their home. Meir was a general
who later went on to head the Mossad. "You are coming to our
party!" they insisted. Both Yitzhak and I were moved by the
adamant invitation, and attended the party.

At the Defense reception, Moshe Dayan sat with us at the VIP
table and carefully steered the conversation to other topics. Dayan
could be a gifted man of gestures. He talked to me about the
Kissingers, and asked whether I thought they were a good couple.
I described what made them a great couple, how they understood
and respected one another and met each other's needs.

"OK, but do they *love* each other?" Moshe Dayan asked.

"What can you say about love?" I said. "It has so many different facets."

Shimon Peres was at our table, too, and he also was friendly.
Then, in a loud voice, to provoke Peres, who never was a soldier
in the Israeli army, Dayan asked, "Yitzhak, are you wearing your

uniform tomorrow for the parade?" They always wore their uniforms once a year, at the Day of Independence parade. Dayan and Peres had always been close, but at this moment Dayan was proclaiming a bond with Yitzhak that Peres could never share.

Many friends stuck by Yitzhak and visited him. Still a major magnet, especially because of his military achievements, he was a very popular speaker at home and abroad. His pension as chief of staff relieved him of financial pressure. We steadily paid off the loan that covered the fine. Yitzhak was more or less content to find his way out of the post-resignation world slowly and methodically. When he spoke of the scandals in the administration and the bank account problem, Yitzhak would say sardonically, "I can't understand why suddenly all the people close to me are in trouble." When people asked him to point a finger as to the cause of his troubles, he simply said that he believed them to be the result of forces "inside and outside" his own party.

As to the general election, Shimon Peres became the Labor candidate and led the party to the first of the five defeats it suffered in general elections with him heading the ballot. In May 1977, the Labor Party was toppled from eighteen years of unbroken rule in governing Israel.

A group of young people almost immediately clustered around Yitzhak, responding to the drastic unfairness of his departure from the peak of governmental authority and his enormous potential to serve Israel. Among our friends, Niva Lanir founded a discussion group called Urim—"the Bright Lights." She truly felt Yitzhak was the best-qualified person to lead Israel and wanted to begin a movement that would see him regain the prime ministership. The group kept him in touch with the key issues and some of the best minds in Israel. Their meetings both briefed him and linked him with fresh, stimulating ideas that could prove important to him in a new administration.

∽ On February 29, 1980, Yigal Allon suddenly passed away from a heart attack. His coffin lay in state in Afula, and the next day we joined the cortege for the huge funeral and his interment at Kibbutz Ginossar. It has been said that Allon had been Yitzhak's only real commander in his career. Yitzhak always thought of him as a highly skilled diplomat and a brilliant military strategist. Allon had served as foreign minister in Yitzhak's government. He enjoyed foreign diplomacy greatly and executed it well. Allon was adored in Israel, and for years people thronged to his grave on the anniversary of his death. Allon's widow, Ruth, encouraged Yitzhak to persevere with the political beliefs that both Yitzhak and Yigal had shared.

But the belief in Yitzhak was fiercest amongst the people. On Saturday, April 9, 1977, Yitzhak attended a Maccabi Tel Aviv soccer match in the city's Bloomfield Stadium. Two days after his resignation from the post of prime minister, Yitzhak was honored with a standing ovation in a stadium full of cheering people. I think they were acknowledging the greatness of an honest and noble man.

Perhaps, already Israel was awaiting his return.

MR. DEFENSE

During all the upheaval in our life during the spring of 1977, our granddaughter Noa was born in Tel Aviv on March 20. Though she has lush, beautiful hair today, Noa was nearly bald as a toddler. Although Yitzhak loved all three of his grandchildren deeply and equally, he spent more time with Jonathan and Noa because they—due to certain special circumstances—spent a lot of time in our house, so much so that they regarded it as *their* home. Yuval's son, Michael, spent about five years abroad, first in Germany and then in the United States. After serving in the armed forces, Yuval was hired by a computer software firm to represent the business overseas.

Yitzhak taught our children and our grandchildren some very basic lessons. "Be totally at one with yourself," he would say, first and foremost. "The more comfortable you are with yourself, the more confident you will be that you are doing the right thing. Pursue your goals, and don't pay too much attention to what anyone has to say about you." Yitzhak loved being with the grandchildren. Whenever Jonathan wouldn't eat as an infant, Yitzhak would personally take over the task of feeding him—just as he had done with Yuval when he was a baby. Suddenly a spoonful of strained peas or applesauce would become an AMX-13 or Patton tank or a personnel carrier moving through the air in front of

Jonathan's high chair. The spoon would follow a wavy, rolling pattern as though it were speeding across desert sand dunes. Jonathan's eyes would bulge with excitement as the spoon "armor unit" readied for a flanking attack and then pounced into Jonathan's unexpecting mouth. It was a maneuver that Jonathan never tired of, and it always worked!

Yitzhak was capable of extraordinary patience and sensitivity. In early 1995 Jonathan was serving in southern Lebanon, and something was clearly troubling him. He wanted to ask Yitzhak some questions about the government's military policies at Saturday lunch. Somehow, other issues dominated the conversation at the table, and Yitzhak never got the chance to answer Jonathan. That evening, Yitzhak and I were invited to the home of the Egyptian ambassador, who lives not far from our daughter's home. On the way to the ambassador's house, Yitzhak said to me, "You know, Leah, I feel really bad about not having talked with Jonathan at lunch. If you don't mind, I shall drop you at the ambassador's house and go to talk with Jonathan for a while." Half an hour later, Yitzhak arrived, having fulfilled the duties of a grandfather who also happened to have been minister of defense and a great authority on military matters. Yitzhak showed patience of a different sort when he started to teach Noa how to play chess when she was only three.

Yitzhak was certainly patient and methodical during his years out of office (1977–1984 and 1990–1992), and he excelled in using this time to his advantage, cultivating relationships and learning new skills and insights. He could not know that he would be prime minister again, he only believed that his odds for a political comeback would be best if he stayed on top of every major issue of the day. I'm sure that he wanted, in the very least, to be minister of defense again. Each initiative Yitzhak undertook in advance of his second term—advocating a phased peace settlement in the Middle East, resolving the quagmire of Lebanon, maintaining the confidence of the U.S. government in his leadership, and shaping a policy that would match the needs of the emerging Middle East—helped create a bedrock foundation for the achievements of his second term. He emphasized time and again in his talks with decision makers in Israeli business and government how Israel must change its national priorities. Surprising for a person whose background was the military, Yitzhak wanted decreases in the military budget and more money invested in the country's infrastructure—especially for transportation, support for industry, and housing and education. All these programs required a patient, long-term view and appealed to his common sense.

∾ In April 1977, Menachem Begin was elected prime minister, heading the first Likud government in the nation's history. Ezer Weizman became defense minister, and Ariel Sharon was named minister of agriculture. Moshe Dayan was offered the post of foreign minister and couldn't resist the opportunity to restore his image. He abandoned Labor and became an "independent supporter" of Likud. Many were very angry at what he had done. Others could understand it and sympathized with him. He was an important component of Mr. Begin's government, in any case.

The rise of the religious parties under the Likud government concerned Yitzhak because of the growing polarization in the goals of Israeli society. The religious parties had gained more seats and were becoming more vocal, for example, advocating closing streets and movie theaters on Shabbat. The Jewish settlement of the West Bank, begun under Labor but intensified under the Likud, was a political incursion that aggravated him to no end and created an unbearable burden on the defense budget. These settlers were not the Zionists of our time, he believed. These settlements were not self-supporting. Rather than extending Israel's defense capabilities, as the settlers claimed, they were a burden upon it. Regarding his opinion of Begin the man, however, Yitzhak was more measured. I recall one Knesset speech where he sharply attacked Likud policy but did not point the finger at Begin, even though he would have had every reason to do so.

Ironically it looked as though a breakthrough was about to take place in the peace negotiations between Israel and Egypt under a Likud regime. We were in Washington, at the home of Polly Wisener, when CBS anchorman Walter Cronkite asked Anwar Sadat if he would go to Jerusalem were he invited. How skeptical the "Georgetown Crowd" was that this visit would ever materialize. Sadat announced that he would go to Jerusalem before the Egyptian parliament. The initiative moved along quickly, and it was revealed that Sadat would arrive in Jerusalem on Saturday evening, November 19, 1977. I was in Washington, while Yitzhak was on the lecture circuit in New York City. When he heard the news on Thursday, Yitzhak dashed to Kennedy Airport and managed to get a seat on the El Al flight to Tel Aviv. On Friday, I took the shuttle to New York and grabbed a Swissair flight to Israel, just missing Sadat's arrival.

When Yitzhak met Sadat at Ben-Gurion airport, he recognized it as a dramatic moment in the history of Israel. In his memoirs Yitzhak wrote of Sadat's bearing:

> *When I greeted President Sadat on the receiving line, there was no time for anything more than a brief exchange of pleasantries. Yet it was the first time I had ever seen him in the flesh, and I was enormously impressed by the poise with which he handled himself in such a unique situation. Here he was meeting all his former arch-enemies, one after the other, in the space of seconds, and he nonetheless found a way to start off his visit by saying exactly the right thing to each and every one of them.*

He also described the brilliance of Sadat's speech before the Knesset and how Sadat disarmed his audience with his acknowledgment, "I understand your need for security, but not for land." No Arab leader had been so forthright before. Sadat made it clear that he would be willing to negotiate a peace with Israel separately from the other Arab nations.

One can easily recall, still, the intensity of the conflict that existed between our two countries twenty or thirty years ago, yet it is amazing how *easily* these barriers can tumble. I have seen this time and again. When Sadat came to Israel, it marked a monumental turning point. The largest and most powerful Arab nation in the Middle East, through the courageous vision of Sadat, reached out to seek peace.

Yitzhak celebrated the achievement selflessly. His openness to sharing such a dramatic success was one of his greatest and most noble qualities. He was a patriot first and foremost. As his aide Shimon Sheves has put it, "Yitzhak was 'Netto Israel' while all the other politicians were 'Brutto Israel.'" The comparison spins off the economic concept of net (netto) versus gross (brutto) national product. To me, this characterization means that Yitzhak's first and foremost priority was always to focus on what was best, bottom-line, for Israel. He didn't concern himself with grand gestures or glorifying actions. He rejoiced when the Camp David accords were signed in March 1979 in Washington, when Jimmy Carter was president and Cyrus Vance was secretary of state, and he never expressed one word of resentment that this achievement fell into the laps of the Likud. He went to Washington to celebrate with the present government, because it was a celebration of all Israel. On the way to the White House signing ceremony in March 1979, he even told the reporter Ron Ben-Yishai, "If this had happened when I was prime minister, there probably would have been blood on the streets of Israel."

Camp David was really the fulfillment of the "land for peace" principle that underpinned Yitzhak's negotiation with Egypt of the Interim Accords in 1975. Henry Kissinger remarked on this after Yitzhak's death. When Yitzhak "went to the airport to greet Sadat," he said, "he must have had some bittersweet feelings because it really should have happened under him."

Yitzhak had only one criticism of the Camp David Agreement— which today seems ironic, given how attitudes have changed. The surrender of the Sinai resulted in the uprooting of a truly meaningful Jewish settlement area called Yamit. Here were settlements that were truly flourishing. These weren't fake outposts, merely political statements. These people had a genuine, fruitful, and deeply grounded life, which was sadly uprooted and removed for the cause of peace. Prime Minister Menachem Begin, in striking this peace, agreed to the removal of about five thousand Yamit settlers so the Sinai could be returned to Egypt. Yitzhak thought that tougher, more exacting negotiation might have prevented it.

∞ In August 1979, Yitzhak announced the publication of his memoirs, which looked back over fifty-seven years. Many praised the book for its candor, clarity, and strategic insight. Others found it to be too harshly critical of other personalities in its examination of Israeli history. In general, Yitzhak preferred to be candid. It bothered him not to be. In his memoirs, he felt what he said about people was justified. The severest criticism came from supporters of Shimon Peres. Yitzhak's description of Shimon Peres as "an inveterate schemer"* was intentional and, he felt, accurate. Many in the Labor Party were enraged. In an interview he gave to the Israeli media, Yitzhak said it was not his style to insinuate. He simply says things directly—*dugri*—as we say in Hebrew slang. Portions of the memoirs were censored; Israeli government officials had to pass their autobiographical accounts before a censorship panel. Later, the *New York Times* published an account supposedly deleted from the book which they contended was obtained from the English translator. The account alleged that David Ben-Gurion had ordered and Yitzhak had implemented the forced ejection of some fifty thousand Arabs from the cities of Lod and Ramla. The truth: There was an expulsion initiated by both Yigal Allon and Yitzhak, during the War of Independence, that appears to have been done to protect troops under their command. That action seemed to be approved by a gesture Mr. Ben-Gurion made with his hand. The censor had burned the story. Out of context, the story was damaging to Yitzhak.

∞ During the late seventies and early eighties, Islamic fundamentalism spread throughout the Middle East. We had new adver-

*A description found only in the original Hebrew edition of the memoirs.

saries such as Iran, which did not share a border with Israel but were dedicated to financing terrorism and violence against us. For Yitzhak, the word *ayatollah* connoted not just fundamentalism, but an arbitrary authoritarian attitude as well. It subsidized insurgency by the domestic population at the local level so as not to look like an international campaign. In this sense, Yitzhak felt, fundamentalism stole a page out of communism in its operating practices.

The downfall of the shah of Iran marked the end of a very strong liaison between Israel and Iran. Overnight a friendly country turned into a hostile one. In November 1979, Shi'ite fundamentalists seized the U.S. embassy in Tehran. For eight years, beginning in September 1980, Iraq and Iran locked horns over the disputed Shatt al-Arab waterway, with staggering casualties on both sides of the conflict.

Egypt and the growingly fundamentalist Arab world splintered further apart, as exchanges between Egypt and Israel became more commonplace. Jehan Sadat now learned what it was like to be rebuffed at an international forum as well. In 1980, most of the delegates at a UN-organized women's conference held in Copenhagen walked out as she was about to speak because her husband had made peace with Israel. (This conference, which takes place every five years, was actually scheduled to be held in Tehran, but it was moved to Denmark with the downfall of the shah.) I didn't hesitate a moment to send her a telegram that recalled my experience in Mexico City: "What a shame that this charade continues. . . ."

∞ In July 1980, Israel declared unified Jerusalem its capital, but international recognition was not to follow, and the international community kept their embassies in Tel Aviv. The Vatican, for example, didn't set up diplomatic relations with Israel until 1994 and it has yet to recognize Jerusalem as the legitimate capital of Israel. After Yitzhak was murdered, my children and I visited the Vatican at the Pope's invitation in December 1995. During the course of our conversation, John Paul II said that Jerusalem had double significance—as the capital of Israel and the capital of three faiths.

My children insisted, "Remember to tell the press what he said," and I didn't forget to do so. The media took great interest in the Pope's remarks. For the Pope to acknowledge Jerusalem as the capital of Israel is a statement of enormous political consequence. Perhaps he didn't mean to say it. (The Vatican immediately published an interpretation that softened the intent of the statement.) But my children and I unequivocally heard the Pope refer to Jerusalem as the capital of Israel.

In January 1981, the international political tide turned once more. Ronald Reagan became America's president, and George Shultz was sworn in as U.S. secretary of state. Nearly the first consequence of this change was the release of the American hostages in Tehran. Throughout his two terms, Ronald Reagan was an excellent friend of Israel. When the Likud protested the United States sale of AWACS reconnaissance planes to Saudi Arabia in the first year of the Reagan presidency, Yitzhak was very concerned about picking a fight with the Americans over an issue with such remote impact for Israel. Issues such as these irritated Yitzhak, and brought him into disagreement not just with the Likud but also with the more aggressive members of the Jewish lobby in America.

In Israel, Yitzhak had thrown his support behind Yigal Allon as a challenger to Shimon Peres for leadership of the Labor Party, but with Allon's sudden death, Yitzhak mounted his own campaign to become the Labor candidate in the June 1981 election. Yitzhak was defeated by Shimon Peres in a vote of Labor's Central Committee during December 1980. Despite the defeat, Yitzhak was still enormously popular. Three factors in particular may have benefitted him: First, Yitzhak was not a professional politician. Second, he had handled his resignation in 1977 with so much dignity and integrity that people felt enormous respect for his strength of character. Third, Yitzhak continually demonstrated such common sense in analyzing the challenges facing Israel. His presence as a candidate with a substantial voting bloc would likely secure him an important cabinet position.

In June 1981, the Likud's Menachem Begin almost guaranteed his reelection when he deployed a unit of F-16 jets to bomb Iraq's nuclear reactor at Tammuz—a reactor that could potentially manufacture fissionable material for atomic weapons. Yitzhak supported the raid, knowing how threatening Iraq's capability to manufacture nuclear arms could be to Israel. Peres denounced it and lost credibility in the eyes of the public as a strong leader. The sortie to Iraq resulted in a brief and immediate turnaround for Shimon Peres regarding Yitzhak's political future. Up until the time of the raid, Peres had given the impression that Yitzhak would not be part of a Peres cabinet. However, after the operation in Iraq and under pressure from many of his advisers who recognized the importance of Yitzhak's candidacy as minister of defense in the shadow cabinet, Peres did an about-face just five days before the election. Yitzhak—more out of loyalty to the party than anything else—publicly announced he would accept the role of defense minister if Labor were elected.

It's unfortunate that the announcement of Yitzhak's potential role didn't come sooner. As it happened, it was too little, too late. On June 30, 1981, Shimon Peres and Labor lost the election to Likud. Menachem Begin continued as prime minister, and Ariel Sharon became minister of defense.

Strains within the Arab world were worsening—especially among those nations trying to pursue peace with Israel. Egypt's president, Anwar Sadat, attended a major military parade in October 1981—an annual event that memorialized Egypt's advance over the Suez Canal in the Yom Kippur War. Sadat was well guarded during this military display, with eight security people around him and countless military personnel on the dais. But a group of fundamentalist officers used the occasion to launch an assassination plot. Sadat was killed almost immediately, as were a number of others on the reviewing stand when they were attacked with a grenade and sprayed with automatic weapons fire.

Three American presidents came to Sadat's funeral and the rest of the West was well represented. Menachem Begin attended on Israel's behalf, but most Arab countries were unrepresented, and television coverage beamed pictures worldwide of people dancing and cheering in the streets, especially in such places as Libya.

Yitzhak felt Egypt had lost a charismatic, farsighted, visionary leader in Anwar Sadat, and I know he was concerned that the tremendous progress realized in Israeli-Egyptian relations might be jeopardized if Sadat's successor were not similarly moderate and able to contain fundamentalist tensions. President Hosni Mubarak fortunately stayed the course, and Israel's phased withdrawal from the Sinai continued. The rift in the Arab world was growing ever deeper, however, and the forces of Islamic fundamentalism were on the rise.

My first visit with Jehan Sadat came in July 1983, some twenty months after her husband's murder. The occasion was an American-Israeli-Egyptian women's conference for peace. The event was mostly show and little substance; Israel's name wasn't even mentioned in the conference announcement. Still, I couldn't pass up this opportunity since it was also my first chance to travel to Egypt. Israeli-Egyptian relations had cooled because of the Israeli invasion of Lebanon, which I shall describe in just a moment. The Hebrew newspaper *Yediot Aharonot* asked me for an account of my visit. Here is what I wrote:

> It's the dead of night and I'm in Cairo—on the road from the airport to the monument. Here, facing the [reviewing] stand on which President Sadat met his death, resides his grave. The stand is floodlit. The monument is pale and now, at night, there is nobody here. Just the soldiers on guard. Suddenly a single car stops. Its passengers, like us, have come to pay their respects.
>
> . . . Sadat was murdered and he is buried here, on the other side of this broad avenue. Were our hopes of peace buried with him?
>
> The brief visit to Egypt . . . was an opportunity, however hasty, to test the meaning of this peace—a peace which wasn't up to our expectations: a process that had begun with a dramatic step and had stopped short at one of the stations en route—no normalization, no visits of delegations, frozen exchange programs in science, industry, and tourism.

But [the people were exceedingly friendly] and this was the staggering thing: I was suddenly wandering around Cairo as in any other city—[perhaps with an even] greater sense of security. The Egyptians immediately seemed much more of a partner for peace than for war. . . . Where had the hatred of thirty years of war vanished to? Had somebody waved it away with a magician's wand?

Shortly after arriving, I let Mrs. Sadat know that I would like to visit with her. She invited me to the family summer palace at Marmora, near Alexandria. Daniella Shamir, whose husband, Shimon, then headed the Israeli Academic Center in Cairo (he later became Israel's ambassador to Egypt and later to Jordan), joined me on the visit.

Security surrounding this expansive seashore home was very tight. The settees were a pale blue velvet, and portraits of Anwar Sadat were everywhere. Jehan Sadat wore an elegant caftan of black silk. Two young granddaughters—one aged four and the other younger than six months—joined us briefly, and Jehan Sadat was very much the affectionate grandmother. We talked for more than two hours. She mentioned how very depressed her husband had been after the Six-Day War. (At that, I could hardly suppress a smile.) Social issues were serious matters for her—from the rehabilitation of wounded veterans to family planning and women's rights. She told one story that exemplifies the conflicting forces that women in the most senior positions in Arab society have had to face. She was doing work on behalf of those wounded in war when her husband decreed, "Jehan, when we are having lunch with the family at two in the afternoon I want you to be home." The first day she was there, and the second day she was there again. But, by the third day, she was a little late. She felt that her work on behalf of the veterans was just too important. Her husband was angry, but she persisted. Sometimes she would come home so late that she would take her shoes off and tiptoe in their room so as not to wake him.

ABC's Peter Jennings had said to me in Mexico: "If you two ever sit on the same couch, you will never want to get up." He was so right. Those moments in Marmora passed very quickly for me, and I found her a fascinating companion.

∞ Impatient with terrorism and violence on the northern border, the Likud government began the invasion of Lebanon (the so-called incursion that was actually a war) on June 6, 1982, when three Israeli divisions moved into southern Lebanon. The operation was dubbed "Peace for Galilee" and it was a conflict that aroused deep discord in Israel. Israel's policy up until that time had been restricted to defending the country from military aggressors, but this mission's objectives were twofold: first, to drive the PLO and the Syrians out of Lebanon, and, second, to empower a government in Beirut that was sympathetic to Israeli interests. The Likud initiated this conflict and presented it to the nation as an advance over forty kilometers, a short-term engagement that would last for only forty-eight hours. This deception culminated in a long-distance attack at the gates of Beirut.

It took some time to resolve the mess in Lebanon. Yitzhak opposed Israel's offensive stance in Lebanon, but he also felt a certain responsibility to support the troops. He never agreed with the idea of resolving the threat from Lebanon by marching into the country in a full-scale operation that would allow Israel to install a handpicked government. The new policy made little sense to many within the country and without—U.S. senators in Washington gave Menachem Begin a chilly reception in June 1982 because of the Lebanese offensive.

Even though he was out of office, Yitzhak could not sit idly by without offering his advice. He couldn't again accept being on the sidelines as events had forced him to be during the Yom Kippur War. He believed that the IDF should take advantage of the progress of troops toward Beirut, while minimizing bloodshed. In a meeting with Begin on July 4, 1982, Yitzhak supported Defense Minister Ariel Sharon's plan to tighten the siege of Beirut by shutting off the city's water supplies. Yitzhak didn't advocate taking Beirut or advancing in Lebanon, but thought it would be a way of forcing the Palestinians and their Lebanese allies to capitulate without further bloodshed. He believed Israel could not guarantee the future stability of a handpicked government and ought not put itself in the position of becoming Lebanon's "policeman." Beware the swamps of Lebanon, he would say.

The advice to close the water taps was to haunt Yitzhak. People were astonished by his position and wondered how Yitzhak Rabin could support this horrible war. He was not a supporter of the war, but he was aware that the IDF had already lost hundreds of lives, and he didn't want this ill-advised campaign to be a total disaster. He believed that closing the taps might help end it faster. Yitzhak was torn by a dilemma resulting from his total dedication to, trust in, and love for the IDF on the one hand and the Likud policy, which he disapproved of strongly, on the other.

There had always been a significant Christian population in Lebanon, and the country traditionally had been Israel's most peaceable neighbor. The Lebanese civil war reached its zenith in 1976 as Muslim forces in the country became more influential. The issue for Israeli leadership was one of method and judgment. Do you best clear a swamp by jumping into it or by recognizing its perils and seeking to manage the situation carefully from its margins? When Yitzhak was prime minister, he was exposed to the same temptations and pressures that Menachem Begin had succumbed to in 1982. The Begin administration chose to involve itself directly, operating with the naive philosophy that one could use the fist of military power to bring about a change of administration in Lebanon. Yitzhak thought this was pointless. The Likud government was inclined to think of Lebanon as a problem that could be resolved in strictly Lebanese terms, but Yitzhak always saw Lebanon in conjunction with Syria and knew that no viable long-term solution for Lebanon could be achieved without resolving the Syrian problem in tandem. The bombing death of Lebanese president Bashir Gemayel in 1982 proved how fragile the situation was. How could Israel control events that were unfolding within Lebanon itself?

For Israel, the toll of the three-year fiasco in Lebanon was enormous. More than 650 Israelis were killed, and the cost of the campaign was estimated at over $5 billion. Those were only the direct, quantifiable effects. Nations branded Israel a genocidal aggressor. The policies tested Israel's bonds with the Diaspora and its strongest allies, America most of all. And the Lebanese invasion created a perfect hothouse for the birth of the Hezbollah, an Iranian-inspired Islamic Fundamentalist terrorist organization.

In September 1983, Menachem Begin resigned as prime minister. He had been deeply affected by his wife's death several months earlier. They shared many very hard years together—years of war in Europe, years in the underground in Palestine (Mr. Begin was the commander of Etzl—one of the armed wings of the Revisionist movement). He and his wife lived very modestly in a small basement apartment in Tel Aviv, but they had a large circle of friends and admirers within Israel and from abroad who would visit them. Aliza Begin, in the words of the Bible, walked with him through a long stretch of "desert." They were a very close-knit couple. Over the years, she suffered increasingly from emphysema—although she continued to smoke heavily—and this eventually caused her death.

Yitzhak Shamir succeeded Begin, but his tenure was short-lived. On January 25, 1984, the Shamir government fell after just four months in office. Meanwhile, Lebanon became a bastion for terrorism. Suicide commandos blew up the U.S. Marine Headquarters in Beirut, killing 241, and a truck bomb killed 58 in an attack on French barracks.

In the spring of 1984, Labor received forty-four seats in the Knesset in comparison to the Likud's forty-one. This was not enough to form a majority government for Labor, so a National Unity government was created—an unprecedented coalition of Labor and Likud. Its premise was power sharing. The premiership would be rotated, with Shimon Peres serving the first two years as prime minister and Yitzhak Shamir as foreign minister, with the roles to reverse in October 1986. The coalition faced two immediate problems—getting Israel out of Lebanon and reining in inflation. The Israeli economy had run aground; by 1985 inflation was galloping at more than 35 percent *a month!* Cost-of-living adjustments couldn't keep pace with inflation and some state-owned enterprises verged on bankruptcy. Every trip to the grocery store became a frightening reminder of the economic disaster.

The National Unity government was to be sworn in on September 13, 1984, and I recall how Yitzhak and I chatted with his aides Niva Lanir and Zvili Ben-Moshe and our journalist friend Aliza Wallach as we sipped coffee in the Knesset cafeteria that afternoon. Dalia and her husband, Avi, also joined us. A coalition was supposed to be announced any minute. However, the opening of the Knesset session was delayed until four o'clock due to last-minute haggling. Then came the interminable debate. Yitzhak's appointment as minister of defense wasn't formalized until eleven-thirty that evening.

Yitzhak thought the National Unity government could work, and he was anxious to become minister of defense, a post he had never held. His appointment was an internal Labor decision and an inescapably obvious one. If Shamir and Peres were to alternate the prime minister and foreign minister posts, Yitzhak was seen as the natural candidate for the defense job, probably by both parties. His role in the new government was more or less a given. Shamir understood Israel saw Yitzhak as "Mister Defense" and gave him a free hand on defense matters. Yitzhak loved the role, as he expected he would, and was more comfortable in it than in any of the other posts he held, meeting as casually with the soldiers as he did with generals. This was his alma mater. The IDF loved him, and he loved them back. I will always remember the look of joy on the face of Yehezkel, Yitzhak's driver, who had been craving to drive the official defense minister's car ever since Yitzhak had been mentioned as a candidate for the Defense post. Seventeen years after shedding his uniform, Yitzhak came back to the Defense establishment. His hair was grayer, but he still had the bearing of a soldier.

Yitzhak was sworn in as minister of defense on Thursday, September 13, 1984. This post was traditionally regarded as the second most important position in the Israeli government. Phone calls and flower arrangements inundated our home, and the reception we held Saturday evening for some fifty friends and well-wishers was a true celebration, and there was a sense of confidence about what the future would bring.

Now Yitzhak could devote himself to the topic that he was prepared to understand the best—the security of Israel and the well-being of our country's armed forces. Yitzhak was a gifted military strategist, but he was never a typical warrior. He believed that the role of power was, above all, a guarantee of our existence and our defense. He believed that the Israel Defense Forces existed merely to defend. He believed that attempts to destroy Israel could be deterred only through a strong Israeli army. He used to say, "Only with a very strong Israel will they be ready to talk peace."

Yitzhak's new job demanded the patient assimilation of endless data. As his staff aide at the Ministry of Defense, Niva Lanir had the duty of reading the telegrams and dispatches that arrived at the ministry. Yitzhak had to initial every document he saw. In advance of his review, Niva would read this material carefully and highlight the documents with a marker. One series of briefings came from the Israeli ambassador to Egypt, who would write long but interesting reports from Cairo. One day, the ambassador, Moshe Sasson, came to meet Yitzhak and started to brief Yitzhak on a technical matter in the course of the conversation. In midsentence, Yitzhak completed the idea exactly as it had been presented in the dispatch.

His inch-by-inch knowledge of Israel's landscape was important to Yitzhak's ability to make effective military decisions. He knew things about Israel that a very senior official would not normally know. With visual images as well as reports, he saw everything and remembered each detail. Once Niva Lanir accompanied him to Petah Tiqva, a suburb east of Tel Aviv where there is a Labor Party building. It's a rather neglected place. Four years later, they went back again. The same place, the same people, the same speeches. On the drive back, Niva noted that there was a cracked window in the building and remarked, "Did you notice that the window is still broken?" And Yitzhak answered, "Did you also notice that over the same corner of the same window, the same spider is curled up in the same cobweb over the same dust?"

Controlling details meant increasing the prospect of survival for soldiers, Yitzhak believed. Even when the nation faced its most tense moments, parents would approach Yitzhak and tell him they were glad their children were serving while he was in charge of the Defense Ministry. They knew that every life-threatening detail would be checked and checked again under his leadership. Yitzhak was also a firm believer in equipment enhancements that were exactly tailored for Israeli needs—such as armored vehicles that had extra plating underneath to resist mine explosions. When Israel bought U.S. Patton tanks, diesel engines were installed for better fuel economy and endurance.

Yitzhak's absolute priority upon rejoining the cabinet was to solve the problem in Lebanon, but he refused to be buffaloed into hasty decisions, though people challenged him as to why it took so long. Yitzhak prepared for every action carefully and meticulously. This included strengthening the Southern Lebanese Army, a militia of Lebanese Christians backed and supplied by Israel, as well as the establishment of a security zone. The security zone was essential if Israel were to protect the border and still have the Lebanese ostensibly in charge of their own territory. Israeli troops would have access to this strip of land, but they would not occupy the territory. Instead, the Israelis would help the Southern Lebanese Army withstand assaults from Iranian-backed Hezbollah guerrillas. All of this took time and—once more—patience.

In January 1985, about four months after taking office, Yitzhak presented his plan for a phased withdrawal from Lebanon that would take place over five to six months. By June 1985, the withdrawal from Lebanon was complete.

As the Lebanon resolution moved forward, Yitzhak turned his focus to Jordan. In March 1985, he held secret talks with King Hussein in London. He presented the King with an Israeli-made Galil assault rifle in a beautiful case made from olive wood. It was well known that Yitzhak had met with King Hussein several times before they had "officially" made contact in Washington in 1994. The first of these private meetings dated back to 1975 or 1976. I went with Yitzhak to Eilat; from there, he left for an undisclosed location—it may have been at sea or in the desert. The press got wind that something was going on. In an Israeli newspaper, a cartoon appeared depicting Yitzhak in Eilat and King Hussein in Aqaba playing tennis across the Red Sea. From Eilat you can see the lights of Aqaba, and vice versa. By car, the two cities are only ten minutes apart, but then they were still worlds away.

Yitzhak had always liked the king greatly and he invariably came home from their meetings with the same comment: "It was delightful, but there were no results." The reason why was simple. The king kept saying: everything or nothing. So it stayed at the point of nothing until the day of the breakthrough, years later, during Yitzhak's second term as prime minister.

On May 20, 1985, 1,150 Palestinians were released from Israeli jails in exchange for the release of three Israeli soldiers who had been held in Lebanon by forces of the Palestinian leader Ahmad Jibril. The inequity of the deal caused people outside of Israel to scratch their heads and Yitzhak came under fire. Whatever the price, he was convinced it was right—a great statement of Yitzhak's loyalty to the IDF.

Could the release have resulted in more attacks, because more terrorists were again free to pursue violence? I don't know the answer. We do know that the guerrilla attacks were becoming more sophisticated. In 1984, Palestinian guerrillas used motorized hang gliders to attack Israel from southern Lebanon, killing four Israeli soldiers in the raid. in September 1985, PLO terrorists killed three Israelis in Cyprus. Later in the month, Israel undertook a reprisal bombing of PLO headquarters in Tunis, which killed seventy-three Palestinians and Tunisians. Yitzhak was involved in every retaliation operation and made decisions as to locations and targets. He had little hesitation about reprisals when Jewish lives had been taken.

The arrest in November 1985 of Jonathan Pollard, a paid spy working on behalf of Israel in the United States in a rogue intelligence operation, strained the U.S.-Israeli relationship in an unprecedented way. Pollard was convicted and sentenced to life in prison. This was an extremely awkward and delicate matter for Yitzhak. He learned about Pollard only *after* he had been arrested. His work had been authorized under the previous Defense Ministry administration at a lower level, and Yitzhak had not been briefed on Pollard when he took office. According to an inquiry commission's findings, other top officials, including Shamir and Peres, were not aware of Pollard's activities, either. Israel had to recover from the embarrassment of a spy working within the defense structure of its closest friend and ally. Still, since Pollard had been employed by Israel, Yitzhak tried to have his sentence reduced. He had once written to President George Bush about the issue, but there was no resolution. However, shortly before his death, Yitzhak did raise the matter of a possible pardon with President Clinton, which was later denied by the president in 1996.

∞ In October 1986, roles were reversed in the National Unity government, with Foreign Minister Shamir becoming prime minister and Prime Minister Peres assuming the post of foreign minister. Yitzhak continued in his role as minister of defense, reporting directly to Shamir. The reporting relationship posed no problems for Yitzhak, a man who respected the hierarchy of government protocol.

By 1986, Arab inhabitants of the Occupied Territories numbered over 1.3 million. The growing numbers of both Jews and Arabs increased the occasions for friction and violence. In 1987, terrorists threw a Molotov cocktail into a car that held the family of Abie and Ofrah Moses. Ofrah Moses died along with one of her children. Abie and two of the children survived but suffered severe burns. Within days, Yitzhak went to the site of the tragedy and was met by a large demonstration of settlers. His remarks to them were clear: "When you came here, you knew the risks involved." The settlers regarded these words as sharp and uncaring, and Abie Moses himself spoke out against Yitzhak in the media. Later, Yitzhak went to visit him and the children in their home. One day Yitzhak, on the advice of Eitan Haber, rode out to Alfei Menasheh, a settlement on the West Bank near Kakilya, with some toys for the Moses children. They reconciled and remained friendly to the end of Yitzhak's life. Abie Moses was one of a long list of people Yitzhak used to call on Jewish holidays. He felt a great moral

Yitzhak at five, with his mother, Rosa, and sister, Rachel, 1927

∞

Yitzhak at thirteen

Yitzhak, Rachel, and their father, Nehemiah, in 1942, after Rosa's death

∞

My parents, Gusta and Fima Schlossberg, in Copenhagen, 1919

My first steps, in Königsberg, 1929

My first "portrait"

*My friend Zohara, whose brief, heroic life ended tragically
on the eve of Israeli independence*

Yitzhak and me shortly after our wedding in the summer of 1948

Yitzhak and Yigal Allon in the Negev Desert during the War of Independence, January 1949

In Rhodes, in 1949, during the armistice negotiations with Egypt: (left to right) Yehoshafat Harkavi, Aryeh Simon, Yigael Yadin, and Yitzhak

The proud father, at Camberley, with little Dalia, 1953

David Ben-Gurion congratulating Yitzhak on becoming chief of staff of the IDF, 1964

Yitzhak and our son, Yuval, at an Independence Day parade in 1964

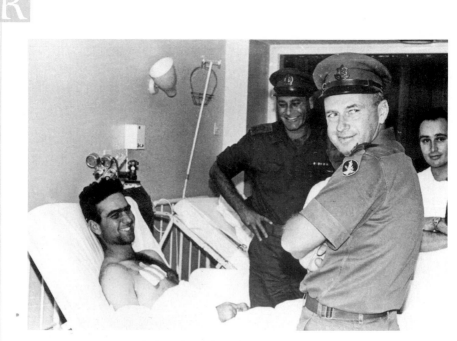

Visiting a wounded soldier after the Six-Day War. The other man in uniform is Yeshayahu Gavish, head of the Southern Command.

Accepting an honorary degree from Hebrew University on Mount Scopus just a few weeks after the 1967 victory

*The Israeli ambassador with President Richard Nixon
in the White House*

*With Henry Kissinger and Golda Meir at a reception in honor of the prime
minister's visit to Washington in 1973*

The only photo you will find of Yitzhak dancing—
with Betty Ford at the White House in 1974.

I found a much more accommodating dance partner
in President Gerald Ford.

Yitzhak, during his first term as prime minister, with former finance minister Pinhas Sapir, the man who backed him for the job, making a gift of two Torah scrolls to a synagogue in 1975. It was a very hot day, but Sapir insisted on carrying the heavy Torah. Within minutes of this photo, he collapsed and died of a heart attack.

The loving grandfather, with baby Jonathan in 1975

With President Bill Clinton in the White House, 1995; the famous handshake with Yasir Arafat, September 1993; signing the peace treaty with Jordan's King Hussein, July 1994; in Spain, receiving the Prince of Asturias Award for International Cooperation, with King Juan Carlos and Queen Sofia, Yasir and Sua Arafat, October 1994; Queen Noor, Hillary Rodham Clinton, and me on the White House lawn; Yitzhak, Shimon Peres, and Yasir Arafat accepting the Nobel Peace Prize in Oslo, December 1994

∞

With U.S. president George Bush in Kennebunkport, Maine; with German chancellor Helmut Kohl in Jerusalem; on China's truly Great Wall; presenting a gift of an ancient urn to Pope John Paul II at the Vatican; Yitzhak speaking on the occasion of the fiftieth anniversary of the Warsaw Ghetto uprising in Poland in April 1993

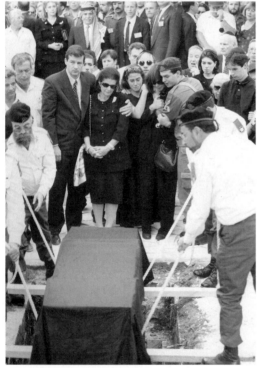

*Singing the "Song of Peace"
at the rally at Kings of Israel
Square, November 4, 1995,
minutes before the fatal shots
were fired.*

∞

*The burial on Mount Herzl.
The family surrounds me:
(left to right)* Yuval, Noa,
our son-in-law, Avi Pelossof,
Dalia, and grandsons
Jonathan and Michael.
Behind us stand King
Hussein and Queen Noor.

Yasir Arafat's visit to our home during the shiva.
Between us sits Yossi Genosar, Yitzhak's former "hot line" to Arafat.

One of the "generation of the candles"
during the thirty days of mourning at the
site of the assassination

∞

Inspired by her grandfather, Noa enrolled in officers' training school in the
year following Yitzhak's death. At a graduation ceremony in October 1996,
she wept as the speaker invoked Yitzhak's legacy.

My favorite portrait of Yitzhak

∞

obligation to keep in touch and to be there for the people who had suffered the most.

The most complex crisis during Yitzhak's term as minister of defense was surely the Intifada. The Intifada (Arabic for "the awakening") began in December 1987, after an Israeli civilian truck driver's vehicle spun out of control, accidentally killing four Arabs in Gaza. The incident set into motion an unprecedented wave of violence and civil disobedience in Gaza and on the West Bank. The Intifada changed the very nature—or at least the perception—of opposition to Israeli rule in the Occupied Territories from isolated terrorist attacks to a seemingly spontaneous outpouring of mass resentment. The Intifada made it wholly clear to Yitzhak that Israel could not govern another people. With Palestinian men in prisons or in detention, women assumed a more active role and youths spearheaded the frontline violence, mostly throwing stones at Israeli soldiers. As difficult as it was for him at the time, I'm sure that Yitzhak would today admit that the Intifada was instrumental in advancing the peace process, because it made it clear that only a political solution could succeed over the long term.

Yitzhak was visiting Dr. Kissinger in Connecticut when the Intifada began. Again, he was criticized at home because his response to the crisis was seen as too slow. But the strikes and violence of the Intifada were utterly new, and a knee-jerk reaction would have been even more dangerous. Yitzhak would say, "Through the use of force, by spitting on our soldiers, you will gain nothing. The solution can come only when both sides sit down and discuss our readiness for compromise. We need to find ways to create the conditions for coexistence in the area."

Yitzhak recognized the intricate public relations problems of the Intifada and from that time on members of the Israeli army were carefully schooled in the appropriate responses to attack. In 1988, Yitzhak said in an Israeli television interview, "It is far easier to resolve classic military problems. It is far more difficult to contend with 1.3 million Palestinians living in the Territories, who do not want our rule and who are employing systematic violence without weapons." The television coverage automatically favored teenagers and children hurling rocks or worse against armed Israeli troops. Even when rubber bullets and wooden clubs were used by the troops in last-case defense, the actions didn't photograph well and made us look unduly cruel. Soldiers fighting children. Yitzhak was sensitive to the impact of TV, just as during the first months of his assignment as ambassador to the United States, he had marveled at how live TV cameras had made American politics so much more reactive to public opinion.

We watched a good deal of CNN at friends' homes during the Intifada, primarily because it was an alternative news source. Our granddaughter Noa, who was only ten when the Intifada began, watched this televised war and saw children her own age, with their faces masked, hurling stones at Israeli troops. "Why, *Saba*, must soldiers hit children in this way?" she would ask. Yitzhak would softly explain that the Palestinians were putting the children up front as a shield while away from the cameras they were harming Jews much worse than the soldiers hurt these children. It's hard to explain a controversial idea to a ten-year-old, but he never brushed aside difficult questions, even when they came from his granddaughter.

Around this time, Yitzhak was widely misquoted with a notorious three-word statement, "Break their bones." This command was supposed to sum up Yitzhak's strategy for dealing with the Intifada. He repeatedly denied ever having made the statement, even addressing it in a speech before the Knesset months later. In fact, his direction was much more subtle. He told IDF officers that it was appropriate to use force—aggressively, if need be—to bring a demonstration under control, but not to use it recklessly. It was not as if Yitzhak was counseling Israeli troops to wantonly beat stone-throwers; instead, he called on our soldiers to make difficult judgment calls. If it was a case of firing a rifle or wielding a club to bring a Molotov cocktail–hurling demonstrator under control, then by all means use the club. But the controversy wouldn't die down, and A. M. Rosenthal, long a backer of Israel, called for Yitzhak's resignation in the pages of the *New York Times*. The Intifada never officially ended but it subsided as peace initiatives became more serious.

In January 1988, Yitzhak proposed expelling Intifada leaders from Israel, and the Knesset approved the program. The Intifada had clouded Israel's relationships abroad. While it was in full force, Yitzhak met with British prime minister Margaret Thatcher for breakfast. She contended we mistreated the Palestinians and was concerned about their misery and poverty. He said to her, "Mrs. Thatcher, we would never object to any kind of support that Britain might like to offer to the people of Gaza. Would you like to build a school, a hospital? We would welcome it very much." Yitzhak said it was the shortest breakfast meeting he ever had.

With all his concern to avoid unnecessary casualties in the IDF, actions were not based solely on that factor. Sometimes he was forced to make choices that were risky or dangerous. Yitzhak never made political or strategic decisions based on the welfare of our children or grandchildren, though he could not forget that we now had a grandson on the front lines. Our grandson Jonathan was a member of a crack paratrooper brigade stationed first on the Lebanese border and later on the West Bank during the Intifada. Yitzhak was always so happy to see him on Friday nights or Saturdays when he was able to obtain leave. "Is Jonathan coming for the weekend?" he would ask anxiously. Jonathan sometimes found himself defending Yitzhak's positions. One time, hundreds of Hamas activists were released from prison in small groups. Each time my husband gave the order to release fifty Hamas prisoners, Jonathan's commander would say, "Jonathan Ben-Artzi! Forward! Your grandfather has now released fifty Hamas, you will now do fifty push-ups in front of the entire unit."

In 1988, George Shultz, characterizing Arafat as an "accessory to terrorism," refused to grant him a visa to enter the United States and address the United Nations General Assembly. The General Assembly then decided to relocate its meeting to Geneva in protest. The next day, Arafat declared that the PLO renounced "all forms of terrorism." That was the gateway to the first meaningful dialogue between the PLO and the United States.

United Jewish Appeal fund-raising in the United States became difficult as Intifada media coverage grew. Yitzhak, however, maintained an active commitment to fund-raising for Israel. He recognized how important it was to secure the developmental funds essential for Israel, and that made him more diligent in making appearances. He was very grateful for the support of the Diaspora over the years, and he always fulfilled his obligations to attend a reception or a dinner—whether at home or abroad.

On a fund-raising trip for Israel Bonds while he was minister of defense, Yitzhak was the keynote speaker at a benefit honoring multimillionaire Arthur Balfour in New York City. Yitzhak also was asked to attend a series of small dinners as a prelude to the big benefit in New York. In these small gatherings, donors committed to the amount they would pledge at the major event to help create momentum at the banquet. He was to meet with *TV Guide* founder Walter Annenberg in Philadelphia, Bob Smith (the son of Charles E. Smith) and his family in Washington, and Mr. Harvey M. "Bud" Meyerhoff in Baltimore. The days were spent with senior U.S. Defense Department officials and the evenings at these fund-raisers.

During the Philadelphia dinner, Walter Annenberg doubled his commitment from one million dollars to two. The entire trip seemed headed for success. But in Baltimore things grew embarrassing. The evening's honoree, Bud Meyerhoff, was very involved with the committee building the U.S. Holocaust Memorial Museum in Washington. His father was the late Joseph Meyerhoff, one of the great princes of our people in the United States, who generously helped me raise funds for the Israel Room at the Kennedy Center. A major backer of education in Israel, Joseph Meyerhoff's name is on the donor honor roll of all the major universities in Israel.

I went to Baltimore with Yitzhak that night. He had a terrible cold. When we arrived, Bud Meyerhoff wasn't at the reception. Mr. Meyerhoff had already left for Washington and had one of his sons attend the reception in his place.

Yitzhak spoke in Baltimore, a dinner followed, and cards were called for contributions. I said to Yitzhak, "Look, you're feeling lousy, and you are in the middle of a difficult, long trip. You have a long day with the secretary of defense tomorrow. Let's leave after the fifth card is called." Yitzhak always saw fund-raising affairs to their conclusions, so it was unusual that he went along with the idea—he was feeling that under the weather. The American secretary of defense had provided him with a waiting helicopter to travel from Baltimore to Washington, and we took off as the fund-raising continued.

On the Saturday following the Balfour dinner, before we were to go back home, the Israeli director of the Bonds organization, Jehuda "Georgy" Halevi, came to our New York hotel room to say good-bye. He started by saying the people of Baltimore were very offended. "Wow!" I said with unmistakable anger in my voice. "What's the matter with you? You know how terrible Yitzhak was feeling. Are you representing the people of the United States or are you representing Israel and its minister of defense? The minister of defense faced an important meeting the next day. Yitzhak left early just this one time, and an Israeli director expresses outrage on behalf of an American organization!" I was furious. I'm not surprised that this same man later became the director of Bar-Ilan University in New York, which is perhaps where he belongs.

I must confess to having experienced some peculiar hospitality during fund-raising efforts for Israel. I keep a kosher home in accordance with our dietary tradition. However, I was once invited to a Jewish fund-raising dinner at Bookbinder's, a famous Philadelphia restaurant, while Yitzhak was prime minister in the seventies. As I entered the dining room, I was shocked to see the almost exclusively male group sitting with plastic bibs around their necks and with nutcrackers by their plates. It was clear that boiled lobsters were about to be served. Lobsters at a fund-raiser for Israel!

Though a gentleman made *"Hamotzi"* and blessed the bread, I was still enraged. In my opening remarks, I said to the attendees: "It is great you didn't forget to make '*Hamotzi,*' so maybe you will somehow be forgiven that you are eating lobster in front of the wife of the Israeli prime minister!"

∞ The 1984 election produced the first rotation government. In 1988, voters gave Likud a very small edge, leading to the formation of a second National Unity government with Shamir as prime minister but *without* rotation of the prime ministership. The cabinet included Yitzhak Rabin as defense minister and Peres as finance minister (a post he held until 1990). That government ended in 1990. This is known as the "Second National Unity Government, But Without Rotation." The relative power of the Labor Party from 1988 to 1990 declined.

∞ While much attention was directed toward the American Jewish community, we never for a moment ignored Jewish communities elsewhere in the world, especially in Russia, where Jews so deeply wanted the right to emigrate to Israel. In November 1989, the fall of the Berlin Wall and the end of the Cold War were to have a profound effect on Russian Jews and on the future of the Middle East. Russian aid to such countries as Syria dried up. Yitzhak certainly felt that the decline of communism was another factor that later enabled him to move the peace process forward.

Not all the effects of the end of the Cold War were good ones, however. In a letter to the *New York Times* on January 16, 1990, then-senator Robert Dole recommended that 5 percent of the annual $3 billion aid budget to Israel be reallocated to countries in Eastern Europe. Fortunately such a measure was never enacted. One of Israel's first and foremost priorities had been "Let my people go"—especially with regard to the Soviet Union. Certainly Israel was doing its part in the reconfiguration of Eastern Europe by absorbing a massive wave of immigration beginning in 1989. Since

1970 more than 700,000 Jews have emigrated from Russia and Eastern Bloc countries to Israel.

∞ Yitzhak was gradually moving toward advocating Palestinian autonomy and self-determination. At the beginning of 1989, he revealed a peace plan based on free general elections for the Palestinians in return for a Palestinian pledge to put a six-month moratorium on the Intifada. In the elections, the Palestinians would choose a negotiating team for talks with Israel. Yitzhak shared his vision of the evolving Middle East on a visit with President Mubarak in Egypt in September of that year. But Yitzhak was about to find his official political position in serious jeopardy.

By early 1990, many in the Labor party were growing impatient with Shamir and the National Unity government. Shamir's intransigence on Jewish settlement in the West Bank and his hard-line position on peace talks with Palestinians had alienated the United States and stood in direct opposition to Labor Party policy. Shimon Peres believed he'd found an opportunity to break the National Unity government by pulling the Labor Party out of the coalition, thereby creating a political crisis in which he could form a new coalition with himself as prime minister. He was already negotiating with the religious parties well before the resignation occurred. When Yitzhak and I talked, it was clear he hated the idea of the government's planned resignation, and challenged its wisdom from the very first moment. Yitzhak would shake his head over what was happening, saying that Peres was playing into the hands of the Likud. Yitzhak nonetheless went along with the plan because of his loyalty to the party. Still, he felt that Shimon Peres was handing the government to Shamir and the Likud on a silver platter.

When Peres as Labor Party leader blocked the funding of eight Likud-favored settlements, the National Unity government fell apart almost immediately thereafter, on March 12, 1990. All Labor Party ministers resigned, and Yitzhak's tenure as defense minister ended. The president, Chaim Herzog, then called Shimon Peres to form a new government. Peres was absolutely certain he would be able to form a governing coalition by the night of April 12, 1990, and intended to present the new government the next day. Peres was banking on drawing the religious party Shas—under the charismatic and youthful leader Aryeh Deri—into the new coalition. He and other Labor leaders had even been making visits in yarmulkes to such ultra-Orthodox rabbis as Ovadiah Yosef, the spiritual mentor of Shas. But there was stiff opposition among the ranks of the rabbis—especially the famous Rabbi Eliezer Schach, the spiritual mentor of United Torah Judaism.

Yitzhak's skepticism was well founded. First Shas bolted from the coalition. The vote to construct a coalition then came down to the slimmest of margins. Knesset member Abraham Sharir bolted from the Likud Party, which seemed to give Peres a majority. But then the scales tipped in the other direction when two members of the orthodox Agudat Yisrael Party dropped out of the Labor-led coalition just hours before the new government was to be presented. After the failure in the Knesset, Peres asked for an extension, which was granted him by President Herzog. A Labor-led government hung in the balance of one or two votes. Even at the time of the nine o'clock news on the decisive evening, the two Agudat Yisrael members wouldn't disclose with whom they would side. Yitzhak and I had left for a state dinner in honor of Václav Havel without knowing how the issue would resolve itself.

At the dinner, I was seated opposite Shimon Peres. At about five minutes to nine, a note was handed to Prime Minister Shamir and President Herzog. Shimon Peres was then informed that it was finished, the Agudat Yisrael votes had swung to the Likud. Peres was not to be prime minister. I must say he remained controlled and continued to make small talk left and right. He was then called outside to speak to reporters and his mood suddenly turned. When he returned to our table, he finally lost control. "What have I done wrong? For forty-nine days I've been fighting to form a new government."

The result of Peres's gambit—which Yitzhak referred to as the "bad-smelling maneuver"—was that Yitzhak Shamir continued as prime minister in a Likud government from June 1990 to July 1992. Yitzhak returned to his tiny office in the Kiryah complex.

Under Likud, relations with the Palestinians only worsened. In the spring of 1990, Ariel Sharon, who had reappeared in the cabinet as minister for housing and construction, pledged Israel would increase the Jewish population in the territories from 100,000 to 300,000 in two decades. This decision was absolutely contrary to Yitzhak's views on settlements. Yitzhak made a clear distinction between *strategic* settlements necessary for Israel's security, and *political* settlements that existed to further a nonessential ideological agenda. When Yitzhak saw the small encampment of a political settlement—an "overnight settlement" or a "sleep-over settlement," as he called them—from a helicopter, his hair would stand on end. "If that's a settlement, then I'm a propeller," he would say, or, "If that's a settlement, then I'm a ball bearing." The incidents and provocations never stopped. One day, for instance, a group of Palestinians threw rocks at Jews praying at the Western Wall. Jerusalem mayor Teddy Kollek pinned at least partial responsibility for the incident on a call by Likud leadership for a new Jewish settlement in Arab East Jerusalem. In the confrontation that followed, twenty-two Palestinians were killed and scores wounded.

On August 2, 1990, Saddam Hussein invaded Kuwait. Many in Israel wondered if Saddam would use chemical weapons against us during the Gulf War, which began the following January. Yitzhak never believed that Saddam Hussein would dare do it, as Saddam knew that Israel could wipe out Baghdad in a single day. Yitzhak knew better than most of us what Israel could do in response.

Israeli government orders to civilians were to seal off a single room in each household with plastic wrap and to wear a gas mask as a defense against a potential chemical attack. We didn't have cable TV yet, but our daughter and her husband had a satellite dish. When they heard on CNN that there were air-raid warnings in Saudi Arabia or that Iraqi missiles were landing on Riyadh, we knew to expect an attack on Israel within minutes. When the air-raid warnings sounded, we would trek into the sealed room with

our gas masks. When I recall the sight of us sitting there in gas
masks, I still feel humiliated. The first time a warning sounded it
was two o'clock in the morning. Security rang the doorbell outside
our apartment, and the guard joined us in the sealed room with his
gas mask on. We could hear the explosions of the U.S. Patriot missiles intercepting the Iraqi Scuds, but we still kept the ridiculous
gas masks on.

The attacks occurred at night. It was winter and darkness fell at
about six o'clock. Everybody tried to be home at that time, and
Yitzhak would rush home, too. It was a very unusual time in our
life to have him home regularly so early. The next evening another
warning sounded. We had guests for dinner. The pasta was on the
stove. We went into the sealed room. Yitzhak and I looked at each
other and at our guests—each of us wearing gas masks. "That's
all. Finished," he said. "When the next air raid happens, we're
going down to the nuclear fallout shelter in the basement of our
building." As our apartment was on the top floor, Yitzhak reasoned, the worst thing that could happen to us would be a rocket
hitting our building—an eighth-floor safe room in an eight-floor
apartment house was nothing less than useless in a missile attack.

When the air raid sirens sounded, we had to quickly run down
eight flights of stairs to reach the shelter before the Scud fell. The
security guard joined us in our downward flight. Normally we arrived after the missiles had already fallen. In the beginning, we
were joined by one or two neighbor families. Eventually, nearly
everyone in the building followed in our footsteps and joined us in
the shelter, but the visits were short. By the time we'd arrive downstairs, we would turn around and be on our way back up again.

Government orders required that no one leave the house without a gas mask. I just wouldn't do it. Can Saddam Hussein somehow see me? I said to myself. I was not going to give this villain the
satisfaction of forcing me to carry a gas mask. I was not about to
be humiliated by this tyrant!

One afternoon, Yitzhak appeared on a popular Israeli TV show
in an interview as a private citizen, and he announced his decision
not to retreat into a sealed room. He explained his reasoning for it

and noted that his views weren't official since he was out of office at the time. Being the authority he was, people asked if he was doing the right thing by contradicting the government directive, but he called things as he saw them.

"This is one conflict in the Middle East which Israel cannot be accused of," Yitzhak used to say. He had great respect for America's resolve to stop Saddam Hussein. That extended to the military and strategic planning of Generals Colin Powell and Norman Schwarzkopf. Foremost, Yitzhak admired President George Bush's determined position. The democratic free world could not permit Saddam Hussein to overrun Kuwait and get away with it. While it was wise for Israel not to interfere, we could have deployed some of our special units and even offered to do so.

Nonetheless, Yitzhak fully supported Israel's restraint in not retaliating. Even though the damage was sizable, it was better to stay the course with the Allied nations and allow them to implement the carefully planned Desert Storm operation. One direct Israeli death, twelve indirect deaths through such causes as heart attacks and asphyxiation, and more than two hundred injuries resulted from the missile attacks. More than four thousand Israeli buildings were damaged. The dangers were real. Dalia and our son-in-law, Avi, actually picked up part of a Scud in their backyard! No one was enthused about the Arab alliance the United States was backing, but American support for Israel was clear.

∞ The guard was once again changing in Israel, with the death of the seventy-eight-year-old Menachem Begin. Yitzhak regarded Mr. Begin, who died on March 9, 1992, as an honorable man, a brilliant and strong leader. When Yitzhak was ambassador to Washington, Mr. Begin, as leader of the opposition party, would come to the United States on visits. Yitzhak helped coordinate Mr. Begin's visits with members of the House and the Senate. Yitzhak would see him to the airport. He gave him all the deference in the world not only because it was something required of him as ambassador, but because he felt a genuine respect for the man. Mr. Begin proved extremely supportive during the Entebbe crisis. After the successful rescue mission, Mr. Begin, a member of the Foreign Affairs and Defense Committee, made a speech at the Knesset in which he said that there were naturally many people involved in an operation such as this and who share responsibility for its success, but there was only one who would have taken the blame if it had failed. Prime Minister Rabin is the one we should be congratulating. Yitzhak was very moved by Menachem Begin's remarks.

Once again, on July 22, 1991, the Labor Party Central Committee confirmed Shimon Peres as its leader. They didn't select Yitzhak, despite the fact that Labor needed a leadership change after the shameful failure to form a government in 1990. Peres got 54 percent, Yitzhak 46 percent. The children and I were terribly disappointed. It was impossible to believe that he lost again. I vividly remember the moment he walked into the house. He had enormous composure. He made us relax and gradually cheered us up. "This isn't the end of the world," he said. He approached his political renewal much the same way he approached the peace process, step by step. A word he always used was *patience*. I lack it. *Savlahnout*—"patience"—was such a pivotal word in his vocabulary, such a crucial trait of his character.

It was becoming clear to Yitzhak that his political opportunities would remain permanently thwarted unless Central Committee control of the Labor Party leadership election could be overcome and a primary system introduced. First, party rules had to be changed—but the party might now be receptive, because it had not won an election since 1974. The next challenge was to register well over 100,000 party members for the primaries. Then, of course, there was an enormous program of campaigning all over Israel to line up party workers and supporters. Yitzhak was not all that confident he would win the primaries, but he felt it was his only chance to win the nomination for party leader.

Yitzhak officially opened his campaign for a return to the prime ministership at the end of 1991, in anticipation of the 1992 elections. It was a response to the continuing groundswell of public support. The advent of internal party primaries, which Yitzhak had first campaigned for in 1990, opened up the selection process to the broad range of Labor Party adherents. Though Peres had been confirmed as Labor Party leader, people were growing uneasy. Could Peres defeat Likud? And if Likud won, what then?

Labor Party leaders began to realize that Yitzhak might have a better chance of winning the election. Throughout the primary campaign, Yitzhak crisscrossed the country again and again, talking to small gatherings in towns and villages, often before audiences inclined to be hostile, in poor neighborhoods, Russian enclaves and Arab towns—winning them over one by one. He made his political agenda clear. As the campaign advanced, he realized how well received his ideas were. At every rally crowds sang "Israel Is Waiting for Rabin"—a play on "Nasser Is Waiting for Rabin," a popular song of the Six-Day War.

The first Labor Party primary took place on February 19, 1992, and with it came the enthusiastic nod (40.6 percent for Yitzhak and 34.8 percent for Peres). Since Yitzhak won the nomination through the primaries, there was no need for any deal making with Peres or anyone else to be assured of the top slot on the ticket, as Labor Party leader and candidate for prime minister.

The Shamir government was pouring more than a billion dollars into the building of settlements. Russian immigrants were pouring into the country, and they felt their needs were not being met because funds were diverted for other purposes. The peace talks were going nowhere, largely—it seemed—because of the Shamir government's foot-dragging. The United States had dedicated enormous resources to the Desert Storm operation in the Gulf and was giving $3 billion a year to an Israel that didn't seem committed to resolving fundamental issues in the Middle East.

Ten billion dollars in loan guarantees from the United States intended to assist Israel in its absorption of hundreds of thousands of Soviet Jews were on the table. We could see which way the wind was blowing across the ocean; it was clear that the Bush administration (in office since January 1989) and Secretary of State James Baker in particular would be more comfortable with Yitzhak's leadership than seeing U.S. support effectively used to underwrite the reckless expansion of political settlements. The United States was also frustrated by the lack of progress in the Madrid peace talks—a Moscow-Washington-sponsored conference launched on the heels of the Gulf War that had gone through eleven uneventful rounds between 1991 and 1993 and whose momentum had ground to a halt. Yitzhak never participated in these talks before the election; the closest he ever got to them were the reports on the television news. Unlike the later phased peace initiatives, the Madrid talks tried to solve all the Middle East issues on all fronts at one time. The Israeli representative for the Madrid talks was the Likud's David Levy. Yitzhak thought Madrid was a big show in which the attendees sat around the same table without getting anything done.

The campaign for the premiership wasn't easy. Yitzhak toured the entire country, visiting almost every spot on the map. Normally, he would come home encouraged by the way he was received. Once again the crowds took up the song "Israel Is Waiting for Rabin." Once I remember him returning with a glowing smile. "You know," he said, drumming his fingertips on the armrest of his chair, "it was really well organized, there was an enormous crowd." He was happy, but, most interesting of all, he was surprised. There were a few incidents of name-calling here and there, but seldom did he meet with abusive remarks or a hostile crowd. He never avoided potential antagonism. In fact, he made it a point *not* to avoid a place where protesters were expected. When he appeared before a crowd that was not necessarily in his favor, he would try and win them over through logical debate.

For example, during the campaign, he met with a group of settlers in the Golan in a kibbutz dining hall. He refused to promise that there would never be an evacuation of the region. When he returned from this meeting, he said it was one of the most difficult confrontations of his life. "But it's nothing compared to what we will face down the road," he said.

The campaign was an exhausting but very satisfying time for him. Election campaigns start late in the afternoon and go deep into the night, because that is when people are free to come to the assemblies. Night after night, one of our drivers, Charlie or

Yehezkel, would drive him to rallies into the late, late hours. Afterward, he would go to the studio to review the video spots prepared for the television campaign. One of the last rallies took place in an amphitheater in our neighborhood. I didn't attend, but the excitement was apparently unbelievable. One of Yitzhak's campaign aides, Yizzhak Matalon, was so moved he called me from his cell phone. "Leah," he said, "I'm in tears. You have no idea what is going on here."

In 1992, Yitzhak was still unsure he could win, but I was more confident, familiar with the attitudes of people on the street, which I learned nearly daily walking through town and in the aisles of the supermarket. "Mrs. Rabin, good luck. We *want* him to be elected," I heard again and again. There was something about Yitzhak that commanded enormous trust. In a televised debate with the Likud's Yitzhak Shamir on June 16, Yitzhak's enormous commitment to Israel's security was evident, while Shamir denied that there was reason to be alarmed about the state of affairs between Israel and the United States. When the debate was over Yitzhak called me. I told him he had been terrific. Yitzhak was fully aware of how important the debate would be in the whole election campaign. He'd prepared for it carefully, defining the views he would present, and he had long rehearsals with his aides. His answers were clear and logical. When he said that it was time to change our priorities and make peace, the nation took him at his word.

CHAPTER
9

ALL HIS SONS

June 23, 1992, was election day in Israel. In the library of our home, we gathered around the television with our children and grandchildren, waiting for the ten o'clock exit poll results to be announced. Many friends had wanted to be with us at the hoped-for moment of victory, but Yitzhak was absolutely firm that no one except the family would enter our house before then. The chatter was subdued but constant. Aides made short, periodic calls to report the latest projections. Once again, Yitzhak was drumming his fingertips on the top of his desk.

Nine fifty-eight. Nine fifty-nine. Then an intense hush. Riveted to the TV, we awaited the results of the exit polls at ten P.M.

At ten o'clock, the television anchorman Haim Yavin appeared on screen and uttered a single word: *"Ma'apach."*

That word said everything to us—everything we needed to know to let loose a joyous round of hugging and kissing. *Ma'apach*: the magic lever that released a river of happy tears.

In Hebrew, *ma'apach* means turnaround. In 1977, Israeli television had used this word when Likud won the election. Until that sultry June evening in 1992, *ma'apach* had terrible connotations for us. But now it meant only one thing: victory.

Pandemonium broke out in our apartment as visitors streamed in, but it was dwarfed by the roar throughout the neighborhood that was rushing in through our open windows—a heavy-throated chorus of high-rises, their windows gaping open like some huge concrete mouths blasting out a storm of approval.

The shouts of joy resounding through the streets came as something of a surprise. The whole neighborhood had wanted this victory? Our eyes and ears flashed between the dramatic live coverage on television and the real-life celebration echoing all around us. It was as if the most crucial goal had been scored in the most important soccer match imaginable. I thought of the ovation that Yitzhak had received at Bloomfield Stadium in 1977, just days after he resigned, but this was ten times louder and relentlessly happier. Vindication, yes. But this was a victory that went far beyond vindication. I was stunned and moved, crying my happy heart out.

There was only one composed person in the room. Only one person who didn't cheer . . . or cry for joy . . . and barely even smiled.

When he heard the word *ma'apach*, Yitzhak didn't react at all. He cautioned us that there might still be a change in the final results. He was right. The first projections claimed that Labor would win three more than the forty-four seats it ultimately did, but in the end it was enough to form the foundation for a coalition.

Yitzhak didn't jump up and down. He quietly answered the first congratulatory phone calls with the words, "Thank you very much." Still, inside I could sense he was a very happy man. We hugged and kissed him, but he never left his chair. "Let's wait and see . . . ," he said.

The phone was ringing off the hook. In mere minutes the apartment was thronged with friends and well-wishers. Our photo albums show the many flower arrangements that were sent in the days that followed; our apartment was like a florist's shop. What an unforgettable sight! There wasn't a square millimeter of table or countertop, carpet or corner that wasn't bursting with dazzling, bright blossoms.

The Labor Party victory celebration at the Dan Hotel in Tel Aviv was in full swing when we arrived at about one in the morning. Music, dancing, and nonstop chanting of "Israel Is Waiting for Rabin." In his acceptance speech at the hotel, Yitzhak praised and thanked all those who worked hard to bring about his return to office. Then he spoke the empowering words that were later often quoted: "I will navigate. I will control. I will lead."

Until 1992, the longest interregnum for a major political figure was de Gaulle's twelve-year hiatus from office. Then came the return of Yitzhak Rabin after an unprecedented interval of fifteen years.

At four A.M., finally, he went to bed, pleased and self-assured, but already planning for tomorrow. Yitzhak said his personal version of good night, *"Ishti,* please wake me up at six forty-five tomorrow morning." The next day Yitzhak got up and went to work. This was Yitzhak—three hours of sleep and off to work like any other day. There was so very much ahead of him. I was reminded of this night years later, when I read Doris Kearns Goodwin's fascinating book, *No Ordinary Time.* I came across a passage in which she writes of Winston Churchill's accession to the prime ministership of the United Kingdom in May 1940: ". . . and when he went to bed that night after the extraordinary day, he was conscious of a profound sense of relief. 'At last I had the authority to give directions over the whole scene. I felt as if I were walking with destiny and that all my past life had been but a preparation for this hour and this trial.' "

In the new administration, Yitzhak would hold two portfolios—prime minister and minister of defense. He knew that he needed direct control of both if he were to advance the peace process steadily. This time, it was to be his show, his agenda. More than anything else, he felt that he was the best one to handle both jobs.

Yitzhak's joint duties were unusual in many world governments, but this combined responsibility had been common in Israel's history, because security concerns overlap with much of the nation's daily business. Both David Ben-Gurion and Levi Eshkol held these two posts in the past. The United States president is also the commander in chief, a situation that approximates what we have had in Israel on a more or less ongoing basis. But Yitzhak never overlooked the irony of his situation, and he would sometimes say in cabinet meetings, "I am now speaking as minister of defense, and I would like you to know that, as minister of defense, I have a problem with the prime minister."

On July 13, Yitzhak presented his government. I wrote these recollections in a diary as we were being driven to Jerusalem for the oath of office:

> *Yitzhak is fast asleep next to me in the car. I am reading the speech he will present in the Knesset. I think highly of this speech. I must admit to being very excited. Can we really be climbing toward Jerusalem—"climbing," as in the full sense of the word?*
>
> *It is fifteen years since Yitzhak's resignation. If there is a hidden force that corrects injustices, then here and now it seems to have worked. Yitzhak is returning in a big way, surrounded by love, supported by leaders from all over the world, and admired by Jews in the Diaspora everywhere. They all look up to him and are so full of hope and expectation.*
>
> *Yitzhak is aware of the responsibility weighing upon his shoulders. He is determined . . . to improve conditions of life for every citizen on every level and, most important, to endeavor to bring peace to the region.*
>
> *The children are with us. Dalia and Avi, Yuval and Eilat, and three mature grandchildren. They were all part of the turmoil of the last few months and today they are rejoicing in the festivities. Aliza Wallach is with us, and so are special friends—Ruthie Goldmuntz from New York, Diane and Norman Bernstein from Washington. Norman and Diane are with us today as they were when Yitzhak presented the government in 1974. My sister, Aviva, has also come, and everyone present increases the sense of excitement and festivity.*

Yitzhak called his speech "A Determined Government," and it was one of the finest he ever gave, as I believe these excerpts demonstrate:

> ... *The government that today seeks the vote of confidence of the Knesset is well aware that everyone in Israel is watching in prayer and in great hope. Many here and abroad wish today for a new road, for impetus, for a new page in the history of the State of Israel.*
>
> *We shall change the national order of priorities. ...*
>
> *Israel is no longer necessarily an isolated nation, nor is it correct that the entire world is against us. We must rid ourselves of the isolationism that has gripped us almost for half a century.*
>
> *We will initiate vigorous steps to put an end to the Arab-Israeli conflict. We shall do so on the basis of recognition, by the Arab states and the Palestinians, of Israel as a sovereign state with the right to live in peace and security. We wholeheartedly believe that this is possible, that this is necessary, that this will come. ...*

Yitzhak went on to propose that peace talks with the Arab states go forward within the framework of the Madrid conference. He invited the joint Jordanian-Palestinian delegation to a conference in Jerusalem to establish a positive climate for working together, though he thought the concept of a joint delegation was ridiculous and wanted to start talking with the Palestinians directly. He reminded the Palestinians that we shared the same land and noted that they had lost so much in life, happiness, and well-being that an offer of self-rule would represent a real opportunity to bring about change. At the same time, he pledged that Israel would concede nothing to terror or violence. He invited other Arab leaders—the king of Jordan and the presidents of Syria and Lebanon—to follow in President Sadat's footsteps and come to address the Knesset in Jerusalem. "Our face is toward the rising sun," as he put it. He pledged continuing partnership with the United States and concluded with a gripping and profound definition of security:

> *Security is not only a tank, an aircraft, a missile ship. Security is also, and perhaps foremost, men and women—the Israeli citizens.*
>
> *Security is also a man's education, housing, schools, the street and the neighborhood, the society in which he grew up. And security is also that man's hope.*
>
> *Security is the peace of mind and the means to live for the immigrant from Leningrad, the roof over the immigrant from Gondar in Ethiopia, the factory and employment of the citizen born here, of the demobilized soldier.*
>
> *It is integration and participation in our experience and culture. That, too, is security. . . .*

Yitzhak's "inauguration" speech was received extremely well, not just in Israel but all over the world. After the Knesset session, the confirmation vote, and the introduction of the new government, we lingered a bit in the new office of the prime minister, where Yitzhak received a congratulatory phone call from President Bush. Then we headed on to the King David Hotel, where we stayed until the prime minister's residence in Jerusalem was renovated.

On July 14, Yitzhak and his cabinet had the customary photograph taken with Israel's president, Chaim Herzog, whose second term in office was nearing a close. I spent most of this day following the swearing-in of the government with our friends from Washington, the Bernsteins. Our relationship, formed long ago during Yitzhak's years as ambassador, truly went on to stand the test of time. It was only natural for us to share these exciting moments with them.

With the transition of leadership in Jerusalem, it would have been a nice, helpful gesture—really almost a routine courtesy—for the outgoing prime minister to congratulate Yitzhak and to wish him well. One would have also expected that my predecessor as first lady would have invited me to see the house and given me background on the staff.

This certainly struck me when we watched the transition of power between Presidents Bush and Clinton that took place in January 1993. Bill Clinton was about to be inaugurated, and television cameras showed the world how warmly he and Hillary were received by the Bush family. After the Inauguration Ceremony at the Capitol, the new presidential couple arrived at the White House. At the same time, news reports showed a van transporting George and Barbara Bush's personal belongings to their future home in Houston. We may have a lot to learn from countries with established codes of etiquette in the transition of their governments. I am sure that President and Mrs. Bush were sad to leave the White House, nevertheless, they welcomed the new couple with genuine warmth and cordiality. As it was, we never received a word of congratulation or an invitation to visit the house from Israel's departing prime minister and his wife.

Yitzhak didn't worry much about the ceremonial niceties that went along with the change of power. Quickly he and his cabinet got down to business. Within the first two weeks after taking office, Yitzhak had already met with U.S. secretary of state James Baker and visited President Mubarak in Cairo. One of the very first measures implemented by Yitzhak's government was taken in July, when Housing Minister Binyamin Ben-Eliezer issued a freeze on new construction in the Occupied Territories. By autumn, Yitzhak had suspended all government-subsidized construction already under way in the Territories. No longer would Israel be funding "sleep-over settlements."

On our first official visit to the United States and Yitzhak's first visit with President Bush, a great deal was at stake. In my opinion, President Bush and Secretary of State Baker had every reason to be angry with the Likud regime. Still, would the United States approve the $10 billion in loan guarantees that had been stalled during the last Israeli administration? Would any other issues stand in the way?

The first meeting was to take place at the president's house in Kennebunkport, Maine. Only a handful of world leaders had been invited to this beautiful site, and we felt especially honored to be among the few. Barbara Bush is a very sensible lady, and she has a commonsense grasp of the implications of events. She showed this side of herself to me early on. Mrs. Bush was waiting for me when we arrived, and we took a long walk around the grounds. I asked her about the upcoming presidential election and she said, "I'm sure the guy is going to win. But if he loses, I shall feel very sorry for him . . . At the same time I'll feel very happy for my children." She knew well the sacrifices that a first family must make.

The strong family feeling of Kennebunkport was perhaps its most memorable feature. We visited George Bush's elderly mother and aunt, who each had separate homes on the estate and were well taken care of by private nurses. In the main house, a dormitory on the second floor had beds for the Bushes' grandchildren. The easygoing, non-manicured look of this dormitory impressed me. Here was an established, well-to-do family that didn't care if all the children's bedspreads matched or not. To the grandchildren, Grandma and Grandpa were the pillars of their lives.

George Bush was charming. Barbara was a wonderful and efficient hostess, not an easy task when you always seem to be looking after a huge entourage. We stayed in the guest house, and I couldn't resist remarking, "Barbara, this guest house is so well equipped, even with a washer and dryer!" She said there were a lot of sports activities at the retreat—tennis, fishing, horseshoes—you name it. She added, with a twinkle in her eye, that she wanted her guests to smell good.

The negotiations over the loan guarantees conducted by Yitzhak and his aides weren't easy. At the end of a long day, everybody's a horse trader. Discussions went deep into the night. Finally, toward the early hours of dawn, the wrinkles were ironed out. The thrust of the American negotiators was to nail down more specifics, to exact certain political commitments from Yitzhak. A position paper was even created to suggest what these might be, ironically termed "The Non-Paper"—an expression of Yitzhak's desire to avoid a formal agreement. Yitzhak prevailed, however, and maintained very general and basic guidelines.

Not long ago, Special Middle East Coordinator Dennis Ross told me about Yitzhak's first meeting with James Baker, a man for whom Yitzhak had considerable respect. One of the first things Yitzhak said to Baker was, "I won't lie to you. If we tell you something you can count on it. We may not always agree, but the one thing you will know is that we are not going to lie to you, we are not going to mislead you." After their initial meeting, Yitzhak approached Ross during a break before lunch. He said, "Dennis, the secretary is treating me as if I'm the last Yitzhak—tell him there is a different Yitzhak now." Ross went back to Baker and told him, look, they are changing their priorities, he told you he is not going to lie to you, we can't act as if nothing has changed. And from that point on Baker did change and the loan guarantees were approved.

President Bush and Secretary Baker were eventually convinced that Yitzhak would use the guarantees for the best of reasons, including immigrant absorption. The Kennebunkport visit acknowledged the refreshing change of policy of Israel's new government. The next morning an open-air ceremony took place granting the loan guarantees. Yitzhak and President Bush were center stage, facing the press. Barbara Bush and I stood off to the side. The president and Yitzhak gave their statements. At this very important moment that meant so much to Yitzhak and his future plans, I was virtually in tears from relief. When Yitzhak finished his comments, the first question by the press was directed at President Bush. "Was it true that you were having an affair . . ." For the press, the loan guarantees were secondary to the latest nugget of mean-spirited gossip. I must credit Barbara Bush for her self-control. She didn't flinch for a moment. For me, this show of bad taste was like an emotional punch in the stomach that brought me sailing back to earth.

All in all, however, the big issues were resolved. We flew on to Washington with George and Barbara Bush on Air Force One— what an experience! Later, Yitzhak met with AIPAC, the leading Jewish lobbyist group. He didn't mince words in criticizing the lobby's overly aggressive campaign to secure the loan guarantees for Israel. It was an important point made by Israel's new prime minister, and it helped clarify the ground rules for the future. Yitzhak and I then flew back to Tel Aviv.

In August, after many hours of hard physical work schlepping and arranging books and furniture, trying to settle into our new residence, and still rebounding from the stress of the election and the U.S. visit, I suddenly took ill during a Saturday-morning tennis game. My arms suddenly became tremendously weak. I sat down in the shade, and this strange episode passed. I wanted to continue playing, but Ziona Leshem, my tennis partner, refused to let me go on. She had lost her husband in a similar situation. While I was still sitting down, the pressure in my chest returned. We realized it must be serious and quickly returned home.

A physician was called, and Dr. Shlomo Segev arrived momentarily. He immediately summoned an ambulance that rushed me to Tel Hashomer Hospital. Commotion engulfed me. The uncomfortable feeling continued, but the minute they injected me with an anti-coagulant, I felt better. I received an injection in order to expand the blood vessels. While I'm sure it helped, it also had the side effect of causing severe headaches, which plagued me over the next few days. I was in intensive care. Late one night, Ephraim Sneh, a Knesset member and later minister of health, suddenly appeared beside my bed. I asked him how he managed to sneak in after visiting hours. "You forget," Ephraim said to me with a smile, "I am a doctor." I was touched by his visit. He has been a devoted friend and remains so today.

Yitzhak and Dalia came to see me in the hospital. They were, of course, shaken by the scare. Yitzhak had a very straightforward bedside manner: "How are you? How do you feel today?" he would ask, matter-of-factly, but I knew it was just his way of expressing himself. He *hated* hysteria! At the same time, after I was out of the hospital and the recuperation was well along, he wanted me on my feet and well again as quickly as possible. He had a hard time with my being sick. He wanted his strong and cheerful wife restored.

The next day the doctors proposed an angiogram. It sounded frightening and I refused! Another day passed, and I was visited by two professors, the managing directors of the hospital. I gathered that they were going to insist on the procedure. I caved in but not before I bargained with them. I agreed to the angiogram if—all being well—they would permit me to travel to Zürich and Berlin in ten days, to do fund-raising on behalf of Shiba Medical Center. They agreed to my terms.

The following day the catheterization was done. Once my mind was made up to undergo that procedure, I stopped being anxious over it. I knew I was in the good hands of the coronary surgeon, Dr. Mulla Ratt. Yitzhak and Dalia anxiously watched the procedure from the adjoining room. To tell the truth, I felt nothing during the angiogram, which was followed by an angioplasty—a "balloon treatment," to enlarge a narrowed artery. After the angioplasty, I was transferred to a regular ward. I spent one more day in the hospital and the next day I went home to millions of flowers. Even President Mubarak sent a floral arrangement to the hospital. Still not a word from Mr. or Mrs. Shamir. Shortly afterward, several days before the Jewish New Year, I was invited to a ceremony at the home of our president. It was a ladies' affair. At the end of the ceremony, as everyone was getting up, I went over to Mrs. Shamir, who also attended. I gave her my hand and said, "Mrs. Shamir, I want to wish you *shanah tova.*" I was very proud of myself for having done the right thing. Since Yitzhak's murder, I still have not heard a single word of condolence from them.

During my hospitalization, Yitzhak was constantly there for me, as he was when anyone in the family was sick. He did not interrupt his working schedule but came to see me several times each day. When my recuperation proved successful and rapid, he settled back into his grueling routine. As the years passed, the people working with him were increasingly astounded by his work habits and his stamina. I often remarked that Yitzhak was a creation designed for heavy lifting. He would get up religiously at six forty-five in the morning and stay in the office until nine or ten o'clock at night. Not one day of illness in his entire second term.

From his co-workers and our friends, all I ever heard was "Can't you stop him? Doesn't he ever need a rest, a day off? Is this a schedule for a man in his seventies?" There was always a reason why, now, he felt he just couldn't . . . there was too much to do. Not one day of vacation in three and a half years. During our last summer in 1995, we were invited to spend a few days with friends in the Berkshires in New England (we had spent vacations there several times before; both of us very much enjoyed those occasions, especially the concerts at Tanglewood). We had to refuse the invitation. "This is not the time," Yitzhak would say. In his first term of office, we had gone to Eilat a few weekends and once or twice to Caesarea. But there wasn't even a weekend off in his second term. He was always traveling somewhere, at least one or two days a week. When the weekend came, he understandably wanted to stay home, but that didn't mean he loafed around the house. Even on Shabbat he would routinely see four or five people. There were the regulars and the irregulars, but there wasn't one Shabbat that someone didn't come to see him and brief him or ask for his advice. I always used to say Shabbat was my working day. There was no help in the house and I would run in and out with cups of coffee, glasses of water, beer or whiskey. Often Yitzhak would give me a hand between visitors, carrying cups and saucers to the kitchen and emptying his own full ashtray.

Observing Yitzhak discharge the duties of his office left many in awe, including the insiders who worked with him most closely. Yitzhak's nature was to address everything in a thorough, meticulous way. He exhaustively reviewed every matter before him and never tired of reexamining the issues. Always flawlessly prepared, he amazed people at how organized he was in his thinking. No matter if it was the Palestinian issue, defense matters, the electricity board, or education. He dealt with them all. He had the capacity to live on so many levels simultaneously! Whether it was the West Bank . . . or the need for high-technology investment . . . or a God-forsaken factory that needed support, or a developing town—like the title of the Arthur Miller drama, they were "All His Sons"!

There was no one subject that interested him less than another. Some have criticized him for that attitude, dismissing it as "micro-management." I think it was a cardinal virtue. He gave the national agenda in Israel more balance than any leader who preceded him.

"We will change the priorities," he had said, but everything was a priority on his agenda. From the political point of view, he knew that he had four years. These four years would end with the 1996 elections. Certainly, he would seek reelection, but "you never know with elections"—this was his view—so he was doing his utmost to achieve what he could in this term of office. Had he been given the chance of another four years, he would have been a very happy man.

Never for a minute did he think that he had done his share and that he was entitled to rest, that he might step down—not for a minute.

For all his many strengths, people were one of Yitzhak's weaknesses. He never had a kitchen cabinet and relied almost exclusively (with some reservations and some criticism) on the people in the official chain of command, behavior consistent with his rigorous military background. Staff aides close to him such as Niva Lanir believe he never fired people even when he should have. Sometimes appointees stayed in their jobs just because he was reluctant to tell them to leave. He relied mostly on instinct in making many of his appointments. If he realized he had made a mistake, he was the one to bear the consequences and make the best of it.

He was always loyal and sensitive to people who worked with him and needed his support. During his second term, a cabinet member, Ora Namir—one very tough lady—faced a devastating crisis. She's a single woman with no children, alone in the world. Yitzhak was angry when she missed a cabinet meeting; he didn't know that she had gone instead to a special medical checkup. She reported back to him with the results. "Yitzhak, I need surgery for a serious brain tumor," she said. He was shocked.

"Whatever you need, wherever you need it; you find the best doctor in the world," Yitzhak told her. "That's what we did when our daughter, Dalia, needed a heart-valve transplant. We looked for the best doctor in the world and found him in London. Don't worry about what people here in Israel will say if you choose a doctor out of the country. Don't worry about the expenses. I promise you that we shall take care of it."

She was so moved. One of the best brain surgeons in the world performed the operation outside of Israel. Her hospital recuperation took four weeks. After returning home, she said to Yitzhak, "Look, I'm in the middle of a long convalescence, and the doctors don't want me to travel to Jerusalem for three months. If you feel that I can't fulfill my duties, I will of course resign immediately."

"What's the matter with you?" he said. "Of course you're not going to resign. We shall wait for you. Take all the time you need."

Yitzhak's reaction was nearly identical when one of the nation's highest-ranking military officers was stricken with leukemia. The officer was shaken and wanted to do the very best thing for the sake of Israel. Yitzhak got all the details on the disease. The physicians said that the prognosis for a cure was good. Yitzhak promised his continuous support to the general. "We are behind you, don't worry," he said again and again to him and his wife in private conversations. The officer was cured, and our nation retained the services of one of its finest military minds.

Yitzhak conveyed this kind of confidence to people on all levels, not just to those who faced illnesses. This came through in a story told to me not long ago on a plane. An Israeli man came over to me and said, "I need to tell you a story. I owe my life to Yitzhak. . . ." He was on the front lines just before the Six-Day War. Yitzhak was personally reviewing those lonely outposts, often manned by a solitary soldier charged with defending the line at a single point. Moshe Dayan had made a similar tour the day before, the man told me. With typical swagger, Dayan had said to the fellow, who was then just a young gunner, "When a soldier manning this sort of post comes under overwhelming fire, it typically takes about four minutes before he is killed." Instead of making him feel like a tough-as-nails daredevil who could stare down death, the remark made the young man feel threatened and scared out of his wits. Sensing this, Yitzhak asked the soldier to describe what exactly was bothering him. The young fellow explained his devastating concern—being so close to the enemy and so exposed. Yitzhak looked around and saw another little hill, a few feet away. He suggested the soldier go over and note whether it afforded him the same view. "So you should move over there," Yitzhak said. Thirty years later, the officer I met on the airplane was still grateful.

Yitzhak was always thinking this way. He believed he held full responsibility for his people and continually sought ways to help them do their jobs better or prevent unnecessary casualties. After his driver Yehezkel had a serious heart attack, Yitzhak promised him he would never smoke again in the car.

As a communicator, Yitzhak had great candor and directness—*dugri,* as I termed it earlier. He was more a statesman than a politician. He realized that you cannot survive in government without being a politician, but he certainly didn't like that part of his job. Eventually he learned how to play the game. This was inevitably the price one had to pay. He would much rather have spent that time differently.

Like most heads of state, Yitzhak ascribed great importance to his speeches. If it wasn't a particularly important speech—such as remarks before the Knesset or at the White House—he would just talk extemporaneously. It might not have been as polished, but the words came directly from his heart and his mind. He was clearly more comfortable speaking off the cuff. He always knew what message he wanted to get across and had a great gift for lining the points up in his head beforehand. He never lost his train of thought, though the sentences were often so long that you expected him to drift away!

For more important talks, he would prepare an outline of the points that he wanted to cover, then his aides would draft the words. Sometimes he would come home, saying that he wasn't happy with the speech that had been written for him. He would invite me to look at it, and I would note my comments and suggestions. Sometimes he would sit down and rewrite the entire speech himself, though most of the speeches written for him were excellent (Eitan Haber was his chief speechwriter).

Henry Kissinger said to me after Yitzhak's death, "I have seen a lot of eminent politicians, and he moved me like very few others have. The thing that to me was so astonishing about Yitzhak was I never thought he was a good speaker—until the peace process started. And then he gave some really great speeches. The key reason was a change in perspective—he raised his sights to history."

After every speech of his I attended, he would come down from the podium and invariably look at me and ask, "Was it OK? Was it bearable?" I was his most severe critic to be sure. Often I hesitated, because you don't want to hurt someone close to you at a vulnerable moment. Sometimes it would hurt him if I said, "You could have done better," or "Your English wasn't so great tonight." Problems arose more often with his English speeches than his Hebrew ones. If he had to deliver an English speech off the cuff and he was tired, he could make embarrassing mistakes. I would take out a slip of paper and note the particular errors. Not that it would help much—he would make the same mistakes over and over again. Though embarrassing at times, my criticism would reinforce my credibility. On the occasions I would say, "Yitzhak, you were absolutely great," he could trust that he truly did a superb job, and I believe it meant a lot to him.

Listening to Yitzhak in public or in private was very natural for me. His opinions and activities were obviously of central importance to my life. Others tell me I'm a very good listener generally. I may be a good listener, but my attention can lapse at movies and at the theater—I easily fall asleep; Yitzhak never did and he would occasionally poke me in the side to keep me awake!

I have always been very curious about literature, art, and music. I count curiosity as one of my virtues, though it's diminished somewhat now. I find myself less interested in things since the murder, less the voracious reader I once was. Something in me has dimmed; my powers of concentration may be faltering, my thoughts keep wandering—always back to *him*. But I believe this is part of the healing process I am undergoing and hope I will once again be able to read as I did before. But will anything be as it was . . . ?

∞ The media were a big influence during Yitzhak's second term as they are everywhere today in matters of government. In Israel we have nationally televised news once a day between eight and nine in the evening on two channels at the same time, so you flip between the two. It's hard to say which network was more supportive of Yitzhak. They are generally out for sensation and blood, to make news and fuel ratings.

Overall, I'm very upset with the Israeli networks. In a society struggling for peace, I do not believe the media have the right to undermine that initiative. The people in the media are themselves more liberal and supportive of the peace process than their programming suggests. Still, to up their ratings, they sensationalize their coverage, and this would often upset Yitzhak—especially with prime-time Friday-night news. He would sit there fuming in front of the screen and say, "What television we have! What a scandal!" Their coverage grew more sensational during the rough period of the Intifada, and it certainly fed on the violent, pro-Likud demonstrations in the year leading up to the assassination. The damage the broadcasters caused didn't seem to register on their consciences.

On some occasions, I confronted the media personally. Dan Shilon is a very famous personality who moderates a highly rated talk show on Israeli television. We knew him well. At times, we were even close friends, with visits between our respective homes and attendance at important family celebrations such as his son's bar mitzvah. I was very fond of his wife.

When Yitzhak's government was experiencing a low point in public opinion, Dan Shilon charged that Yitzhak's government had lost touch with the people of Israel. I saw red. I'm not sure where Yitzhak was traveling, but I'm certain that we weren't watching the show together. I called Dan Shilon the following day at his office and said, "I assume that you support the peace process and basically support the government. So why are you taking this position? You yourself are fully aware that this government is not detached from the people. You know that statement is untrue, but you don't really give a damn for anything other than the ratings of your program."

He was speechless. How dare I question what he had said on television? He said that, out of respect for me and my position, he wanted to forget our conversation ever took place. In fact, he ran—I'm sure he couldn't walk fast enough—to a press meeting to tell them the whole story: Leah Rabin had the nerve to call me up and accuse me of being interested only in the ratings of my program. A friend called and asked if I was aware that Dan Shilon leaked the story to the press. He also supposedly said, "We are friends? I hardly ever see her."

Several months later, Dan Shilon wanted to interview both Yitzhak and me. Yitzhak asked what I thought we should do. I said, "You go. I'll keep my boycott." The show aired in the spring of 1995. Shilon had promised to make this the best show possible. And he did. He had a wonderful group of guests. I remember Shilon asking an Israeli youngster what he wanted to do when he grew up, and the boy said he wanted to become chief of staff of the IDF! The young pop singer Aviv Geffen also was a guest on the show. Yitzhak was relaxed and had lively, interesting exchanges with the other guests. The audience applauded him constantly, and the program was a great success.

As prime minister, Yitzhak had to communicate a message that linked peace to prosperity. He had to show people that peace would have tangible benefits for their everyday life. Yitzhak was committed to the growth of a market economy, but he also understood that the budgets had to include outlays for medical care, social security, and education. While he was concerned about working conditions, he abandoned early the strict socialist belief in equal pay, no matter what the work. People should, he felt, be compensated for more demanding or more sophisticated work. An item on his agenda was to make Israel a totally modern economy with modern attitudes.

In his second term, Yitzhak's policies realized 6 percent economic growth and sharply reduced unemployment from 12 percent to 6 to 7 percent. Still, he wanted more money invested in industrial development, housing, education, and infrastructure improvements. This also included solving the immigration-related problems of jobs and housing.

The peace process stimulated economic growth. After the loan guarantees, foreign investment surged by American companies such as Johnson and Johnson and McDonald's. Great gains in real growth and declining inflation helped the standard of living to improve dramatically. The signs of prosperity were everywhere; one barometer was the growing number of personal cars, with 150,000 purchased each year. There also was an incredible surge in the number of Israelis traveling abroad—about a half million every summer.

Yitzhak constantly fought outmoded social attitudes. Israelis still subscribed to the notion that signs of prosperity were considered unacceptable. In the early days, when offices were designed, the rule of thumb often was, "Do anything you want, but make it look modest." For many years, Israelis drove primarily Japanese cars because they were smaller and cheaper. American cars were considered too luxurious, too showy. The government adhered to this idea and continued to buy Japanese cars, even when the value of yen soared. There is now no difference in the price/quality equation between Japanese and American cars. Yitzhak fought this bias vigorously and would question, "Why can't we help the American automobile industry when Americans are constantly helping us?" When I last purchased a new car, Yitzhak insisted I buy an American car to serve as an example. Change comes slowly, but Israeli attitudes are changing.

Yitzhak saw the importance of developing Israel's high-technology sector and ambitiously tried to learn more about emerging industries. Unless a crisis was taking place, he would select a different industry to visit each week. As I like to put it, he was always getting into the batter to help others bake their cakes.

The Ministry of Defense is located in Tel Aviv but the cabinet and Knesset meetings are in Jerusalem, so Yitzhak divided his week between the two cities. Yitzhak greatly respected his hard-working defense department staff. When the phone rang in the middle of the night or early in the morning, you could be sure it was Yitzhak's military aide Danny Yatom and that the news was not good. Danny would convey the message in a very understated, matter-of-fact way. He was both dispassionate and genuine, and Yitzhak truly appreciated that.

Having spent twenty-seven years in the military, Yitzhak always had a great rapport with the troops. He loved to meet with them under any circumstances. His visits returned him to his past, a past that he never really left. Yitzhak knew the names of most commanders and their units. He knew where they trained and camped. He was acquainted with the life of an Israeli soldier to the last detail. After a serious incident, he would visit the site, generally within hours, and talk with the soldiers. He would find out exactly what, how, and why it happened. If morale was shaken, he would be there with the chief of staff to help restore it.

Unnecessary casualties caused him the greatest pain. If a risky operation were done according to the highest standards and it didn't go as planned, he might not have liked the result but he could live with it. But he couldn't live with the loss of young lives due to lack of discipline or order. Yitzhak couldn't tolerate human life lost in vain.

Not long before the murder, a mobile Israeli patrol in the southern Lebanese security zone detonated a mine, and the tank exploded. Special half-track tanks with extra-fortified bottoms are now routinely used for these kinds of patrols. They can run over an exploding mine without blowing up. The command unit had two such half-tracks but they were both sitting in the shop awaiting mechanical repairs, so the patrol used the regular half-tracks. When he heard about this, Yitzhak said, "This really drives me out of my mind. We are investing so much effort and thought and developing so many means to protect these young lives . . . and these guys just left the extra-armored vehicles in the workshop, didn't see to their repair, they used the other ones, and got killed."

Yitzhak had a longtime friend in Moshe Netzer of Kibbutz

Ramat Yohanan. They attended kindergarten together. They were
pals in grade school and at the Kadoorie Mandatorial High School.
They even competed for the Agricultural School's top prize, which
Yitzhak ultimately won. They had a very strong bond over the
years. Moshe's son was killed one night due to negligence. Someone had thrown a container he thought was empty into a campfire,
not realizing it contained a live shell, and it exploded. When he
learned the news, it was one of Yitzhak's saddest days.

A great tribute to Yitzhak's philosophy on defense and security
came from his colleague Lieutenant General Amnon Lipkin-Shahak,
the IDF's chief of staff, at the thirtieth-day remembrance ceremonies following Yitzhak's death. Here are some of the most
poignant moments from that moving speech:

> *In agonizing pain and with awesome respect, we meet
> again, on this quiet hilltop of tombstones, facing a fresh
> grave. . . .*
>
> *Thirty days have passed, only thirty days—yet they seem
> an eternity, or perhaps already thirty days, for it seems like a
> fraction of a second since that terrible night. . . .*
>
> *How could this thing happen among us?*
>
> *We have a saying that it is not the armor which will over-
> come but the man, and Yitzhak Rabin, who commanded us
> and led us on the battlefields and in the roads of peace, was
> such a man. . . .*
>
> *Security, according to Yitzhak Rabin, is made up of seeing
> the complete and overall objective, just as much as paying
> attention to the details. In his speech to the Command Staff
> and College, in August 1992, Defense Minister Yitzhak
> Rabin addressed the graduating class, and sent a message to
> the entire army: "One of our most painful problems has a
> name—a first name and a family name. It is the combination
> of the two words Yihye beseder, 'it will be all right.' Behind
> those two words are usually hidden all the things that will
> not be all right: arrogance and excessive overconfidence, un-
> justified power and authority. Yihye beseder is the hallmark*

of lack of organization and discipline, of nonexistent profes-
sionalism, of idleness. . . ."

He went on to say: "And what do I feel that I have the
right to demand of you? Firstly responsibility. What else do
we demand? Professionalism, initiative, and innovation—to
be human beings, to report the truth, to set a personal ex-
ample, discipline, pride, and motivation."

In essence, Yitzhak Rabin required that we should be like
him, for all that he demanded was there in him. We saw him
ponder, consult, then finally decide alone. . . . And thus it
was he said, "All my life in the Palmach and the IDF, from
when I was a squad leader through my service as regional
commander, chief of staff, prime minister, and defense min-
ister, before any decision for a raid, a battle, a war, I always
had before my eyes the eyes of warriors asking, Is this sensi-
ble, is there no alternative? And the eyes of the mothers, the
fathers, the wives and children, who wait at home. . . ."

And the children were before his eyes. As he told us, "The
State of Israel has no natural resources—no coal mines or oil
wells. Our greatest resource is our children." The children
that he thought about, spoke of, and acted for are the sol-
diers of today and tomorrow. They who have understood
that he fought for them, worked for their welfare, and be-
lieved in their future. Those children always responded to
him with love, and have done so in overwhelming might in
the last thirty days.

Shalom, commander, we shall miss you. . . .

∞ The social side of state affairs was never as important to
Yitzhak personally as his dedication to detail on the battlefield, but
he recognized that both were important in the life of a stable nation. During the second term, my role as the wife of Israel's prime
minister had strikingly different dimensions than during the first
term. The peace process was the constant center of international
media and political attention. Israel's acceptance abroad was
greater than it had ever been. As a result, I had the good fortune to

be at Yitzhak's side as the mightiest nations in the world accorded Israel newfound respect and admiration.

Still, other aspects of how we entertained remained unchanged—no matter if the guests were heads of state or dear friends we had known since childhood. I've always felt entertaining at home is a very important element in building friendly relations with state guests. Over the years, the whole idea of having company within Israel changed. When we were young, we would be invited to a friend's home for coffee and cake after dinner. As our standard of living rose and our obligations changed, we would invite people over for dinner parties, more or less formal ones. We also used dinners as a means to bring people into the house earlier. In the current Israeli lifestyle, friends might arrive as late as eleven. Yitzhak had to get up early every single morning. The trick was to have them arrive for dinner at eighty-thirty and see them leave by eleven or twelve. When we were invited out, sometimes Yitzhak would smilingly use the expression, "Let's go home or else we shall have to wash the dishes."

I personally very much appreciate being invited to a person's home—in Israel and abroad. It always gives me extra insight into people's customs and preferences. Yitzhak also felt that you can learn a lot from a person's home. Very seldom is a head of state invited this way abroad. Either it's a guest house or a designated room in the official residence. I remember how special it was to be invited by King Juan Carlos and Queen Sofia of Spain to lunch at their private residence outside of Madrid. We saw how warm and comfortable they were with their family and experienced their personal tastes firsthand. If you are privileged to be entertained in a private home—by a king, head of state, or simply a friend—you always retain a special kinship.

Former U.S. secretary of state James Baker, after having endured difficult and embarrassing moments in attempting to work with the Likud government that preceded Yitzhak's administration, had developed a fine working relationship with Yitzhak. When he and his wife came to Israel after he left office, we hosted them a private dinner at our home in Tel Aviv. Little things emerged at the dinner—we discovered we had the same china pattern, and the Bakers taught me about the customs of Lent. After Yitzhak was murdered, the Bakers gave generously to help establish a chair in his memory at the James A. Baker III Institute for Public Policy at Rice University in Houston, and many recall that Secretary Baker wept publicly when he heard of Yitzhak's death. Seemingly small touches can mean so much in fostering a strong human relationship and strengthening the bonds between people and their nations. The Bakers have become dear friends of mine.

Generally, Yitzhak left matters of our home life up to me. If a guest had a question about our art collection, he would invariably say, "Ask Leah, that's her department." When people came to the house, he wouldn't let them go before showing them our rooftop garden—"Leah's Garden," he proudly called it. Our home meant everything to him.

While most decisions on the home front were mine to make, Yitzhak surprised me when the question arose as to whether we should redecorate our private residence in Tel Aviv. In September 1992, when I first brought up the idea, Yitzhak thought it unnecessary. "Why do we need to do it?" he asked. "We have a beautiful home already. Why must we go through all the trouble and expense?" After twenty-three years, I said, it needs to be done. Once we decided to do it, he became totally absorbed in the project. He amazed both me and the interior designer with his involvement, inspecting and overseeing the project over the two and a half months it took. The decorator told me how much she envied our relationship and our togetherness.

As part of the renovation, we planned a new library. The designer laid out the blueprints and corrected them according to our suggestions. Still, Yitzhak insisted on approving every adjustment. At ten-thirty one Saturday night, when we returned to Jerusalem to start the new week, she came to review the plans. Yitzhak wasn't able to join us until eleven o'clock, but once he arrived, he sat with her for another three-quarters of an hour. She couldn't get over how he could find the time and the presence of mind to look at the plans in such a concentrated way. Here again, he did not leave anything open to doubt. He needed the assurance that the work would be up to his expectations. He was a perfectionist on every level.

Coming back from the office every Friday, he would stop into the apartment to have a look. After a while, he was comfortable with the transformation. "It looks great," he said, "but it will never be ready on time." I promised him it would be. It was.

Yitzhak enjoyed relaxing with an hour of television viewing in the evening—he loved soccer and tennis matches or mysteries. When I mentioned getting a large-screen television for him just before our wedding anniversary in August 1995, he suggested we wait until the Jewish High Holidays in the fall. I said to myself, Why wait for the holidays? He will enjoy it now. I took the initiative and surprised him. He was overwhelmed with joy! For months afterward he said, "I'm so grateful you bought me this television." It was the biggest toy of his life. Had I waited, it would have shortened the time he would have had to enjoy it.

Yitzhak never really wanted anything—he was so modest. When I asked "What can I bring you or buy you?" he would answer, "I need nothing, I want nothing, I'm really a very happy man." But when I came back from a trip and brought something for him, he clearly appreciated it, even if it was just a shirt. In a quiet way, he liked the attention. Normally, he was mildly and humorously critical of my shopping adventures—especially when it came to buying shoes. When he'd ask me what I bought, I would say, "I better not tell you. You will be angry, because I bought shoes."

"After the television, I will never be angry again," he'd reply.

Every wife of a political leader elects a different role for herself. In contrast to countries that have established protocol in such matters, the role of the Israeli prime minister's wife has been very individualized by those who have occupied it. Whatever I did in either of the two terms was a mixture of my personal inclinations and priorities, though I would usually discuss my plans with Yitzhak.

One part of the role I have always given special attention to is the choosing of state gifts. I generally handled it with the *chef de bureau,* Eitan Haber—sometimes I did the shopping, sometimes he did. Some years ago, when an American first lady came to visit, I found myself in a limousine with her and the wife of Israel's president, our first lady. The wife of our president thanked the visitor for the gift she and her husband had received. Then came the embarrassing response—the American first lady did not know what the gift from America had been. "The chief of protocol handled state gifts," she shrugged. At the same time, she confessed she had not even seen what she received from our president. "It's probably already been shipped back home," she said. Wow! The lack of personal attention baffled me. I learned a long time ago that one does not refer to state gifts at all. Send a thank-you note to acknowledge the gift but it's too risky to bring it up in the course of conversation. Once when French president François Mitterrand visited Israel, we commissioned a fine artist to paint his portrait, based on four excellent sketches. I don't believe we ever received an acknowledgment. Maybe he didn't like the way he was depicted—or maybe he never saw it.

I would generally volunteer to accompany a visiting first lady to the museums or other places of interest or to entertain the visitor in our home. On the visit of a foreign head of state, our president would host the official dinner and we might invite the first family to a luncheon. If the visiting dignitary was a prime minister, we would entertain. If the guest list were longer than twenty people, we would need to hold the function at a hotel. Our choice for such entertaining was the King David Hotel in Jerusalem. In collaboration with the King David staff, I was about to bring about some memorable events.

One truly unforgettable occasion occurred just several months before Yitzhak's murder. When Germany's Chancellor Kohl visited Israel in June 1995, I wasn't scheduled to be in the country. I was to leave for Paris on a mission for the Tel Aviv Museum. Yitzhak didn't ask me to change my plans because the chancellor was coming without his wife, Hannelore. Nonetheless, I decided to stay, primarily because I realized the chancellor was the strongest European leader at the time, and I felt it was my duty to be there for Yitzhak on such an important visit. It was also a delicate time in

German-Israeli relations. A major topic of debate was negotiation with Islamic fundamentalist regimes like Iran; the Germans felt we should talk with them, but Yitzhak strongly disagreed.

Though 150 guests were to attend, I decided to hold the event on the beautiful patio of the prime minister's residence in Jerusalem. In the summer one could easily plan an evening in the garden with no danger of rain. The King David Hotel supplied the tables, the place settings, and the food. We usually had after-dinner entertainment for state events. On the morning of the dinner, I called one of Israel's finest singers, Ora Zitner, who was scheduled to perform for us, and asked her to sing songs about Jerusalem. Initially she protested that these songs were not in her repertoire. "Ora," I said, "I beg you—you have all day to prepare." She said that she would have needed two weeks, but I told her that Jerusalem was a controversial subject, and such a program would be especially meaningful tonight. At last, she agreed.

After the guests passed through the receiving line, I took the chancellor out to the garden, beyond the place where the tables were set.

"What, here one doesn't eat yet?" he said.

"No, here one drinks," I replied. He was *hungry*. It is our practice to get the speeches out of the way before dinner is served. First Yitzhak spoke, then Chancellor Kohl. It was getting very late. The chancellor, Yitzhak, Shimon Peres, the speaker of the Knesset, the president of our Supreme Court, and I sat at the head table. When Ora began to sing, the Israelis seated throughout the garden began to sing along, filling the garden with magic.

After the singing, Chancellor Kohl insisted on coming back up to the podium. In German (which is the only language he speaks), Chancellor Kohl said, "I want you to know, I'm a very experienced, longtime politician, but you have moved me to tears, and I have no words to respond to what I have just witnessed." When he came back to the table, I gave him a kiss and said, *"Sie sind ein Schatz!"*—You are a dear. To myself, I said, Leah, well done! You have moved the rock of Gibraltar.

When Warren Christopher came to visit once, I also had a long-established commitment to be in France. Yitzhak insisted I go, but decided that he would entertain the secretary of state at our home nonetheless. Something told me that I should have stayed home that time, too. I anxiously waited until eleven that evening to call Yitzhak. "Everything went great!" he said. I later learned that a waiter had dropped a drawer of silver on a shelf of my best china and that he had opened a treasured bottle of 1967 Bordeaux I had been saving for the 1997 anniversary of the Six-Day War, pouring it along with the other red wine served that evening. I learned my lesson.

Every first lady in the United States and elsewhere also chooses projects to sponsor. These projects are often far more ambitious and time-consuming than is widely realized. For example, Lady Bird Johnson was a strong activist for the beautification of the American landscape and environmentalism. When Mrs. Johnson published her memoirs, a critic in Israel attacked them as a typical example of a first lady who sees the world from the kitchen window of the White House. I took exception to that. Mrs. Johnson is a businesswoman who has skillfully managed a chain of broadcasting stations. Her interests are wide-ranging, and she was anything but the first housewife when Lyndon Johnson was president. I have great admiration for her. Lady Bird is a very intelligent and interesting lady, in addition to having been a wonderful wife.

I'd met Jacqueline Kennedy only once, during a small private showing of the Scythian gold exhibit at the Met in New York in the mid-1970s. She looked radiant and impressed me with her knowledge, interest, and enthusiasm for fine art. After her death, I read a magazine article about her life and was particularly impressed with the meticulous plans she'd made for her own funeral, including the reading of a passage of Cavafy's poem, "The Road to Attica." The poem struck me so deeply, I later presented a copy of it as a gift to Queen Sofia of Spain, who is of Greek origin.

Patricia Nixon was a totally different person from Jackie Kennedy and Lady Bird Johnson, but also a thoughtful and important partner for her husband. Betty Ford unfortunately suffered great physical pain but I always found her an enormously likable woman.

Rosalynn Carter was quite unlike her immediate predecessors. She tried hard and put a lot of effort into entertaining us. She hosted a big tea party for me, to which I was asked to invite all my American friends, and took me to see the musical *Annie* at the Kennedy Center on an evening when a stag dinner was being held at the White House, but somehow I always found it difficult to communicate with her. She never asked me one question about my children or my life in Israel. So how long could I go on asking about Amy?

Nancy Reagan and I have met only twice. Once was at a light-hearted celebration of publisher Kay Graham's seventieth birthday. Mrs. Reagan looked beautiful . . . and enviably skinny. Barbara Bush, as I've said, was always so natural and efficient.

When I first met Hillary Rodham Clinton at the White House, we discussed her deep involvement in national health care reform. I shared information about Israel's national health practices and attitudes. I found her intelligent—a perceptive listener—and endowed with beautiful blue eyes.

Yitzhak not only encouraged me in my various causes—the Autistic Society, Shiba Medical Center, the Tel Aviv Museum, and others—he made a concerted effort to attend major functions for those activities with which I was involved. While these involvements were personal concerns of mine, there's no doubt that they dovetailed with Yitzhak's own agenda. As for the arts, Israel has a thriving cultural life, and it has always been central to the nation's morale and well-being. In many respects, I was Yitzhak's personal ambassador for cultural affairs and I took that role very seriously. My passion for art was always highly appreciated by the various museum directors. In me, I know they felt they had a real advocate who was always ready to lend a hand.

∞ The peace initiative went into high gear in 1993. Even as the Madrid talks went through round after round in Washington, Israel opened a secretive "back channel" to the PLO in a series of meetings held mostly in Norway. With a dramatically different future before us, we took time out to make an unforgettable journey to the past. In April we traveled to a place that ignites in the heart of every Jew the absolute necessity of a peaceful and secure homeland.

Our visit to Poland began in Warsaw to commemorate the fiftieth anniversary of the uprising of the Warsaw Ghetto, which took place on April 19, 1943. In front of the capital, Polish troops paraded in our honor, "goose-stepping" in the manner still common in ex-Communist states. We visited locations in the Muranów-North quarter of the city and the bunker of Mordechai Anielewitch, who commanded the uprising and met his death at Mila Street 18. Yitzhak was to lay a wreath at the Warsaw Ghetto memorial and pay tribute to the valiant members of the uprising. He climbed the memorial stairs, his back to us, and stood at attention. From there we walked to the notorious Umschlagplatz, where Jews were assembled and sent to the concentration camps. A staff member of our Ministry of Defense had himself passed through that point fifty years earlier.

Polish president Lech Walesa attended the evening ceremonies, as did Polish prime minister Hanna Suchocka and U.S. vice president Al Gore. Erected in 1948, an enormous relief wall in Warsaw commemorates the uprising. Apartment buildings surround the memorial square. The square was festively lit, but I couldn't understand why all the windows in these large apartment houses were dark. At a given moment, candles were lit in every single window in memory of the uprising. It was truly breathtaking.

Lech Walesa, Al Gore, and Yitzhak each laid wreaths at the site, and each spoke as well. The Poles had made an enormous effort to create a memorable occasion. A Polish military choir sang the famous Yiddish song *"Es Brennt, Kinderlach, Es Brennt"* ("It Burns, Children, It Burns"). A memorial fire had been lit behind the monument, and the flames accidentally started to spread toward the wooden platform where the cantor was conducting the singers. What a horrifying symbolic moment—we feared they might go up in flames! Fortunately, the fire was contained before it could do any harm.

The next morning, the entire group from Israel went to Auschwitz and Birkenau. The horror that still surrounds these sites of unfathomable atrocities remains unabated. Yitzhak placed a wreath at the memorial in Auschwitz, in remembrance of our people who perished in the camps. We were a large group—Yitzhak's entourage included members of the prime minister's office and the Ministry of Defense, many members of the press, and above all fifty survivors of Auschwitz and Birkenau. Being there with the survivors was the most meaningful part of our visit; we were fully aware of what it meant to them to visit Auschwitz with the prime minister of the Jewish state. We passed through the gate, beneath the words *Arbeit macht frei*—work makes you free. Our guide was an attractive young Polish woman. Yitzhak listened to her comments intensely. The press pushed so close, I could barely hear the guide, but what we saw spoke for itself.

The barracks. The shoes. All the shoes. The hair. The children's clothes. The evidence of a cold, calculated horror. *Their* hair. *Their* shoes. *Their* eyeglasses. All in separate showcases. *Ordnung muß sein!*

Among the group of survivors was Samuel Gogol. He came to Auschwitz as a child with Dr. Janus Korchak, who headed an orphanage and was known as an outstanding educator with a great influence on children. When the Poles eventually discovered the orphanage and took the children to an extermination camp, Dr. Korchak would not let them go alone, even though he himself was not Jewish. Today there stands a beautiful statue of Dr. Korchak and "his" children but I was saddened to see that the statue was made of fiberglass, simply sprayed with bronze-colored paint. Can't we, the Jewish people, do better in commemorating this unique, great man?

Dr. Korchak made it a practice of giving his children a coin under their pillows each time they lost one of their baby teeth. As a boy, Samuel Gogol saved his coins and asked Korchak to buy him a harmonica with the money. Gogol developed quite a talent with the instrument, and he was ordered by the Nazi authorities to play his harmonica while lines of Jews were marched into the gas chambers. He credits his survival to that harmonica. At Birkenau, he again played the harmonica at our ceremony. He died within a month of our visit—as if the circle of his life could now close.

When Yitzhak spoke at Auschwitz, he spoke the words of a strong man. Only a man fully aware of the sufferings of Jewish history could capture a worthy vision of peace:

> *Every handful of earth in this accursed place is soaked in the blood of the victims. Each of the now-silent huts in this terrible camp has heard the cries of the tortured. Each partition here is a wailing wall. Every rusting barbed wire in this city of death bears between its barbs the emaciated bodies of our brothers, and the wind here will always carry on its wings the smoke of the ovens. In the face of starvation, isolation, humiliation, cold, and tortures—who could have behaved differently? They did not go like lambs to the slaughter. An abandoned nation, a solitary people, went to its death here.*
>
> *Fifty years later, and the cries still rend our ears. Even though the well of tears has run dry long ago, we do not forget and we do not forgive. The fearful eyes of our brothers who departed the world of the living not knowing why, the hidden glances that sought a redemption that would not come, their shouts and tears and muted weeping still cry to us today. Our entire annals, from the dawn of our days and forever, recede into the shadows of this—the most horrible crime in history.*
>
> *Wherever we go in Israel, the memory of the Holocaust, its distress and its lessons, walks with us.*
>
> *We did not break. In the face of the helplessness that was here, the terrible despair and the march to the walls of death—the gallows, the gas chambers, and incinerators—the*

nation of Israel lives! We have arisen out of the ashes of the victims and have created a nation and a state of moral quality, of culture and intellect, of military power.

Fifty years later, we have today enough might and spiritual reservoirs to stand in the imperatives of time, to repel enemies, to build a home, to grant asylum to the persecuted. And we have both the strength and the spirit to smite all the seekers of evil—and to extend the hand of peace to our enemies.

CHAPTER
10

ISRAEL THE
PEACEMAKER

I t is often said that Yitzhak was a soldier who late in life became a man of peace. I consider that an incorrect assessment.
Even while serving in the military, he drew the greatest satisfaction
from pursuing the course of peace. He first talked peace in 1949 at
Rhodes, when he was just twenty-seven years old and a veteran of
the War of Independence. From then on he viewed the evils of war
as a means to coerce combatants to come to the bargaining table.

On July 25, 1970, Yitzhak wrote me the following letter:

Dear Leah,

I'm taking advantage of the fact that Motke Gazit is
passing through Washington on his way home to send this
letter with him. There's a great deal of activity here. The
problems are especially great since Egypt gave a positive answer to the American initiative.** The fact that Egypt has
agreed to this initiative has created quite a few substantive
problems and PR concerns for us.*

There's no doubt that we now face not Arab but Soviet

**A member of the Israeli Foreign Ministry.*

** *The "American initiative" was to keep the Suez Canal open through creating a de-
militarized zone, ten kilometers wide on either side of the canal.*

thinking, which is much more sober and at a world power level. There's also no doubt that Soviet military presence in Egypt gives the Soviets the possibility of exerting considerable influence on Egypt, though this is a tactical move that does not represent a substantial change. At the same time, we cannot ignore the fact that the Egyptians have strayed from the line that was traditional—that the condition for renewal of the Jarring* mission, even in the presently proposed format, is prior Israeli agreement to comprehensive withdrawal [from the Sinai].

In practice, Egyptian and Arab PR here is beginning to say that we accepted renewal of the mission, albeit indirectly, but without any preconditions. We don't deny that we have a clear and finalized approach, but we are not presenting it as a condition to start talks. Moreover, by formally accepting the American proposal, the Egyptians are ready to admit that the purpose of the talks is peace between Israel and Egypt. They do indeed have a plan that will result in a changed image for Israel, even within the June 4, 1967, lines. This by way of the demand for free choice on the part of the Palestinian refugees between return to their homes or compensation.

The choice, according to the Egyptian plan, is in the hands of the refugees (to our great discomfort, there is also a UN resolution along those lines). The Americans don't accept this approach. At any rate, the Egyptians are not insisting that the start of Jarring's mission is subject to preconditions. If it's also true that Syria has accepted the initiative, our PR situation will become most difficult.

Israel has been able up to now to proclaim from the rooftops that we want peace, but the Arabs have not. Now it will be more difficult if the government of Israel decides to continue not deciding. It's a complex problem and I am not convinced that we have people in Israel who are thinking

---

* *UN Ambassador Gunnar Jarring was heavily involved in Middle East peace initiatives during the 1960s and 1970s.*

seriously and comprehensively. Golda, in my opinion, understands the issue perfectly. Moshe D. is a national disaster. I would be much calmer if I knew that Yigal [Allon] was now in the country. In my opinion he's much brighter and more capable of understanding this reality than are the other two. Nevertheless, I hope that Golda will overcome Dayan's opposition, despite Eban's chattering. [It] does not help her—only does damage.

In brief, decisions are difficult given a badly composed government. It's much more noticeable that we lack a man like David Ben-Gurion, with vision on the one hand and ability to maneuver despite internal opposition on the other. Without this capability, Israel has no chance in the present circumstances.

This places me in an awkward situation. In practice there is no possibility to answer any questions. All the TV stations want to interview me, and I'm refusing. Luckily, my appearance on Meet the Press *is behind me. We are talking generalities, but everyone is asking what the Israeli position is on the American initiative in light of the Arab response. I hope that the decision-making process will not continue for long, otherwise we will lose favorable American—including Jewish—public opinion.*

From all the above, I am worried that the holiday might get a little complicated. I did cable the Foreign Office yesterday, announcing that I intend to take home leave on August 5. So far there is no comment on that. Accordingly, I hope to be in Israel in ten days' time. Meanwhile, [we are drowning in work]. This week, too, I have dinners every evening. I had intended to play tennis with Paul Berger* today (Saturday), but I had to meet with [Joseph] Sisco. Most of the day I'm in the office. I did go home for lunch. Vikki** is looking after

---

*A lawyer and friend of the family.
**Vikki was our loyal African-American maid through most of our five years in America. We loved her very much and she loved us back.

me and preparing good food. Incidentally they did bring the two dining room carpets, properly cleaned. The carpet from the big room hasn't come yet. I'm even spending today in the office.

I hope that you and the children are continuing to enjoy life. Do your utmost to enjoy as much as you can. Since I can't take part in it with you, the fact that you are enjoying yourselves gives me great satisfaction.

*Lots of kisses
to you and
the children,
Yitzhak*

The letter is obvious in its criticism of Golda Meir, who didn't advance the pursuit of peace during her administration. She placed absolute trust in Moshe Dayan's ability to maintain our nation's military readiness—a failing that, to some extent, invited the 1973 Yom Kippur War. When Yitzhak succeeded her as prime minister, he changed the national agenda, negotiating the interim peace agreement with Egypt, and laying the groundwork for the Camp David Accords.

In 1984, as minister of defense, Yitzhak devised the plan for a phased withdrawal from Lebanon and the creation of a security zone, at last extricating Israel from its disastrous direct military involvement there. It was also Yitzhak who changed the method of confrontation during the Intifada, after it became painfully evident that this had become a war waged through the media. He also recognized the Intifada battle would never be won through conventional military means, and that Israel would have to find a political solution to Palestinian grievances.

Some of Yitzhak's favorite expressions—the ones he believed in most deeply and repeated most frequently—reveal his attitudes toward war and peace:

"The best war is the war that can be prevented."

"The coldest peace is better than the warmest war."

"A destroyed house can be rebuilt. A burned-down tree can be replanted. But a young life cannot be replaced."

No statement, however public, or accomplishment, however noteworthy, matches Yitzhak's achievement of making peace with the Palestinians and Jordanians and putting into place a structure that one day, we hope, will bring about lasting peace with Syria and Lebanon.

Of course what made a new political reality in the Middle East possible was resolving the Palestinian question, the key Middle East conflict that could unlock peace with Israel's other Arab foes.

After the 1991 Madrid Peace Conference, Israel held round after round of talks with the Palestinian delegation, which was composed of Palestinian leaders from the Occupied Territories, none of whom held any official PLO title. Arafat and his PLO officials were based at PLO headquarters in Tunis and were barred from participating in the negotiations. But these talks had made little headway, partly because Arafat nevertheless had control over the delegation and often purposely dragged his feet to demonstrate the impossibility of progress as long as he and his aides were formally excluded. Many Israelis, particularly academics and left-wing intellectuals, began to believe that a substantive breakthrough was dependent on opening a direct dialogue with the PLO.

However, for the moment, talking directly with PLO officials was a formidable taboo in Israel, as the organization was still widely identified with terrorism against Jews. The government knew that if it was to open talks with Arafat's senior officials it would have to be done in extreme secrecy.

In January 1993 Foreign Minister Shimon Peres approved an initiative by some Israeli academics to put out feelers to senior PLO officials about setting up a secret peace process. This quickly developed into what became known as the "back channel"—negotiations that went on in private, usually in Oslo, with the help of senior Norwegian Foreign Ministry officials. The back channel, eventually widened to include members of the Israeli Foreign Ministry, went forward as Israel continued public talks with the Palestinian delegation in Washington.

Yitzhak was first informed of the back channel in February. He didn't object to it but remained skeptical about its chances of success. However, as long as it remained "officially unofficial," he allowed it to proceed.

After the breakthrough of the Oslo back channel, Yitzhak appointed Yossi Genosar, a former General Security Service (Shabak) division director, as his chief contact with Arafat. Yitzhak would say, "Yossi Genosar is my back channel to Arafat. I don't need others." Throughout 1994 and 1995 Yossi had weekly meetings with Arafat to maintain the relationship, the trust, and the open lines of communication. The meetings continued until Yossi resigned his post in September 1995, about six weeks before Yitzhak was murdered.

Yossi's meetings with Arafat were not public knowledge although on one occasion Arafat announced to his cabinet that he had established a hot line with Yitzhak. The story was leaked to the press. Yitzhak asked Yossi, "What is this hot line?" So Yossi went to Arafat and asked him, because he didn't know, either. Arafat said: "You are the hot line, but I didn't want to tell my cabinet that." Everybody thought there was a little red telephone sitting beside Yitzhak. Afterward, Yitzhak took to calling Yossi "the hot line."

As the Oslo talks progressed in early 1993, Yitzhak took an active role in the discussions. Yitzhak first confided to me that secret talks were under way in March. Despite the decades-long rivalry between Shimon Peres and Yitzhak, the two of them never struck a better, more successful partnership than in their pursuit of the Oslo agreements. One of Yitzhak's aides once told me he felt the reason why they overcame their "history" was because Oslo was such a great triumph it could easily be shared between the two of them. They were like two actors playing leading roles in an important play. Apart from one incident that occurred immediately before the famous Washington "handshake" with Yasir Arafat— an event I'll describe later in this chapter—Shimon Peres was certainly a positive and supportive partner for Yitzhak in his later years.

The road to the peace agreement between February and September was not an easy one. Yitzhak subscribed to Henry Kissinger's philosophy that diplomacy can be successful only when there is military might to back it up. Never for a moment did Yitzhak support diluting Israel's military strength. "If you want to make drastic concessions for peace, you must show the public you can take drastic measures for security," was how his aide Eitan Haber described Yitzhak's policy. On the issue of land, Yitzhak often said, sure he would like to make the West Bank part of Israel, but that would also mean making 1.3 million Arabs Israeli citizens, thereby changing the raison d'être of a Jewish state.

While logic would have argued for making peace with the Jordanians first, there was great wisdom in resolving the Palestinian question at the heart of the Middle East conflict. This step not only settled the most complex problem first, it also created an incentive for Jordan to reach a clear accord with Israel. Yitzhak's office conducted polls to gauge the Israeli desire and readiness for peace. The majority of Israelis were in favor of it. One of the pollsters—Kalman Geyer—explained that the watershed had been the Gulf War, when the Scuds came raining down on Israel. "For the first time," Geyer said, "the Israelis saw the peace process as a component of security."

The next six months were anxious and intense ones. Yitzhak oversaw the negotiations, but was never very confident that they would result in success. He skillfully involved (or decided not to involve) certain players. Although he kept Secretary of State Warren Christopher and President Clinton informed of major developments, Washington was less active in this peace initiative than it had been in any previous talks. Yitzhak also didn't involve the IDF until the implementation stage, fearing that they would slow down the negotiations by being too focused on logistical details. He knew that, unless he kept the discussions moving forward at a brisk pace, he ran the risk of destructive leaks that could force the participants to harden their positions.

The Americans were very supportive of Yitzhak's approach to the peace process. The relationship Yitzhak had with President Clinton was, he felt, the best he had had with any U.S. president. Yitzhak developed a strong rapport with Warren Christopher early on—they were alike in their diligence, patience, and determination—and it went far beyond a working relationship. Often when Christopher came, we entertained him at home. He liked the "Rabin Restaurant," whereas Henry Kissinger thought the food *chez* Rabin during the middle seventies was too heavy. We had a Hungarian cook at the time, so he may have had a point!

Finally, by September, Israeli and PLO negotiators had hammered out a breakthrough agreement. The agreement called for the establishment of Palestinian self-rule in the Occupied Territories over a five-year period during which time Israel and the PLO would work toward resolving all issues in dispute, including Jerusalem, borders, statehood, and the fate of Palestinian refugees.

On Wednesday afternoon, September 8, President Clinton called Yitzhak in his office. After congratulating Yitzhak on reaching the Oslo agreement, the President told him he'd like to host the signing in Washington, but it was evident to Yitzhak that he was uncomfortable at the thought of inviting Yasir Arafat. How could Yitzhak go if Arafat wasn't going to be there? Who would be the signatories if not Yitzhak and Arafat? Yitzhak's own staff was divided. Eitan Haber believed the Israeli public was not yet ready for such a gesture and advocated lowering the level of the representatives attending to Foreign Minister Shimon Peres and the PLO's Abu Mazen. Shimon Sheves, who was the director general of the prime minister's office, disagreed and felt that a handshake between Yitzhak and Arafat would lend weight to the occasion. Sheves felt that Yitzhak should be identified strongly with the agreement, and the handshake would symbolize it. Yitzhak had, of course, never met Arafat face-to-face.

While the United States wanted an agreement, neither the State Department nor President Clinton's advisers showed much enthusiasm for Arafat visiting the capital. They did not want the "complications" of hosting Arafat, until then persona non grata in official Washington. Like Yitzhak's staff in Israel, the Clinton administration was internally divided.

On Thursday morning, Haber sounded out a dozen people about whether or not Yitzhak should attend. The majority opposed his going, but, when pressed, aides confided that the agreement would be less likely to hold without the personal endorsement of Yitzhak and Arafat. At that stage of the discussion, the balance shifted in favor of Yitzhak's going, nevertheless it still seemed to Yitzhak that President Clinton was reluctant to invite Arafat.

On Thursday afternoon, during a lunch meeting of "the Table"—an informal group of friends, political figures, and journalists who met weekly at a Tel Aviv restaurant—a fierce debate took place on the issue. I was, perhaps uncharacteristically, reserved.

Niva Lanir, a close friend and a former adviser during Yitzhak's days as defense minister in the 1980s, held the same opinion as Shimon Sheves—that Yitzhak's presence was needed to lend credibility to the agreement.

"Rabin has to lead this move," she told me.

"Tell it to Yitzhak," I answered. Others were hesitant or opposed his going. Lunch ended without consensus.

On Friday morning, September 10, Arafat signed a document in Tunis recognizing the state of Israel, and Yitzhak signed a document in his office recognizing the PLO. Yitzhak used an inexpensive Pilot pen,* and I remember everyone in the office smiling over Yitzhak putting his name to such a momentous document with such a modest pen. We were still not certain if we were going to Washington. Later in the day, I called Yitzhak's office, while the staff was in the midst of yet another discussion. I talked with Sheves and asked what the current feeling was.

"Yitzhak," he told me, "leans toward not going, and I think it is a mistake."

"If this is what Yitzhak thinks," I said, "don't press him. Leave him alone."

An hour or so later Sheves called me and told me that more advisers had voiced their opposition to the trip to Washington. At

---

* After his death, I donated a pen that Yitzhak had used to a charity auction, and it fetched a handsome 58,000 NIS (approximately $19,000) for a good cause!

five-thirty P.M. Yitzhak decided that Shimon Peres would go to Washington instead of him. With that, Yitzhak called it a day and left for our apartment in Tel Aviv. But the matter didn't end there. Yitzhak wrestled with the implications of his decision well into the evening. There were countless phone calls between him and his advisers. I tried to be a sounding board but realized it was best to leave the matter up to him. The question that remained in Yitzhak's mind was what President Clinton really wanted to do—invite Arafat or not.

At ten in the evening, Yitzhak called Sheves to say he was reconsidering the whole matter. "I am not clear on the exact position of President Clinton," Yitzhak said. He also was not sure of Arafat's position, so he asked Sheves to check with his Palestinian sources and to report back.

Warren Christopher called a short time later and said the president would very much like Yitzhak to come. "I cannot come if Yasir Arafat is not coming," Yitzhak said to Secretary Christopher.

"Yasir Arafat *is* coming!" Christopher assured him.

At midnight, Shimon Sheves called Yitzhak to report that Arafat had received an invitation directly from President Clinton and was planning to go to Washington. Before climbing into bed at around one, Yitzhak decided that we would go to Washington.

The phone rang at five A.M. On the other end was Israel's ambassador to the United States, Itamar Rabinovich, calling from Washington. The ambassador was relaying a "heads-up" that he had received a formal invitation from the president to take part in the signing ceremony on Monday. Immediately afterward, Yitzhak called Sheves to arrange a staff meeting at our home at nine A.M. Yitzhak did not call Shimon Peres, but it was pretty clear by then that Yitzhak was intending to go to the United States. The question was whether he alone would represent Israel.

The announcement that Yitzhak was going to the United States was made at eight A.M. by the government press office. The announcement was made early to avert further debate; instead it blew the matter sky high. A few minutes prior to the broadcast, the Israeli author Amos Oz called Niva Lanir. Oz told her that he had just received a call from Shimon Peres. The news was serious. Peres told Oz he was going to resign. Peres, the initiator of the Oslo process, felt slighted in his exclusion from the discussions about the Washington ceremony. Yitzhak now had to weigh Israel's international objectives against the volatile political situation at home.

All that day, talk of a feud between Yitzhak and Shimon Peres spread like wildfire. Could a meeting between the two be arranged? A mediator, Giora Eini, was called in. Eini was a lawyer who had worked with the Labor Council, the Histadrut, and had acted as a voluntary mediator over the years in resolving disputes between Yitzhak and Shimon Peres. Why was a mediator necessary? Perhaps because Yitzhak and Peres both recognized the need for someone with absolutely no vested interest to consider the matter. Both Yitzhak and Peres trusted Giora Eini. He could be counted on to be absolutely impartial and to keep the matter totally confidential. In fact, Yitzhak's staff never really liked Giora, because he was *so* impartial.

Our apartment and the Peres home are in the same neighborhood, just a few blocks apart, so Giora practiced a funny sort of "shuttle diplomacy." We could see him strolling up and down the street in his effort to cut a deal. Giora went back and forth several times; when Yitzhak learned Giora was on his way back, he would alert the security guard downstairs, motioning with the palm of his hand to the base of his neck, as if to say "the guy with the long hair"—Giora wore his hair down his neck—"is coming back."

They reached a straightforward agreement: If Washington approved, *both* Yitzhak and Shimon Peres would attend the ceremony. That's how the list of invitees to the ceremony grew to include not only the heads of state but also their foreign secretaries—Foreign Minister Peres, Secretary of State Christopher, and Abu Mazen for the Palestinians.

After a flurry of tie-picking and suit-packing, we left for Washington on Saturday night! We flew with Shimon Peres in an Israeli Air Force plane. Dalia and her husband, Avi, were with us. Yitzhak's speech was essentially written before we left—Yitzhak always found it hard to do paperwork on a plane or even while traveling in a car. En route to the United States, we made a refueling stop in Holland, and the Dutch cabinet met us at the airport at one in the morning to congratulate us—their beards a bit stubbled and their clothes a bit rumpled, but extremely happy nonetheless.

On September 13, 1993, the Declaration of Principles was signed by President Clinton, Yasir Arafat, and Yitzhak on the White House lawn. The Declaration stated the end of the "confrontation and conflict" between the state of Israel and the Palestinian people and laid the framework to achieve genuine reconciliation and a "comprehensive peace settlement" by setting forth the step-by-step process by which the Palestinians would be granted autonomy.

After the actual signatures were in place, Yitzhak said to President Clinton and Yasir Arafat that this was a very important moment in all their lives. *"This is a truly important moment,"* Yasir Arafat responded with emphasis. Then he turned to President Clinton and said, "Mr. President, it is now your role to support this peace process, and it will be up to you to make it work."

Did Yitzhak intend to shake Yasir Arafat's hand? Surely, he had mixed feelings—after all, this was the leader of an organization that had, over the years, taken the lives of countless Israeli civilians and soldiers. But peace is something you make with your enemies, not with your friends. And making peace means moving past bloodshed, beyond anguished memories. The look of discomfort on Yitzhak's face was unmistakable; he looked as if he'd swallowed something large and painful. He was shaking the hand of a man he said he would never dignify with direct contact. He was breaking a vow. How could he forget the victims of terror, even at this historic moment? Had it not been before the eyes of the world, he might not have felt so deeply conflicted. I imagine he was thinking, The whole world has heard me say *never,* and now I *am.* . . .

After the handshakes, Yitzhak addressed the crowd on the lawn, his people, the Palestinian people, and the television cameras of the world:

Today here in Washington at the White House, we will begin a new reckoning in the relations between peoples, between parents tired of war, between children who will not know war. . . .

We have no desire for revenge. We harbor no hatred toward you. We, like you, are people—people who want to build a home, to plant a tree, to love, to live side by side with you in dignity, in affinity, as human beings, as free men. We are today giving peace a chance and saying again to you, "Enough . . ."

Let us pray that a day will come when we all will say farewell to arms.

At the conclusion of the ceremony, Yasir Arafat and Yitzhak went down the first row of attendees, shaking hands with everyone. I was sitting in the center of the row. I turned left and shook the hands of the people on my left and then turned to the row behind me. I shook the hand of the Palestinian spokeswoman Hanan Ashrawi, who had played an important role in keeping the Palestinian-Israeli dialogue alive in 1991–1992—her joy was palpable.

At the end of the day, Yitzhak was absolutely convinced he had done the right thing. Surely there were risks involved, but he realized they were risks we had to take. The signing had such a profound impact on the way Israel was perceived internationally, not even Yitzhak could anticipate the dramatic extent to which this was to happen. The signing took place two days before Rosh Hashanah. What an auspicious beginning for the new year!

∞ On our way home from Washington, we stopped in Morocco as an expression of gratitude to King Hassan II, who had been an important player in bringing about this peace. As far back as 1975, Yitzhak had visited the king disguised in a toupée, glasses, and a dental prosthesis. Hassan had been an important facilitator in the peace process over the years and had always expressed a deep respect for the Jewish people. The 1993 visit was brief, with an official reception, the playing of "Hatikvah" at the airport, breakfast and lunch at the guest house, and then a visit to the summer palace, where Yitzhak and Shimon Peres met with the king, while I had a very pleasant conversation with the crown prince.

The wave of international approval made itself felt soon after. Our first major trip abroad was to China in October, the first time an Israeli prime minister was invited to the country. The focus was economic development, especially in the agricultural sector. Yitzhak felt that we could teach the Chinese how to make their vast deserts bloom, and in fact, the visit put into motion agricultural development projects that remain active today.

Staying at the dignitary guest house in Beijing was quite an unforgettable experience. It is situated in a compound that reminds one of a large, elegant park. Even though we arrived late at night, we received an official greeting at the mansion. To the right of the guest house stood a row of gorgeous girls posed like models in a fashion show—all tall, all wearing red silk dresses slit high up their legs, each one more beautiful than the next. To the left stood boys dressed in tuxedos and bow ties. They were obviously picked from China's massive population with great care.

The guest compound was appointed with beautiful Chinese lacquered furniture. Walking down a long corridor, we finally arrived at a magnificent bedroom with a large bed and vast closet space. It was just the *first* bedroom, however. Realizing we were to be provided with two separate quarters, I grabbed our "bundles" and made my way to the second bedroom, where we settled. Beautiful kimonos were set out for each of us. Yitzhak had a private library and living room. Meals were served in a large dining room. The secretary of the cabinet at this time was Elie Rubinstein, an Orthodox Jew, and the Chinese respected the rules of kashruth, serving fish throughout our stay. We had fish from A to Z . . . we had fish coming out of our ears!

Who could have imagined we would hear "Hatikvah" ring out across Tiananmen Square? We visited all the important sites—among which the Great Wall impressed us the most, although I must admit that climbing the wall was quite exhausting. When we reached the first plateau, Yitzhak declared, "OK, we got the idea. Enough climbing!"

After Beijing we went to Shanghai. We saw Chinese rural life firsthand at the Chinchung Project outside of the city, a program that couples market economics with agricultural development. In the little village we visited, both the husband and wife in a typical family have jobs, but they also have a little patch of ground in which they grow rice or durum wheat.

From China, I flew to New York, but Yitzhak's destination was far more exotic. The Mossad had cautioned Yitzhak that if there was any leak *whatsoever* of the next destination, the meeting would have to be canceled. The meeting was with President Suharto of Indonesia, the leader of the largest Muslim nation in the world, and it took place at the president's residence. The agenda was again economic development. The Israeli press was enraged that they didn't know Yitzhak's destination, but his hands were clearly tied if this diplomatic advance was to take place at all. After Indonesia, they stopped in Singapore so as not to travel on Shabbat.

In December 1993, the Vatican established formal diplomatic relations with Israel. Yitzhak was not to meet with the Pope until the following year, when he presented a beautiful ancient jar to John Paul II.

On February 24, 1994, the peace process was dealt a temporary but severe setback when an American-born physician and West Bank settler, Baruch Goldstein, armed with an automatic weapon and wearing an army uniform, massacred twenty-nine Arabs praying at the mosque in Hebron, the heart of the West Bank. The episode shocked and infuriated Yitzhak, who saw it as the work of a single deranged individual. After the incident, Yitzhak made a thorough tour of the mosque, inspecting its security and reviewing how Goldstein was able to enter the mosque with a loaded weapon. As a result, changes were instituted that restrict the presence of Israelis within the mosques during services. For Yitzhak, the murders were not only a disgrace for Israel, but a stain on the armed services, since Goldstein was wearing a uniform when he carried out the brutal attack.

∞ In May, I traveled with Yitzhak to Cairo, where he was to sign "Oslo-A," the agreement that established self-rule for the Palestinians in Jericho and Gaza. We stayed at a hotel on the Nile. In the evening dinner was served on a cruise ship to those who did not participate in the talks, while last-minute negotiations continued until the early hours of the morning. U.S. special Middle East coordinator Dennis Ross told me afterward about some tense moments that Yitzhak defused.

During the night, a four-way meeting was held in Mubarak's office between Yitzhak and his delegation, Arafat and his, Mubarak and his foreign minister, and Secretary of State Christopher and Special Coordinator Ross. After hours of often heated discussion, the parties felt a viable compromise had been reached that would permit them to finalize the agreement. All the parties but Arafat, it turned out, who began to raise the same issues he had raised hours before. A couple of the Israelis started to laugh—in a derisive way. "Do you think I'm a joke?" Arafat said.

"No," Yitzhak cut in very quickly. "We take you very seriously. Let's settle this."

Ross later remarked that he found Yitzhak's response clear-headed and sensitive for someone with such a tough reputation. Arafat then dropped the points he had raised, agreed to the compromise, and the agreement was finalized.

The next morning the signing ceremony was to take place. There was some lingering anxiety over the compromises struck just hours before, but as Yitzhak and I rode to the beautiful, modern congress center in Cairo, I noted that I was in a way more excited now than I'd been at the Washington ceremony because this agreement was more substantive. The Declaration of Principles was the blueprint for peace, but this agreement spelled reality. The symbolic handshake was now materializing in this first step.

The mood was festive in the hall, but as the signing went forward, Yitzhak noticed that Arafat hadn't initialed several maps.

"What is this?" He was indignant. "I'm not signing any more documents."

Then the *commedia dell'arte* began, with members of each delegation scurrying back and forth across the stage. The event was being broadcast live all over the world. I sat in the audience next to Susan Mubarak, who suddenly grew very tense. She said that she was getting a headache, so I supplied her with an aspirin. Mrs. Mubarak whispered to me that they ought to get offstage and straighten matters out. The signing had become a spectacle. Yitzhak was standing off to the side, cool and determined. Soon the dignitaries onstage realized that they ought to withdraw for a few minutes. I used this interlude to go to the ladies' room, thinking that I would have plenty of time. It was farther away than I thought. By the time I returned to my seat, the problem had been solved, and the parties returned to the stage and resumed the signing.

Later, Yitzhak told me that he was, of course, quite upset by this. He thought Arafat's initials might have been intentionally omitted. Though the process had come so far, Yitzhak's innate skepticism remained intact. President Mubarak, as the host, may have been even more angered than Yitzhak and apparently used some very tough language to set things right. We all chatted happily at lunch, but I suspect Arafat felt a little isolated since the anger of the group was directed at him. But this was just a temporary spat. As I like to think of it, basically we were "going steady" with Arafat at this point.

As his relationship with Arafat matured, Yitzhak's comments to me reflected his increasing respect for the veteran Palestinian leader as a strong and intelligent man who was nevertheless not easy to work with. Yitzhak believed that Arafat tried hard to control Hamas. Was he confident that Arafat did enough to rein in this violent terrorist organization? I don't know. It was, perhaps, still too early to judge by the time Yitzhak was murdered.

Yitzhak's relationship with Shimon Peres also grew and deepened during this time. Yitzhak and Peres had never before realized how great a contribution their cooperation could be to the Labor Party and to the nation as a whole. With his election to the office of prime minister, Yitzhak accepted the importance of the foreign minister's position and granted Peres great authority. He also began to trust Peres as he never had before, as long as it was clear that Yitzhak was in the driver's seat and he alone held ultimate responsibility. Though they were never really friends, they were comrades in peace. Destiny had thrown them together.

∞ In June 1994, the first of the international accolades was presented jointly to Yitzhak, Shimon Peres, and Yasir Arafat in Paris. The distinction was the UNESCO Peace Prize awarded in memory of the longtime president of Côte d'Ivoire, Houphouët-Boigny. Following the long afternoon ceremony, a large dinner party was held at an elegant restaurant in the gardens bordering the Champs Elysées near the Rond Point. The Palestinian leadership, the UNESCO officials, and the Israelis all sat around one huge oval table. My daughter, Dalia, leaned over and whispered, "Mother, do you realize we are having dinner with all of the Palestinian leadership?"

Between Yitzhak and me sat an official from Senegal. Faisal Husseini of East Jerusalem, one of the leading figures of the Palestinian movement, sat across the table. His father had been one of the highest-ranking commanders of the Palestinian volunteer units in 1948. During Israel's War of Independence, a long, bloody battle was waged along one of the cliffs on the road to Jerusalem that took the life of Abdel Kader el-Husseini. His significance to the Palestinian movement and his importance as a military commander was so great that his death led to a collapse in Palestinian morale and, ultimately, their defeat. During the dinner in Paris Faisal Husseini leaned across the table. "Does your husband know that I am the son of Abdel Kader el-Husseini?" he asked.

I looked at him in amazement. "But, of course," I said. "What a question!" I passed the baby to Yitzhak. "Yitzhak, Faisal Husseini asks if you are aware that his father was Abdel Kader el-Husseini." Yitzhak then praised his father for the important role he'd played and the great symbolism his father held for his people. Faisal Husseini was pleased and honored by the recognition.

∞ On July 25, 1994, a very hot and humid day, King Hussein, President Clinton, and Yitzhak signed, on the White House lawn, a declaration that ended an official state of war between Israel and Jordan. Just before the signing ceremony, I met King Hussein and his wife, Queen Noor al-Hussein, for the first time.

I was standing beside Vice President Gore's wife, Tipper, when the queen and I were introduced. The Princeton-educated queen, the daughter of an American airline executive, struck me as both articulate and surprisingly down-to-earth. (I was even more impressed when Yitzhak and I were guests of the king and the queen of Jordan, and Queen Noor personally served us at the table as a special gesture of respect.)

Resolving the agreement with Jordan meant that soon Jews from all over could at long last visit Petra—the dream of many young people who literally risked being killed just for a glimpse of the spectacular red rock formations. I couldn't wait to see it. "Your Majesty, are you aware how much Israelis always wanted to visit Petra?" I remember saying to Queen Noor at this first meeting.

"And, do you know how worried we are already?" she replied. She was making reference to the Israeli reputation for "storming" tourist sites. Months later, before the opening of an important bridge between our countries, Queen Noor sent me the most beautiful gold pin with a relief of the red rock of Petra.

King Hussein and Yitzhak addressed the U.S. Congress on the twenty-sixth of July. In his speech Yitzhak noted, "Only a seventy-minute journey separates these cities, Jerusalem and Amman—and forty-six years."

That afternoon, Yitzhak was invited to meet the king alone at his hotel. Shortly before the meeting, an unexpected message was delivered: Would Mrs. Rabin please join us? Of course I came along, figuring that Yitzhak and the king would talk while the queen and I would spend time together, but I was surprised when His Majesty asked me to join the three of them. They were to discuss the financial implications of the Israeli-Jordanian treaty. I quickly realized that the queen was totally aware of the issues, and

I was pleasantly surprised. We spent an amiable hour together. That evening President Clinton hosted a large reception.

The Friday night after we'd returned from our trip, we were sitting in the living room of our Tel Aviv apartment when the phone rang. It was the king calling from his airplane, en route from Washington to London, thanking Yitzhak for his insight and his friendship.

∞ In October, Yitzhak and Yasir Arafat were co-recipients of a second honor: the Prince of Asturias Award for International Cooperation, bestowed at a ceremony in Oviedo, Spain. King Juan Carlos and Queen Sofia—whom we had met twice before during their visit to Israel and our state visit to Spain—invited us and the Arafats to their private residence at Moncloa, near Madrid. Juan Carlos and Queen Sofia are most delightful people and I very much enjoyed meeting Sua Arafat for the first time. I found her friendly, warm, and intelligent. We were growing more comfortable with the Arafats. During the ceremony, we shared a common bond: Neither of us understood one word of what was going on, since the entire ceremony was in Spanish!

At the ceremony I was told that the novelist Gabriel García Marquez, a previous recipient of the prize, was in the audience. I have always loved the novels of García Marquez—he is such a strong, sensuous, colorful writer. I got very excited at the prospect of meeting him and did something I never did before or since: I asked the official Israeli photographer to snap a photo of us when we met.

At the large cocktail reception afterward, I introduced myself and said how delighted I was to meet him. Not even a smile. He could barely bring himself to extend his hand. This was clearly not shyness; it was coldness. García Marquez had been a vocal supporter of Palestinian rights over the years, and when he saw Yasir Arafat, the two fell into each other's arms. The next time I saw Arafat, I told him how embarrassed I was by my chilly encounter with the writer, while the two of them had embraced like old kindergarten buddies. "You know something," Arafat confided. "It was the first time I ever met him."

Sua Arafat and I spent time together in Spain and later in Oslo. We got along very well from the start. She's wonderfully accessible—a very natural, disarming person. Not for a moment does she set aside her role as a representative of the Palestinian people, nor does she forget that Palestinian women are still sitting in Israeli jails. She felt passionately that my husband grant their release. As we say in Yiddish, *Zi midarft, zi midarft nisht*—when it fit in or when it didn't fit in, she would remind me again and again that my husband had to release these women.

In the same month, Yitzhak learned that he was to be a co-recipient of the Nobel Peace Prize. However, on the day he received the news, he was in the throes of a national crisis. An Israeli corporal, Nachshon Wachsman, had been kidnapped by Hamas terrorists. The ransom the terrorists demanded was the release of about two hundred Arab prisoners. A major search for Wachsman was launched by the IDF, and the house near Jerusalem where he was being held hostage was soon located. A special rescue unit tried to force the kidnappers to surrender. A gun battle followed, and Wachsman was killed along with a member of the Israeli assault team and all the kidnappers. What a very sad Friday night that was.

Yitzhak assumed full responsibility for the failed effort. This was an unbearably difficult moment for him. He appeared on television to explain that sometimes there is no alternative and one must take the risk, even in doubt. I remember Yitzhak wearily rubbing his forehead with the tips of his fingers after learning of Wachsman's death. He said he would gladly have forgone the Nobel Prize if he could have exchanged it for Wachsman's life. His heart was bleeding.

The following Saturday night, Yitzhak and I visited the home of Nir Poraz, the soldier killed in the rescue effort. I had known Nir's mother and her sisters for many years, which only made the situation more painful. The soldier's two sisters were weeping. Yitzhak and I would have embraced the parents, but tension was evident in the room, and we shook hands as we offered our condolences. Yitzhak sat near Nir's mother and talked with her. Nir's father had been a pilot in the Israeli Air Force who was killed in 1973. Now his widow, the mother of three children, lost her son. Also present was her longtime companion, who, more than the boy's own mother, expressed enormous bitterness at the young man's death. How could you have sent him on this dangerous operation? he asked Yitzhak. Nir was about to be discharged from the army. He was in the process of leaving at the time of the rescue. The truth is that only the best are taken on an operation like this, Yitzhak told him, and reminded the man that all the participants had volunteered. The encounter with this family was heart-wrenching. Following the visit to the Poraz home, Yitzhak went to see the Wachsmans on his way to Jerusalem. I knew this visit would be even more difficult, given the especially tragic circumstances of Wachsman's death; Yitzhak called me later and confirmed just how hard it had been.

At a press conference following the incident, Yitzhak again assumed responsibility for the mission. His aide Eitan Haber said that Yitzhak asked to be left alone to wash up before the session, and at that moment he believed he saw tears in Yitzhak's eyes. Had that been so, and I believe it could well have been, these would have been Yitzhak's first tears since his mother's death.

∞ On October 26, 1994, the formal, comprehensive peace treaty with Jordan was signed in the Arava desert, on the Israeli-Jordanian border near Aqaba and Eilat. It was a most joyous occasion— thousands of brightly colored balloons were released after President Clinton, King Hussein, and Yitzhak signed the documents. We drove from there to the king's summer palace in Aqaba, on the Red Sea. At the celebratory luncheon the men ate on the first floor of the palace, while the women were served on the second floor. Even with Americans at the table, Yitzhak encouraged the king to have a cigarette. "After all, this is your home," Yitzhak said. The king lit Yitzhak's cigarette and then Yitzhak lit the king's. No such luck upstairs, where the evils of secondhand smoke were endlessly discussed.

Among the ladies at lunch, I recognized Mrs. Fawaz Sharaf, whose husband had been the Jordanian ambassador to Washington when Yitzhak was posted there. Back then, of course, we never met. Upon their return to Amman, her husband became the Jordanian prime minister but died soon after. Mrs. Sharaf was now a senator in the Jordanian parliament.

These last months of 1994 were exciting, memorable times for us, culminating in the awarding of the Nobel Peace Prize on December 10—an event I shall never forget. Upon our arrival in Oslo I was taken to the marvelous building that houses memorabilia on former laureates and prize committees of previous years. From there I joined Yitzhak, Shimon Peres, and their entourages and went to a general rehearsal that prepared us for the official ceremony. In the evening, we attended an intimate dinner party for the laureates, their closest associates, and the members of the prize committee. The next day we toured Oslo. The prize ceremony usually takes place in the morning, but since it was Shabbat, the event was postponed until after dark. King Harald V and Queen Sonja were seated at the front of the hall. The chairman of the committee spoke first, then the laureates.

"At an age when most youngsters are struggling to unravel the secrets of mathematics and the mysteries of the Bible," Yitzhak began, "at an age when first love blooms; at the tender age of sixteen, I was handed a rifle. . . ." He continued:

> *The profession of soldiering embraces a certain paradox. We take the best and bravest of our young men into the army. We supply them with equipment that costs a fortune. We rigorously train them for the day when they must do their duty—and we expect them to do it well. Yet we fervently pray that day will never come—that the planes will never take flight, the tanks will never move forward, the soldiers will never mount the attacks for which they have been trained so well.*

After the ceremony, there was a gala black-tie dinner, though Arafat—as expected—appeared in his khakis and kaffiyeh. The next day, a formal luncheon was held in the beautiful Akershus Festning—an ancient fortress on the peninsula to the south of the city that offered a breathtaking view of the Oslo Fjord. We sat around a long, long table, in the style of a traditional banquet, with everyone facing the water. Before lunch was over, Arafat stood up to say good-bye. "I must leave for Helsinki," he said. "But I'm leaving you my wife." Forget protocol. Yasir Arafat is always his own boss. And with a big smile he gets away with it.

In the afternoon, we were the honored guests at a concert of Israeli, Palestinian, and Norwegian musical groups in the presence of the king and the queen among the magnificent acoustics of the Oslo Konserthus. At the end of the concert, the laureates were invited onto the stage for an open interview. Sua Arafat stood in for her husband, and she handled herself beautifully. The whole affair was gloriously managed by the Norwegians from start to finish.

Yitzhak and Shimon Peres decided to put their share of the considerable prize money in a fund that would advance the cause of peace. Yitzhak was certainly very honored by this distinguished recognition, but I'm sure that he would not have regarded it as one of the most important or remarkable moments of his life. Shaking hands with Yasir Arafat and with His Majesty King Hussein would have meant more, because these acts symbolized their changing the course of history.

From Oslo we flew to Japan, and from Japan to Korea. In Japan, talks were held on how the Japanese could best extend financial and technological support to both the Palestinians and the Jordanians. In Korea, the talks focused on opportunities for expanding high-tech industrial cooperation. In both of these countries, Yitzhak was asked to provide his analysis of Middle East affairs—world leaders greatly esteemed his insight and clarity.

The Imperial Palace in Tokyo is a typically austere Japanese structure. We walked down a very long corridor and through a door, behind which stood Emperor Akihito and Empress Michiko.

We exchanged bows, and the emperor sat down with Yitzhak, while I joined the empress. The empress had obviously done her homework and asked me some very informed questions about kibbutz life.

Both dinner with Prime Minister Morihiro Hosokawa on the night of our arrival and lunch the following day featured Franco-European cuisine of the highest quality. The background music was performed by a live chamber orchestra, creating a lovely atmosphere. The table was set in the most glorious way. We also met Crown Prince Naruhito and Crown Princess Masako—who had been married the year before. She had attended Harvard and Oxford and had worked as a trade negotiator. Her father had been foreign minister. Upon the marriage of his daughter, the Japanese constitution required him to leave his post. He then went on to serve as Japan's ambassador to the United Nations—where we later had a chance to meet again.

On December 14, we flew to South Korea. In the morning, I met with the wife of the president while Yitzhak held talks with the president and members of the government. Korea's President Kim Young Sam was intensely interested in how Yitzhak had been able to make peace with longtime foes, in light of his fears about Korea's northern border. He told Yitzhak that he was the first South Korean president who was not a general, and Yitzhak pointed out that he was the first Israeli premier who had been a military man. He just couldn't get enough of Yitzhak and spoke to him almost exclusively throughout the state dinner. Schedules are strictly adhered to in the East, yet the dinner lasted half an hour longer than expected because President Kim didn't want to let Yitzhak go.

The next morning, Yitzhak was scheduled to get up at seven to review the situation on the country's northern border with South Korean military officials, but as we left the dinner, the president suddenly asked, "What are you doing tomorrow morning? May I invite you to a private breakfast at the pavilion next to the palace?" Yitzhak was surprised by this spontaneous invitation and said that he would have to rearrange his schedule, but he would gladly do so. The border tour would have been fascinating, but who can turn down an invitation from the president?

The breakfast conversation continued the theme of the previous night and was devoted to the fine points of border strategy. According to custom, we had to take off our shoes and put on those funny-looking slippers which never look right on your feet. Later in the day, I attended a lunch at the Israeli embassy in Seoul. As my Israeli hosts changed into slippers, I said, "Forgive me, but this is Israeli territory. Forgive me if I don't change my shoes." The embassy staff was so used to this custom, they didn't question it for a moment!

∞ In the months following our trip to Asia, Yitzhak immersed himself in the details of moving the peace process forward. On the eve of the Israeli Day of Independence in May 1995, Israeli television presented a dialogue between King Hussein and Yitzhak in Aqaba. Before the interview, we at last visited Petra. We were a large group, including Yitzhak's aides and our children. Petra was even more magnificent than I had expected.

One walks down the narrow *siq* between sheer red rock faces. The limestone cliffs surrounding you almost obscure the sky, their fantastic shapes rich in pinks, reds, and grays. At the end of the *siq* is a clearing with a marvelous temple carved out of the pink limestone. But the real excitement, Yitzhak and I both felt, was to be found in what God, not man, made. Yitzhak enjoyed the monumental scenery of Petra, but he may have savored more the implications of Israelis now being able to see Petra freely for themselves.

On June 8, 1995, Yitzhak appeared on Larry King's television show on CNN, along with President Clinton, King Hussein, Shimon Peres, and Yasir Arafat. The interview reflected the rapport these men now shared, but Yitzhak typically did not mince words when asked to state his position on a united Jerusalem. "I was born in Jerusalem," he said. "For me, Jerusalem [is] united, it will [remain] under Israel's sovereignty, it will be the capital of Israel and the heart of the Jewish people. Whoever would like to raise the issue, to talk about it, no problem. At the same time, we are committed to free access and free practice to the members of the other two religions, to the holy shrines in Jerusalem, to the Muslims, and to the Christians."

Peace was being celebrated around the world, but it didn't always reign on the streets of Israel. On July 24, 1995, a Hamas suicide bomber blew up a bus in the Tel Aviv suburb of Ramat Gan, killing six and wounding thirty-one. We were in London for a fund-raising dinner. Yitzhak wanted to fly back to Israel immediately, but there weren't any flights. He had to hire a small plane to rush back home.

This bombing was devastating to him. He inspected the scene of terror. It was as if a bomb had gone off in New York's Times Square. He looked at the casualty list and shook his head over the names of innocent victims. He saw the charred and twisted metal and the shattered glass and he asked the keen, methodical questions that he always posed after any such incident. Investigators combed the wreckage. The crowds tried to press close, and boom microphones and TV cameras bobbed everywhere. Yitzhak didn't sleep easily that night. For a long time he remained awake, anxious, but he never lost his perspective. The peace process could not fall victim to acts of terror.

∾ Building relations abroad remained a priority. On a two-day visit to Ukraine on September 12 and 13, 1995, we met Prime Minister Yevgeny Marchuk and his wife, Lydia. The visit acknowledged the geographic nearness of our two countries. From the southern border of Ukraine to the northernmost border of Israel is roughly 800 miles—the flight time from Tel Aviv to Kiev is about two hours. Sections of the former Soviet Union are much nearer to the borders of Israel than one is inclined to think.

This particular trip was designed to strengthen commercial and agricultural ties. Arms exports are significant for Israel. Ukraine has had to find other sources for armaments since the USSR was dissolved, and especially since the squabble erupted between Russia and Ukraine over the ownership of the Soviets' former Black

R A B I N

Sea fleet. During the visit, Yitzhak publicly criticized Russia's sale of nuclear reactors to Iran. Agricultural exports, so important to Israel, presented an opportunity for development in Ukraine, and so the talks also covered agricultural technology. In addition to visiting with government officials and business leaders in Ukraine's nascent market economy, we also attended the inauguration of a cultural center at the Israeli embassy that would reach out to Ukrainian Jews.

I found Mrs. Marchuk an educated and active woman. She heads an initiative for the development of dairy products in Ukraine. With a large percentage of the workforce employed in agriculture and vast stretches of rich, arable land, this is a very important position. Chernobyl devastated the already poor Ukraine, and the people faced the challenge of rebuilding their country— something to which we could so easily relate. Come to Israel, I told Mrs. Marchuk, and I will take you around. You will see what can be done in less than fifty years. You will not believe your eyes. Our dairy industry has grown and prospered remarkably, producing and exporting the whole range of cheeses, yogurts, ice creams, and other specialized products. I couldn't wait for her visit.

We had a good time, but conversation conducted through an interpreter is naturally clumsy. Still, it wasn't hard to detect an inquisitive, perceptive woman. We found ourselves waiting for our husbands to conclude their talks before we were to leave for the airport, nibbling hors d'oeuvres, killing time. "We always have to be on time," she huffed. "Never mind about *our* schedules. They assume we have the time to sit and wait." So I suggested we join the men. I walked over to Prime Minister Marchuk.

"Listen, the saying 'Behind every strong man is a strong woman' is total baloney," I said. "You guys just happen to be very lucky."

"You know we have been married for forty-seven years," Yitzhak said to Marchuk.

"And we have been married for twenty-seven years," Marchuk replied.

The Ukrainian speaker of the house then asked to tell a story.

Abraham and Sarah are celebrating their twenty-fifth wedding anniversary. Sarah asks, How shall we mark the day? Abraham responds, With one moment of silence . . .

This memorable visit included a somber journey to Babi Yar, on the outskirts of Kiev. Thirty-four thousand Jews were brutally slain there by the Nazis in a two-day massacre in 1941. In 1961, the Russian poet Yevgeny Yevtushenko evoked that horror in a poem of the same name. Yitzhak spoke these words in memory of the victims:

Here, in Babi Yar, the men of Sonderkommando A4 smashed the dreams of small children and the hearts of their parents, who tried to shield them with their own bodies. Here the roar of gunfire drowned the cries of tens of thousands of Kiev Jews and of many others. And here, in this pit of death, ended the history of a magnificent Jewish world— the Jews of Ukraine who had brought forth from their midst the first dreamers of Zion, the best of Jewish poets and writers, the great leaders and trailblazers of Zionism.

The Nazis and their helpers tried here, in this tranquil landscape, to eliminate any memory of their crime and any recollection of the Jewish people. They ground tens of thousands of their victims' bodies into dust and sowed it on the wind. No vestige of them remains.

The Jewish people were shot and killed here, but out of the trenches of death we were reborn, and now we must tell the entire world: let our tragedy be a warning sign to every human being that danger has not yet passed over the land. In these very days despicable successors arise, even in the countries that spawned the master murderers. Anti-Semitism breaks through frontiers. The contagious disease of racism threatens to wreak havoc on us. If the world does not awaken in time, if it does not smash the monstrous head of anti-Semitism and racism, we will be taken by surprise and unable to say: We did not see, we did not hear, we did not know.

Citizens of Israel, members of the Jewish nation: Jewish destiny impels us to return again and again to the killing ravines of Poland, Russia, Ukraine—to every place where Jewish blood was spilled: we return to these horrible places to remember, not to forget—and we will never forget—and also to draw strength and moral might from the terrible tragedy, to learn lessons for the future, and to know that no power on earth will again smite the Jewish people that have survived in exile for two thousand years. The nation of Israel will live forever.

We then met six elderly people—three survivors and three Righteous Among the Nations—Gentiles who helped save Jews during the Holocaust and who are remembered by trees planted at the Yad Vashem Memorial in Jerusalem. The life stories of these six people were devastating, and as we listened to them in Babi Yar, they were so immediate, so vivid, it was as if a half century had not passed.

Upon our departure from Kiev, the entire government, including Prime Minister Marchuk, saw us off. For some reason, our Israeli Air Force plane had not yet started its engines. The entire government would be locked in formation until we were airborne. Yitzhak could have throttled the pilot, who should have known better, and he let fly a barrage of questions: "Why don't you take off? Can't you see that these people are standing in the cold waiting for our departure? Why didn't you start the engines before we boarded? Why must it take so long?" He was so embarrassed that these dignitaries were made to stand in deference to him.

∞ On September 28, 1995, Yitzhak, Yasir Arafat, King Hussein, President Mubarak, and Bill Clinton met again on the occasion of signing the second Oslo agreement that extended Palestinian autonomy to the bulk of the Arab population on the West Bank. The ceremony in Washington was perhaps the culmination of all their hard work. I felt that this agreement was certainly the most successful single collaboration between Yitzhak and Shimon Peres during the peace process.

This signing took place inside the White House. The foreign ministers of all the countries who participated in forging this agreement, including the foreign minister of Norway, were in attendance. The many speeches were rather long, and it was getting late. When it was Yitzhak's turn to speak he said, "I have good news for you—I am the last speaker." And then he continued:

> *Now, after a long series of formal, festive statements, take a look at this stage. The king of Jordan, the president of Egypt, Chairman Arafat, and us, the prime minister and foreign minister of Israel, on one platform.*
>
> *Please take a good, hard look. The sight you see before you at this moment was impossible, was fantastic, just two or three years ago.*
>
> *Only poets dreamed of it, and to our great pain, soldiers and civilians went to their deaths to make this moment possible.*
>
> *Here we stand before you, men whom fate and history have sent on a mission of peace: to end, once and for all, one hundred years of bloodshed.*
>
> *Our dream is also your dream. King Hussein, President Mubarak, Chairman Arafat, all the others, and above all President Bill Clinton—a president working in the service of peace—we all love the same children, weep the same tears, hate the same enmity, and pray for reconciliation. Peace has no borders.*

By now, Mrs. Arafat and I had become good friends. As Yitzhak made his address, she leaned over to me and whispered yet again, "Tell him to release those Palestinian women in Israeli jails."

On the fifth of October, the Knesset debated and ultimately approved the second Oslo agreement. The way seemed clear to tackle the next item on the peace agenda—peace with Syria. That evening, the Likud and other right-wing parties mustered a crowd of 20,000 to 30,000 to Zion Square to protest the latest Oslo accords, chanting, "Rabin is a traitor" and, "Rabin, go home before you give it away." During the rally, demonstrators burned posters of Yitzhak in an SS uniform or a kaffiyeh, as Benjamin Netanyahu stood on a balcony overlooking the crowd.

At home, we watched the news coverage of the protest. The children and I were horrified by the frenzy, the vehemence of the demonstrators screaming their hate directly into the cameras. The passion and volatility reminded me of fundamentalist demonstrations in Iran. When the children and I expressed our concern to Yitzhak, he waved it away. "What's to be done?" he said. "We are living in a democracy."

On October 20 we flew to New York to participate in the ceremonies commemorating the fiftieth anniversary of the United Nations.

Boutros Boutros-Ghali, UN Secretary-General since 1992, was never considered a great friend of Israel but became much more of a supporter after the peace process started rolling. The change in attitude toward Israel within the United Nations was dramatic. At these celebrations, we found ourselves seated at the most honored places and with the most important leaders. In recent months we had hosted many of the world's leaders in Israel, including Holland's Queen Beatrix, Austria's Chancellor Franz Vranitzky, Kenyan president Daniel Arap Moi, British prime minister John Major, Chancellor Helmut Kohl of Germany, French foreign minister Alain Juppé, and many others.

The United Nations is like a window on the world. For years, we were isolated behind a curtain, and condemned within its walls. The abbreviation for the United Nations in Hebrew is "Um." David Ben-Gurion was known to say, "Um! *Schmum!*" in disgust—his inimitable response to our seemingly hopeless relationship with the institution. We were reprimanded again and again, and at times it seemed as if we might be ousted from its membership. When an Israeli delegate would address the UN, it was not unusual for two-thirds of the audience to walk out.

In his remarks before the UN in October 1995 Yitzhak noted our "historic turning point." "Just as we came to you to protest," Yitzhak said, "we now come to praise." He quoted the words of the prophet Isaiah: "They shall beat their swords into plowshares and their spears into pruning hooks." And his determination to achieve peace ran clear as always: "The road is still long. However, we are determined to continue until we have brought peace to the region. For our children and our children's children."

So many world leaders wanted to meet Yitzhak during this trip. He never got carried away and never took the attention personally, instead seeing himself as a privileged representative of all those who worked to bring about this peace. At the first big gathering of all the heads of state, Yitzhak stood in a corner, looking like a bashful boy on his first day of school. Within ten minutes, however, he was surrounded by a dozen leaders wanting to talk. Yitzhak's staff tells me that as many as eighty heads of state tried to secure appointments, though it was possible for him to see perhaps only forty of them. In a meeting with China's president, Jiang Zemin, Yitzhak began the conversation with typical modesty, pointing out how tiny our country was compared to the vast, mighty China. President Jiang waved his hand, dismissing the idea in midsentence. "To us," he said, "the quality and might of a nation is judged not by the size of its population, but by the culture and technological advancement of its people. By those standards, Israel is indeed a superpower."

The last of these meetings was with King Hassan II of Morocco on Friday afternoon. By the time it was over, night had already fallen and it was Shabbat, so Yitzhak and his entourage walked from the Plaza Hotel to the Regency in the pouring rain.

After the UN ceremonies, Yitzhak received the "Intrepid Freedom Award" from the governors of New York and New Jersey at a celebration on the USS *Intrepid*—an aircraft carrier that has been decommissioned and turned into a floating museum moored on the Hudson River.

Yitzhak met with President Clinton in Washington on October 25. That night we were all to attend a black-tie ceremony on behalf of the United Jewish Appeal. The pace of the day's events had been hectic—we were leaving for Israel that night—and Yitzhak was obsessed, as usual, with being punctual. He rushed from Capitol Hill, where he'd addressed an event commemorating the three thousandth anniversary of Jerusalem's founding, bypassing our hotel, to meet the president so they could proceed to the ceremony together. Better to arrive at a formal affair in a business suit than to keep a president waiting.

Seeing Yitzhak in his suit and tie, President Clinton came to the rescue, magically producing a black bow tie, which he helped Yitzhak to tie on. (Just as Yigael Yadin had provided timely tie assistance in Rhodes in 1949! *Plus ça change . . .*) The scene resulted in a terrific picture of President Clinton helping Yitzhak—a picture that radiates such warmth and mutual esteem.

Warm and respectful as their relationship was, Yitzhak and President Clinton had their share of heated disputes. Yitzhak's aide Shimon Sheves once observed Yitzhak pound his fist on the table at a frustrating moment in his negotiations with the president. Bewildered by having seen Yitzhak so comparatively mild-mannered and polite when dealing with an unruly cabinet minister back in Israel, Sheves asked Yitzhak how he could be so demonstrative and determined in addressing the president of the most powerful nation in the world. Yitzhak pointed out that the cabinet minister was just an aggravation, but when he spoke with the president, he had no choice but to assert and defend the interests of Israel to the fullest. In those moments, he said, nations were speaking to each other, not individuals.

Yitzhak attended a conference in Amman, Jordan, on October 29, another stop on the road to peace. These were such exciting times and Yitzhak was so committed to the cause of peace he wouldn't let violent demonstrations or terrorist bombings deter him from his mission. When we returned to Israel, Yitzhak again immersed himself in his work. His calendar remained the same throughout his second term—leaving our home at seven-thirty each morning, never really eating a proper lunch or having a nap, coming home around nine (if not later) to catch the evening news.

Relentless and indefatigable. Yitzhak was not oblivious to the threats to his personal security (such as the incident at Wingate) or to the hecklers outside our home, but he was not shaken by these events either, because he genuinely believed that peace was the only alternative for the future of his country. The rally of November 4, 1995, at Kikar Malchei Yisrael was to be an affirmation from the people of his hopes and his vision.

As he walked off the speaker's platform that joyous night, he heard what he needed to hear: the love and the blessings of hundreds of thousands of voices, young and old, too long silent, now ringing out as one, urging him forward in the name of peace. Descending the stairs to his waiting car, I am sure his thoughts, as always, turned to the hard work of the days ahead—to Syria and beyond. But a nobody with a 9-mm Beretta and a mind littered with hate interrupted the song of his life—*shirat chayav be'emza nifseka*—and my world, our world, was never to be the same.

ALL HIS CHILDREN
GRIEVE

December 7, 1995

Airborne over the Atlantic

So many times we made this flight together. We would have a whiskey and enjoy time out, in the way that only a flight can offer. We would share one sleeping pill and try to sleep for as many hours as possible side by side. You would be on your way to new challenges, and I—to satisfy my curiosity, meeting new people, seeing new places. All the many ceremonies and dinners as well as our breakfasts together. Those private breakfasts we never gave up.

Tonight I am alone in the first class cabin of El Al, drinking my whiskey alone and crying.

I take the half pill and its solitary mate remains on the tray.

From now on, I shall always have to face those challenges which your death has left me on my own: to meet people who seek new ways to commemorate you or simply wish to visit with me since they loved and admired you. And, always now, to remember.

There were many times that I traveled alone, of course, while you stayed at home. But it was never this kind of solitude. We would speak every day, and I would know how you were and you would know how I was. After so many years together we required so few words. Oh, Yitzhak, when will we speak? I carry on a one-sided conversation; still, in some way, it is a comfort to me in my burning pain.

DECEMBER 8, 1995
NEW YORK CITY

The cold rosy sky of a December daybreak surrounded us as we eased onto the runway of Kennedy Airport. Waiting cars sped us to the Consulate General of Israel, at Second Avenue and Forty-second Street, so that we would be there by nine A.M. *The night you were shot, crowds of people gathered at that site. During the* shiva, *mourners lit candles in your memory and stood in long lines to sign the condolence book at the consulate.*

New York's City Council decided to name this part of Second Avenue "Rabin Way," and the children and I were invited to the dedication. Mayor Rudolph Giuliani, City Council members, Consul-General Colette Avital, and I stood on the improvised stage before a crowd of hundreds who came on this chilly morning. The tributes in your memory were many.

Colette had not warned me that I would have to speak so I was forced to improvise, but I've grown used to this after thirty days of interviews and speeches, so it is no longer so difficult for me. What is *difficult is that there is so much pain and so much grief, and I am the checkpoint through which it all passes. To whom can I turn?*

DECEMBER 10, 1995
NEW YORK CITY

On Sunday there was a large rally at Madison Square Garden. There were many concerns before the event: about the security arrangements; whether President Clinton should at-

tend; how to discourage the demonstrations of the ultra-Orthodox; whether enough people would show up to fill the arena.

In the end, there was no cause to worry. The hall was packed! From eight in the morning, nearly 20,000 people stood in line in the bitter cold to pass through security checks. Shimon Peres, Edgar Bronfman, Chief Rabbi Yisrael-Meir Lau, Leon Levi, the new head of the Conference of Jewish Presidents, all addressed the audience. When I spoke, the audience seemed very moved. Aviv Geffen sang his song, a children's choir sang the "Song of Peace," and Marvin Hamlisch performed "The Child of His Child," a song he wrote for Noa. Vice President Al Gore spoke exceptionally well. A sea of people . . . the impact was overwhelming. But the picture of you that they hung from the rafters . . . well, it simply wasn't you. Perhaps this awful picture actually helped me a bit. When I sit opposite a good picture of you, I can't hold back my tears because it is you before my eyes—so good-looking and with such a kind expression—and I can't bear it. Here you looked like someone's uncle, a complete stranger!

Mayor Giuliani hosted a reception afterward at Gracie Mansion and remembered you eloquently. Shimon Peres, Al Gore, and Rabbi Lau also spoke. At first I did not want to speak, but then changed my mind and asked to say a few words after Rabbi Lau. The children and our friends ask again and again where I get the strength to do this. The strength comes from only one source; that your leaving us must somehow be made to matter.

I referred to remarks Shimon Peres had made earlier at the rally, about continuing along the path of peace, and said that if you could have spoken to him, you would have said, You must continue what we started together.

December 12, 1995
Washington
From New York, we flew with the vice president to Washington.

My Yitzhak, my darling—the honor that is bestowed on you through me has taken me to places I never dreamed of. I spent the night at the White House. I never thought that Lincoln's large bed was for real! But there I was in it, alas, alone. Lincoln and you, both felled by fanatics.

The Clintons couldn't have been warmer or friendlier hosts. We felt so very welcome. The Gores joined us for dinner—everyone was relaxed and it almost felt like a family affair. The next morning, the children and I sat down to breakfast at the White House. The president stopped by, dressed in sports clothes, on his way to his private office. Dalia was wearing a White House bathrobe and President Clinton said to her, "You look so good in it, you must keep it." Then Hillary stopped by. She, for her part, admired my cashmere robe. Her secretary came in a few minutes later to find out where I bought it. We told the housekeeper how much we had enjoyed the soup served the previous evening, and within five minutes, we were given the recipe in the chef's handwriting.

This is the warmth and the generosity in which we were received. Though they live in the White House, the Clintons remain so gracious, giving us the feeling that we were the guests of a very amiable American family.

December 13, 1995
Rome
We flew directly to Rome from the United States. No European country seems to have taken your assassination harder than the Italians—perhaps because they are such an emotional and outgoing people. In November, President Oscar Luigi Scalfaro was one of the first heads of state to arrive at

the funeral, with news that the grief in his country was like a period of national mourning.

The police presence upon our arrival at the Rome airport was gigantic, and we were surrounded by bodyguards, as though we were heads of state. Our schedule was chock-a-block with TV and newspaper interviews. Again and again, I retold the moment of your assassination. Again and again, I related my vision of the future—expressing the hope that support for the peace process would only grow as a result of the outrage at your death.

We visited the Great Synagogue in Rome in the presence of the chief rabbi. It was a somber occasion in more ways than one. The Jewish population of Rome has dwindled to poor, elderly people. The young and more affluent Jews have moved north to Milan and Turin. The very simplicity of the people and the synagogue made everything so poignant and so endlessly sad.

A memorial ceremony at the Opera in Rome was most dignified. The entire government, many members of Parliament, the diplomatic corps and public figures attended. President Scalfaro spoke with tears in his eyes. I sat beside him on the stage and could not hold back my own tears. I read my speech, which had been translated into Italian. Excerpts from some of your speeches were read. Ahinoam Nini sang "The Song of Peace," followed by an uplifting concert conducted by Daniel Oren. All the artists volunteered their participation.

It was hard to walk through the streets of Rome. Everyone, it seemed, recognized us and came up to shake our hands, as if we were in Tel Aviv.

DECEMBER 14, 1995
VATICAN CITY
Today the children and I had an audience with the Pope, an extraordinary gesture! When you told me of your meeting

*with the Pope you described him as a formidable yet pleas-
ant man. You were right. The strict rules of protocol permitted only the children, our ambassador, and me to attend the
audience.*

*He told me that I was sitting in the same chair you had
sat in during your visit the year before. He said that, to his
mind, you had become a saint by your death. Yitzhak, even
in our country, in the eyes of the thousands who continue to
visit your grave and the site of the assassination, you have
become something of a saint—certainly a martyr . . . so terrible a fact to come to terms with.*

*The Pope then spoke of the Chosen People, and here I
expressed my opinion that this was a choice we ourselves
had made when we accepted the Ten Commandments. "Thou
shalt not kill" declares the sanctity of life supreme. It was always that way for you. And now a Jew has murdered you.
And we are shocked and ashamed.*

*I told the Pope that you regarded the unification of
Jerusalem in 1967 as one of the proudest moments of your
life, and how important it was for persons of all faiths to
have free access to their holy sites. It was then that the Pope
said that he regarded Jerusalem as a city with double meaning: the capital of Israel and a holy city for three faiths. How
delighted you would have been at that moment! In parting,
the Pope presented me with a beautiful painting of a
Madonna framed in ivory.*

*After we left, a well-attended press conference probed
our conversation with the Pope, and its implications made
headlines around the world. On our last night we had dinner
with our ambassador, Yehuda Milo, and the embassy staff so
that we could thank them for the hard work they put into arranging our visit.*

*Yitzhak, how difficult it is to come home, to know that
you will not be there waiting for me, beaming and ready
with your warm hug. I was always so happy to return after
every trip—to you, to our home, to the comfort of our to-*

getherness. And now there is the house and your pictures.
The emptiness. The never-ending sadness.

∞ In the months following Yitzhak's death, the nation paid tribute by naming many structures and facilities in his memory. In December alone several dedications occurred. There was a sports
center in Herzliyah. My beloved secondary school, Tichon
Hadash, which both our children and our grandson Michael attended as well, became the Yitzhak Rabin School. Beilinson Hospital and Sharon Hospital were now united and called Rabin
Medical Center.

On December 21, 1995, the power station in Hadera was renamed the "Rabin Lights." Yitzhak was at the power station for
its inauguration, four days before his assassination. All the light
the station generates now bears his name.

As I walked through the plant on the day of the ceremony, I
learned much about electrical power, just the kind of details
Yitzhak always hungered to know. Through the workers themselves I was reminded of a different kind of power. They stood
with tears in their eyes—remembering someone they loved so
much, a brother.

To Yitzhak, this plant was another rung on Israel's ladder of
progress. Once again songs were sung, and once more I sat there
with an ache in my heart and tears that could not be stopped.

Long after the *shiva,* many people from different walks of life
continued to pay their respects. In late December, for example, the
actor Ben Kingsley spent a few hours with me at home. A month
before the assassination, Ben was invited to Jerusalem by Uzi
Baram, the minister of tourism. At a dinner for a thousand people—most of them publishers and editors of tourist magazines
from the United States—Uzi and Ruthi Baram, Yitzhak, Ben Kingsley, and I were seated at the same table. Ben sat on my right, and I
enjoyed our conversation about books and theater immensely.

After dessert was served, the seat next to Yitzhak was free for a while and Ben moved over so they could chat. They talked about our upcoming visit to Camberley, and about Ben's role in *Schindler's List* and his study of mid-century European anti-Semitism. In our living room, Ben described their talk as a "three- to four-cigarette conversation, which is how you measure time with Rabin." I asked him what about Yitzhak struck him most, and he captured it in two words: "His stillness."

On January 6, 1996, the trauma unit of Tel Aviv's Ichilov Hospital was renamed the Rabin Trauma Unit. Attending were King Hussein and Shimon Peres, members of the Knesset, and the hospital staff, including Professor Gabi Barabash and the trauma unit team. It was King Hussein's first visit to Tel Aviv.

I expressed my thanks to the trauma unit team under the leadership of Dr. Yoram Kugler and Dr. Motti Gutman, who were by Yitzhak's side from the first moment he was brought there to the very last, when they realized they could do no more. The shock of that night for the hospital staff had been enormous—to have the prime minister brought in in critical condition, trying everything possible to save him, then having to make the decision to take him off life support and declare him dead. I should have thanked them that night in November for their efforts, but I was dazed—I just was not thinking at all. In conclusion, I expressed my gratitude for King Hussein's presence by quoting scripture: "Blessed be he by coming and by leaving us on his way home."

FEBRUARY 5, 1996

LAUSANNE

Again I am on a plane. This time to Switzerland. I will speak on behalf of Keren Hayessod* in Lausanne and Geneva.

Yitzhak, I am often asked: "How are you?" Such a simple, polite question, though one I dread. I try to answer vaguely, "Thank you, OK," but it sounds hollow. Some-

---

**An organization that raises funds in Europe for Israel.*

times I even tell people not to ask because they do not want to hear how bad I feel, how much it hurts.

Before I left, a photo exhibit was unveiled in Ramat Gan. One hundred eighty wonderful photos from your life. Images of the man you were: the soldier, the chief of staff, the diplomat, the statesman, the leader, the friend, the father who embraced his children, the grandfather who hugged his grandchildren, my husband. In one photograph you were helping a handicapped soldier to rise from his chair, and your concern was so obvious. In another you were laughing heartily during a press conference with Warren Christopher . . . Yitzhak, what was so funny?

Yitzhak—I want so much to overcome my pain. I am very concerned that I am not succeeding. I cannot concentrate, I cannot read. I want to be strong, for you and for our children, but my strength is diminishing, and I am frightened.

FEBRUARY 9, 1996.
GSTAAD

Many times I was in Gstaad without you. At home, in Israel, you would say, "Enjoy yourself!" You always encouraged me to ski—something you repeatedly refused to try. "One broken leg is enough," you would say. "I have enough risks in my life." In a sense, skiing is now, as it was when you were alive, a way of being with you while being without you.

You are always with me. It seems that I am smoking your last cigarette before bed. Good night, my darling.

FEBRUARY 10, 1996
GSTAAD

We brought the snow with us to Gstaad. The hours of skiing were like medication for my aching heart. The beautiful, rich scenery enlivened me, and the hours on the slopes have done me a world of good, even if it is merely a temporary escape.

But something that happened in Israel is making me cut this visit short. The abominable family of the subhuman that killed you stood on a street in Jerusalem, surrounded by supporters, holding signs that proclaimed: This Is Blood-Libel. He Is Innocent. A demonstration—with a police permit! How much longer can we withstand the madness of our system? The murder trial has been under way for three long months. You were always very critical of our slow justice system. And now, after a murderer has assassinated you before the eyes of the world and confessed to the crime, we still await his verdict. I cannot understand this.

Yuval spoke out about this on the radio in Israel. Many tell me his remarks were strong and articulate. You would have been proud of your son. What a terrible thing to say . . . you would have been . . .

∞ In the week before what would have been Yitzhak's seventy-fourth birthday, two terrorist attacks struck our country. In the first, a Hamas suicide bomber boarded bus 18 near Jerusalem's central bus station. The bus exploded, killing twenty-four and wounding fifty.

Forty-five minutes later, another Hamas bomber detonated an explosion at a crowded hitchhiking post outside Ashkelon, killing one and wounding thirty-four. The intent of these attacks was clear: by killing innocents, Hamas was out to prove that this peace did not bring security, hoping to frighten the people away from peace. How the nation needed Yitzhak to reassure them, to comfort them, to convince them of the need to persevere. . . .

On his birthday, March 1, we were to unveil Yitzhak's tomb on Mount Herzl. I asked our friend, the architect Moshe Safdie (who had created the hauntingly beautiful Children's Memorial at Yad Vashem) to design the monument. I wanted the headstone to be made of basalt, a glassy, volcanic rock found in the Golan Heights, and to carry only his name on the front and the years of his life on the back.

The tomb has simple lines, befitting a great and straightforward man. The stone has a commanding presence—its two sides meet in a V, with one leg of the stone a pale ivory in color, the other black. In front of the headstone rests the eternal flame.

It was raining when we arrived at the cemetery, and the flame would not light. Was this somehow symbolic? I wondered. Shimon Peres noted that some of the victims of last week's terrorist bombings were buried on Mount Herzl and that the *shiva* for them had not yet concluded. He said that Yitzhak had "taught us not to yield to terrorism, not to deviate from peace."

Fighting back tears, Dalia recalled how her father had enjoyed celebrating his birthdays. "On your birthday, we come again," she said. "But we are honoring your birthday without you." Yuval recited the Kaddish. And I spoke to you.

Yitzhak, this is the second time I am talking to you before a crowd, knowing you cannot hear. My need to talk to you persists. As does my need to remark on the cruelty of this one-way conversation.

On that terrible night, when the first shot was heard, you looked back, as if to say, "One moment, what's going on here?" And then I saw you fall down, and the others fall on top of you. I thought, and so strongly wanted to believe, that you were thrown down for protection against bullets that missed you.

You would have refused to believe that a bullet shot by an evil Jew was aimed at you.

Why did you fall, the hero of my youth, the hero of my life? Why did you fall and not get up?

We are gathered here today around your headstone. Today, the first of March, your seventy-fourth birthday. And you are no more!

It is already four months that we have been hurting. You are missed at every moment. We cannot comprehend that we will continue to be without you, always.

"The storm will blow around us," says the Palmach's anthem. Hamas, suicide attacks, bombs, and the heat of elections. The storm rages.

All this does not affect you anymore. You are here, forever.

∞

MARCH 4, 1996
NEW YORK

After your birthday I left for the United States. I was invited by Fairleigh Dickinson University in New Jersey to accept an honorary doctorate awarded to both of us. Sixty people have died in suicide bombings in Israel in recent days. Yesterday another Hamas bomber blew himself up near Dizengoff Center, in the heart of Tel Aviv, killing twelve and wounding over one hundred, many of them children. Indeed two New Jersey families have lost daughters to terrorist acts in recent years. In addressing the university crowd, I spoke words you would have wanted me to say at such a critical time:

In the past week we have been given a terrible reminder of the terrorism used by Islamic extremists. Exactly one year ago a similar act of terrorism took place at Beit Lid. I would like to quote what my husband said then. "To our enemies we say: As in the past, we will continue to fight you, both now and in the future. We will continue building our homes and our families here. We will continue our search for peace, and at the same time we will pursue you and hit you hard. No border will stand in our way. We will eliminate you. We will overcome you. No enemy will defeat us."

Then as now, we must fight against terrorism while pursuing a real peace. And now another bomb in Tel Aviv. . . .

In hundreds of thousands of letters I've received since Yitzhak's death, people tell me what they've lost, what he meant to them, what he stood for, and how much they will miss him.

Now, four months later, when the candles are out and the flowers have wilted, as the first letters are filed while more continue to arrive, the whole country, and many other countries, cities, and universities all over the world, wish to honor and commemorate him. Now Rabin is a road and a square and a medical center and a sports center and a kindergarten and a school. There are foundations and scholarship funds in his name. He has become a myth. But what is a myth if not a legend for the generations ahead?

When I am asked whether I have an agenda, I say I do indeed. As the person closest to him, who loved him all his life, who was beside him at all the crossroads, who knew intimately the workings of his great mind and his courageous heart, I feel an acute responsibility to carry his message forward, to ignite again and again the brilliant light that was so brutally extinguished.

I am here to remind you of him.

MARCH 7, 1996
BOSTON

Today, Yitzhak, I spoke at the John F. Kennedy School of Government at Harvard in a televised address. You were to make this speech last November 16; I am your humble stand-in. The hall was filled to capacity—more than 800 people. A friend tells me the silence was such that you could hear the people breathe. After I talked, there were questions. One of the students, an Arab, had saved a question he'd prepared to ask you last November, but now he was forced to ask me instead. I shaded my eyes with my hand as I looked into the audience to find him. "I can't see you," I said. "But if you want to ask Yitzhak, let's try and see what happens. . . ."

MARCH 10, 1996

LOS ANGELES

Tonight I attended a benefit at the Beverly Hilton for the Shiba Medical Center, which is building a rehabilitation center that will bear your name. The evening was conducted in typical Beverly Hills style. The actor Rod Steiger was asked to talk for two to three minutes—during which he called you "Rubin" four times. When my turn came to speak, I said to the actor, "In faraway India there was an old man who said he had a friend who died for peace whose name was Rubin. He is entitled to say Rubin, but I expect you to call my husband by his right name."

Natalie Cole—Nat King Cole's daughter—also was on the program. She has her own style, which that evening was to appear more or less topless. I didn't feel that it was in very good taste. When I spoke, I said that there was magic in Jewish life, how we live in different parts of the world and adjust to the different ways of life of those around us, yet remain one people. As I attend ceremonies around the world in honor of my murdered husband, I told them, I see the diverse ways people choose to memorialize him. I'm sure Yitzhak would have enjoyed Natalie Cole very much!

While Dalia and I were on the plane to the United States, an Inquiry Committee published its conclusions about the functioning of security on the night of the murder. The findings were critical of Shabak. Since the murder, my feelings on the subject have not changed. The murderer managed to get to you and kill you. The climate leading up to the murder encouraged him to act. You could never believe that a Jew might kill you—a view you expressed time and again. How can we expect those in charge of your security to feel otherwise?

I have not wavered in my attitude toward the security people who protected you. You trusted them. You trusted them for so many years—and I too have always respected

their dedication and hard work. If they made mistakes, they
are paying for them now. But I cannot think that they failed
you. Whatever I think will not bring you back.

ɔ Spurred primarily by the rash of terrorist violence in Israel, a
global terrorism conference was convened in Sharm el-Sheikh, Egypt,
on March 13, 1996. President Clinton attended, along with many
other world leaders, including President Mubarak, King Hussein,
Helmut Kohl, Jacques Chirac, John Major, and Shimon Peres. The
conference reminded many of the gathering of heads of state that
had come together for Yitzhak's funeral just five months earlier.

After the conference, President Clinton came to Israel. He announced the American commitment of $100 million in advanced
technology to help combat terrorism. He visited the grave of
Nachshon Wachsman, the kidnapped soldier slain by Hamas, and
spoke with his bereaved parents. Then we went on to Yitzhak's
tomb on Mount Herzl. The president and I stood facing the grave,
hand in hand. Total quiet reigned as the president placed on the
grave stones from the White House Rose Garden and a wreath of
red, white, and blue flowers with a ribbon that read, *Shalom,*
Chaver. He is indeed a wonderful friend to us.

Later that afternoon, President Clinton attended a huge youth
rally at the Tel Aviv Opera House. When I entered the hall, I was
stunned by the ovation I received from the "Generation of the
Candles," as the young people who grieved for Yitzhak have come
to be called. They gave the president an equally warm and rousing
reception. As always, President Clinton spoke with great eloquence,
urging our youth not to abandon hope in the face of adversity and
to fight to fulfill their dream of a better future. He gave Shimon
Peres powerful support in his election bid for the premiership.

On March 25, 1996, the Labor Party primary took place. Shimon Peres was once again voted Labor's candidate for prime minister. We had to feel hopeful that this time his bid for the
premiership would succeed.

MARCH 25, 1996

TEL AVIV

I am at home. Everything here is about you. Your photographs are everywhere. Your closets still hold the belongings which you had left behind on that cursed day. The ties, the shirts, the beautiful blazers. Your shoes, the tennis shoes—the tennis drawer—I cannot bring myself to touch anything. It all remains yours, and in this way I keep you with me. Here at home it is as though you will reappear at any moment and you will find everything just as you had left it behind. You were always so thoughtful to those around you. You used to come home and say: "Whenever it will be convenient for you, please make me a cheese sandwich," and I did it at once knowing you must not have eaten all day. It is so painful to remember even this after five cursed months. No, I no longer expect you just to walk in, but sometimes just thinking it makes it easier for me to cope. Will I ever feel differently?

Like the emptiness of this primary night without you, many things that used to hold meaning now fill me with dread—the approaching Pesach, my birthday, Independence Day. My Abba'le, it is terrible to think that nothing again will ever make me truly happy. That every happy day, every holiday will be so terribly sad without you.

∞ When the verdict and the sentencing of Yitzhak's murderer was announced on March 28, 1996, the phones never stopped ringing. I refused to follow the trial, but people told me about the murderer's smirking, his unrepentant attitude, and his gum chewing in the courtroom. Who needed this?

However, now that the verdict has been rendered, I support the petition efforts under way in Israel to make the sentence forever exempt from commutation or pardon. That the murderer will be allowed to vote in the national election is an abomination!

MARCH 31, 1996
LOS ANGELES

Three more pleasant days in Los Angeles. Beverly Hills is one of the loveliest places on earth—isolated as it is from bitter realities. Beauty, wealth, glorious weather, and perpetual flowers.

Sunday noon, we participated in a moving ceremony to name the square at the entrance to Universal City in your honor. The mayor, members of the city council, Lew Wasserman, and a group of hechalutz Jewish pioneer youth. A square named "Rabin" even here—in the middle of the make-believe movie world.

A big Jewish Federation event was held that evening. Fifteen hundred people at Century Plaza. Monte Hall coordinated the evening with charm and dignity. I was introduced by Richard Dreyfuss. I have never before been introduced with so much emotion and originality. I was enchanted by him and his style. I spoke a little longer than usual, and it was apparently successful, judging by the response. Again and again I talk about the night of the rally and its aftermath. About you—and more about you—and, finally, about your commitment to the Jewish people, and your expectations of their commitment in return.

∞ Of all the many expressions of condolences received after Yitzhak's death, none stood out for me more poignantly than that of a fifteen-year-old girl, Bat-Chen Shahak. She called her poem "A Letter to Rabin."

Three shots and it's all over—
Now one talks about him in the past tense.
Suddenly the present becomes the past,
And the past is only a memory.
We are standing, crying,
We want to believe it never happened,

That it is all a nightmare,
And when we wake up the next morning—it will not be so.
Instead, we wake up to a warped reality,
Where pain is laced with hate.
We cannot digest the enormity of this loss,
And we cannot comprehend its severity.
How can we understand such a tragedy,
In a civilization and not in the jungle?
It is like that first fallen domino,
That provokes a chain reaction.
We were beheaded, in every sense of the word,
And now it all crumbles.
As though he were the head, and we the body,
And when the head does not exist—the body dies!
It is impossible to build with parts that do not fit,
It is impossible to build with mismatched bricks.
It is an art to build a straight tower,
But a single kick can shatter it all.
And then,
One can destroy a State!
I do not know why they search for guilty parties,
I think we are all guilty for not showing how much we
*   loved him.*
Like the children that grow up,
And only then understand their parents,
And sometimes it is too late. . . .
They ask for forgiveness, they write and they cry.
Maybe I am too naive,
But I cannot understand,
How people,
Take the law into their own hands.
How can we take the best gift ever given,
Life. . . .
I mourn with you and I hope you will never experience
*   further grief.*

I would have loved so much to thank Bat-Chen for her words. But I shall never have that chance.

Bat-Chen was killed on her birthday in the terrorist bombing at Dizengoff Center in March 1996, along with two of her girl-friends. Several weeks after the bombing, I visited the families of these three fifteen-year-old girls. Even after the devastating loss of his daughter, Bat-Chen's father had the courage to say—to me personally and publicly on Israeli television—that he supported the peace process as passionately as his daughter had.

April 3, 1996

Tel Aviv

My dearest loved one, when you were assassinated it was au-tumn and now it is spring. Everything is blossoming—the poppies, the acacia.

The long winter has passed, but not its sadness. One long wintry night drenched in longing, in which sunshine rarely flickered.

It is Pesach eve, and the flow of flowers and phone calls is never-ending. People do not know what to say. Should they wish me "Chag sameach"? Many say it, but the very thought is impossible for us. The house drowns in flowers. How we loved the festive seder nights at Dalia's in-laws, the Pelos-sofs. You used to dress up for these occasions and we felt the special honor of your presence.

Yesterday we went to Mount Herzl at a time we hoped no one else would be present. Indeed, for the first time we were there alone—Avi and Dalia, Yuval and Tali, and Jonathan and Noa. We sat by your grave and we cried—together and alone. We are standing on the edge of an abyss and we try not to fall. . . .

APRIL 8, 1996

TEL AVIV

Dalia and Tali threw me a birthday party in Dalia and Avi's beautiful new home. You would have had so much joy seeing them in such a lovely setting. Our friends, their friends, and those of Noa and Jonathan—three generations—came to celebrate.

Yitzhak, for a short while I indeed felt better. I was engulfed with life, love, and support. The people to whom I am closest were all with me—all but one. As I left our home on my way to the party, about 150 youngsters were waiting for me downstairs to wish me a happy birthday. They sang the "Song of Peace" and other birthday songs. The youth shower me with love, yet I could hardly voice my gratitude to them through my tears. They called to me: "Be strong . . . we need you." I am not strong and I do not know what exactly I can do for them. A void has been left that no one can fill.

APRIL 14, 1996

GENOA

We landed at a small airport bathed in sunlight. Mayor Sansa, bearing a huge bouquet of tulips, and the director of the Primo Levi Cultural Center were both there to greet me. The mayor—a man with piercing blue eyes—immediately struck me as impressive. I traveled to town in his car. He called your assassination "a Greek tragedy."

The center awards its Primo Levi Prize annually, commemorating a distinguished humanitarian, and I am to receive it on your behalf. It's a great, prestigious honor, and because it is in Levi's name, it speaks to my heart.

After lunch I met members of the Jewish community, which dates back to the expulsion from Spain in 1492. They had been persecuted and expelled from Genoa, only to return again. The community consists of only five hundred souls, but they maintain their Jewish identity and their at-

*tachment to Israel. Disturbing, though—I saw few young-
sters among them.*

*Both the Primo Levi award ceremony and the honorary
citizenship of Genoa took place in a venerable and elegant
hall, built in opulent style: marble pillars with ornate capi-
tals, painted ceilings. Every seat was taken and people stood
along the walls. In a neighboring hall, the overflow audience
watched the event on closed-circuit television.*

*I spoke about Primo Levi and his works and mentioned
that my grandfather had perished on his first day in
Auschwitz. I spoke of our life in Israel in terms of history's
high and low tides—a notion familiar to a port city that had
seen its own ebb and flow over the centuries.*

*The mayor of Genoa told me that I must become the next
president of Israel. I don't think I have mentioned this to
you in my letters, but many people have urged me toward this
role. Leah, your wife, president of the state? Yitzhak, doesn't
that sound absurd? When I'm asked about it in interviews, I
reply, "I won't fight for it—and because nothing is ever
handed to a person on a silver platter, it follows that it simply will not happen!" I was partner to all your battles, and I
know how hard you fought. I have had my share of fights.*

*Tomorrow I will be in Florence to receive yet another
award. Do you remember how we loved Florence on our
first visit in 1953? For five days we reveled in the length and
breadth of that beautiful city. And we left knowing that we
would return, which we did time and again—and now I will
return and think of you. . . .*

April 15, 1996
Florence
Dear Yitzhak, so beloved yet so far away . . .

*There are some beautiful moments. Today in Florence,
you were given the annual Pegasio d'Oro Award by President Ghitto of the province of Tuscany. And then, a visit to*

the mayor of Florence, Mario Primichario, in the Palazzo Vecchio. He touched me deeply with a story he told. He had visited Israel to create a sisterhood between the cities of Florence and Nazareth. "The first thing I did was go from the airport to your husband's grave." Then he went to meet Yasir Arafat and told him about having been to the grave. Arafat jumped to his feet and embraced the mayor, saying, "Thank you for going to my brother's grave!" He repeated the story when he introduced me to the city council. After the meeting, we went for a walk on the Ponte Vecchio surrounded by a veritable army of police. Yitzhak, if only you could have seen the scores of people lining the roadside. It was a warm, sunny day and we enjoyed every minute, despite the vast entourage of policemen. I am showered with respect, always surrounded by heavy security that builds a human wall around me—all because I belong to you.

APRIL 23, 1996

NEW YORK

My first Independence Day without you.

For forty-seven years we celebrated this day together, from those first Independence Days with the IDF parades that grew bigger and more ceremonial year after year. I remember our excitement as the parade passed before us—the pride and joy at the sight of the army, marching to the tunes of our youth, the navy in their sparkling whites, the tanks— with new, bigger, and stronger models each year—the flights of the air force overhead.

Over the years, Independence Day took on a new quality, with the parade giving way to picnics, with family and friends gathering in every park and forest grove, under shady trees. In the evening, there would be parties. We had our own tradition, attending a reception at the President's house and the finals of the Bible Contest,* stopping by a

---

*An annual quiz competition for young people gauging command of the Bible.

few home gatherings and picnics, then heading back to Jerusalem for the Israel Prize ceremony. At night we would go to the reception at the Defense Ministry, ever larger each year. Thousands of hands to be shaken. A long day of running like mad from place to place, yet a day of so much joy. The flags, the songs, the whole of Israel celebrating—and for forty-seven years we were at the center of it.*

And now, how am I to pass the day without you? Every flag, every song, every event is full of thousands of memories. Forty-seven years in the life of Israel. Forty-seven years of struggle for survival, for peace, for security. Forty-seven years of a wonderful marriage that ended all too soon.

On this Independence Day you are missed by many everywhere. On the Lebanese frontier, the katyushas *have been falling for two weeks, while Warren Christopher shuttles back and forth between Jerusalem and Damascus.*

I knew that I wouldn't be able to cope with it all and happily accepted an invitation by the American Association for the United Nations, a fund-raising group. Last year's honoree was Colin Powell, and this year they had decided on you, which means me. . . .

Noa, Jonathan, Avi, and Dalia came with me. Back home, on Remembrance Day, our closest friends visited your grave, as did Yuval and Tali. They were with you when the sirens sounded at eleven A.M. There were many at the graves of their dear ones in the military cemetery.

Yuval tells me that banks of flowers covered your grave. On that afternoon visitors saw a young naval officer in dress whites snap off a sharp salute and lay a bouquet of red roses before your monument. A solitary tear trickled down his cheek, and his jaw quivered as he sought to keep his bearing.

---

*Prizes awarded for exceptional achievements in a variety of fields, such as medicine, the arts, and philosophy.

MAY 23, 1996

JERUSALEM

Mount Herzl on the eve of a Shavuot was deserted when we came to wish you a happy holiday, to place a plant and light a candle. How the sadness becomes even more oppressive at festivals.

Again that feeling that we have abandoned you, on Mount Herzl, under the monumental stone. We returned home, to a picture of you in every corner. Your absence cries out to the heavens.

I'm parting from you here and going to the synagogue, to see a sefer Torah *installed in your memory on this the celebration of the giving of God's law.*

∞ Quickly the election was upon us. On May 26, Shimon Peres and Benjamin Netanyahu engaged in their only debate of the campaign. Most observers said the outcome was close. Closer than many had predicted.

Throughout the campaign, the polls gave Shimon Peres a 4 to 6 percent edge. Then the election became too close to call. I wondered why the Labor campaigners not been more aggressive in invoking Yitzhak's memory. Why had they not utilized me more extensively in the campaign? I had certainly offered to help. In retrospect, I feel I should have perhaps insisted, but I was so reluctant to push myself and so sure they were going to succeed anyway.

On the night of the election, Yael Dan from Israeli television interviewed me at home. I told her I was confident that Labor would win the election. But what if they don't, she pressed me. I said if, God forbid, that happens, I was eyeing my suitcases. Predictably this statement caused an international furor. As I explained shortly afterward in an interview in *Newsweek:* "I was joking. I said I'll feel like packing my bags if Shimon Peres lost the election. But this was not said seriously. I can never leave my country. This is my country. My children are here, and here on Mount Herzl Yitzhak is buried." Could anybody take that comment seriously? Apparently there are those who lie in wait for such opportunities.

The initial exit polls on May 29 predicted a victory for Shimon Peres, but the balance gradually shifted in favor of Netanyahu. It took three days to finalize the result, which was announced on Friday, May 31, shortly before sundown. Up until the final day, the results of the election could have been determined by absentee ballots—those of soldiers and hospital patients . . . and by the ballots of imprisoned felons, even one who assassinated the incumbent candidate in cold blood and in plain view.

June 5, 1996
Tel Aviv
My Yitzhak, beloved and so far away . . .

The elections are behind us, but the shock of failure remains. The murderer did an enormous thing. He brought you down, even in the afterlife, and now he's laughing. They're celebrating, for without you it is impossible to acquire the trust of the people. Bibi won by a mere twenty thousand votes, but already he is chattering about peace and his commitment to the Oslo agreements. You were the traitor and murderer, but now he is going to make peace—your peace. The man who stood in Zion Square and watched them burn your name.

How could it happen? We were promised victory. But some members of the Labor Party were, it seems, too complacent. They waged a very weak campaign. They decided that the campaign should be kept low-key: no friction, no accusations. So they didn't want to bring up your murder or the frenzied Likud demonstrations and their wild incitement. . . . They were afraid of clashes, of even more killings, so they avoided mass election rallies in the city squares. They were "sleepy, vegetarian, and anemic," as you would say. They ran a campaign from two different headquarters that fought with each other, then blamed each other. There were public opinion polls that never reached the people who needed to see them. The gap in Peres's favor—experts all wrote and spoke about 4 to 6 percent—seemed to be constant. Now I don't know whether in fact there ever was a gap.

On the other hand, Bibi fought a focused and professional campaign. The Likud brought in an expert from the United States and did everything that he advised. They succeeded in frightening the voters with the specter of terror strikes: "Since when have we been scared to ride a bus?" "Bibi will make 'peace with security.'"

I was sure—and in many trips abroad I said—that we have only one option: to remain strong and united in the face of attempts to undermine the peace process. The angry demonstrations that usually followed terror strikes faded away after the murder. The style had changed and I was optimistic. I wanted to hope that the assassination, and your terrible sacrifice, had in some way contributed to the peace process, to the shift in so many people's attitudes.

Then came the election and trumped all the cards. I was asked after election day whom I was angry with, since everyone here is angry with someone. I said that I only had one thing to offer: If you had lived, you would have won—for they elected you and said they trusted you. You radiated to the public that same thing that you took with you to the grave: credibility. There was a desire to believe you, to trust you because you would do the right thing. And, if you had lost, you would have taken responsibility for it, as you have done all your life. Some people interpreted my words as a call for Peres's resignation. I said no, I wasn't commenting on what Shimon Peres should do, only on what you would have done. You, Yitzhak, would have immediately claimed responsibility for the failure. Of that I am absolutely sure.

Where are you when I need to share all the sorrow and pain? You have become like a distant planet—ours, but only

*a star. I read the poems and letters of Shabak personnel,
written after the murder. I read letters mailed to me after the
election failure and my eyes brim with tears.*

*The days are divided between pain and apprehension.
The few hours that I spend with people somehow succeed in
breaking the chain of anxious thoughts, but the many hours
of solitude only leave me to the nightmare, to that which has
yet to be grasped. . . .*

*It was a cool evening in Jerusalem. The wind toyed with
the treetops and we stood facing that silent tombstone, so
helpless and so in need of you.*

∞ Nearly a year later, a woman still comes every morning to clean
the area where Yitzhak was killed. She removes the faded blossoms and the candle wax and weaves fresh flowers into the fence
surrounding the site. We do not know who this woman is.

AFTERWORD

We have come to you, Yitzhak, to report for roll call . . .

We have come to you, as a big family, and we have come
    one by one
And you were commander to us all, already destined for
    great things
And not only commander, you were comrade and you were
    brother

In the billet over the cowshed, in the stuffy hut, in the
    damp tent
On desert marches, with but one canteen
Looking to "the small immigrant boats, Captain, we'll
    meet on the water"

And in the nights of skies reddened by dynamite
In the days of bread and jam, shorts and sandals
With that oath of brotherhood, still living among us

Unwritten, wordless, wonderful, a true oath
That ties us, your living comrades, to you in your grave . . .

For you were to us a loyal brother, a true brother, never pretending

And we sang, "Where, oh where, are there others like that man?"

∞ At a memorial service on Mount Herzl, Hayim Hefer, Yitzhak's comrade-in-arms from the Palmach, spoke these words. The passing months only sharpen the sad truth of the question posed in that song from our youth. What was it that made Yitzhak so special—so widely adored, so trusted . . . so cried over, so sorely missed, and so utterly needed?

In response, I can begin only by recognizing how blessed I was to have met him when I was but sixteen and to have known even then how unique he was. I spent a lifetime with this great man—sharing joy and sorrow, ups and downs, good and bad. How privileged we were to be side by side at every crossroad of our country's short history. As one, our countrymen held on with an enormous sense of mission. We shall overcome. We shall fight and not let go and not give in. We shall survive.

After the War of Independence, Yitzhak declared in an interview, "I will dedicate all my energy all my life so we shall never again find ourselves defending Israel in such a vulnerable position." From then on he committed himself to molding the Israel Defense Forces into one of the strongest, best-equipped armies in the world. In his total dedication to our nation's survival, there was never a pause. At the end of every long day, he would always ask himself, Have I done enough? What have I missed? On his commemorative medal are engraved the words, "I devoted all my life to security and peace." How true!

But for him, a strong defense was the first step toward the peace table. A few days after his murder, Henry Kissinger wrote in the *Washington Post,* "A gentle soul, Rabin steeled himself to acts of conspicuous toughness; a military man, he taught himself, step by reluctant step, the grammar of peace. . . . His funeral was a testament to how well he had succeeded in elevating security to a moral dimension."

Recently, Yasir Arafat was asked to reflect on what, in his opinion, made Yitzhak unique among the ranks of world leaders. "The courage that Rabin showed in searching for the political solution surpassed—in the eyes of his people, the world, the Palestinians and the Arabs—by many folds his courage in war," he recalled. "Rabin's peace was the peace of the brave. He was honest with himself and with his people. He was not a prisoner of the magic of power and might. For all these reasons, Rabin occupies this distinguished place among the great leaders in history."

Yitzhak considered himself a fortunate man if rarely a happy one. Seldom would he allow himself the luxury of happiness. Something would always intrude to prevent him from giving in to such a feeling. Not after the victory of the Six-Day War. At no point during the peace process. Not even when he was victorious in his quest for a second term as prime minister. He was content to appreciate the magnitude of the moment. Content and realistic. For there was always work to be done, unfinished business on the agenda, tomorrow's concerns awaiting him.

What did not escape his gratitude was the acknowledgment that history had bestowed on him more than one second chance: A chance to unify Jerusalem in 1967 after leaving her divided in 1948. A chance to secure the future of the nation he'd fought so hard to establish. A second term as prime minister that afforded him the opportunity to change the priorities of the country, and over three and a half years, he'd realized so much of his promise— doubling the budget for education, quadrupling foreign investment, bringing about health reform, reducing unemployment by half, absorbing hundreds of thousands of Jewish immigrants, overseeing a whole new road network for Israel, revamping the electrical grid, modernizing the telecommunications system, and launching "technological hothouses" that would put Israel's industries at the vanguard in the years ahead.

But most important, history graced him with the chance to

usher his country into a time of peace. To prove himself a warrior for peace and not just a warrior. Alas, it was not enough.

The business left unfinished by his death cries out for his wisdom and perspective. Jerusalem, Syria, the ever-volatile, still-fragile peace, not to mention the rifts within our own country, the violent forces that brought him down still aflame—all this and more beg for his clear head, his firm hand, and his pure heart.

It's hard for me now not to see these cherished attributes as being responsible in part for his demise, like the tragic flaw of an ancient hero. Yitzhak was too capable, too strong, too willing to go it alone. Whether he felt this deep down inside himself or not, this is what he projected—to us, his family, to his supporters and detractors in the government and amongst the people. We were guilty of believing him and trusting his assurances that it was safe to send him out there virtually alone.

On Yitzhak's *yahrzeit,* the one-year anniversary of his death according to the Jewish calendar, our grandson Jonathan spoke at the grave site. "A year has passed," he said. "And everyone has asked forgiveness. The great men and the little people, the sensitive and the indifferent, secular and religious . . . They have all come to beg forgiveness.

"Only we are left. Till today we have not asked your forgiveness. . . . So here we are. We who are so close to you wish here and now to ask your forgiveness.

"Grandfather, forgive us. Forgive us for believing you, forgive us for falling into your net, forgive us for succumbing to your charms, forgive us for closing our eyes out of pride. Forgive us for not protecting you as we should have. . . .

"Please understand, we were different, we were mistaken.

"Forgive us, Grandfather, for letting them take you from us."

∞ A terrible irony has emerged over the last year—one that is painful and at the same time promises hope. It has to do with our children and the children of Israel as well. It is what Jonathan was referring to when he said, ". . . we were different, we were mistaken." For our children *were* different when their father and grandfather was alive.

Throughout their lives, our children had been private people—earnest and responsible but averse to publicity and loath to speak out. They preferred to leave the limelight to their father, who, though shy himself, fulfilled the obligations that came with political life with the sense of duty and dedication of a military man. In his absence, however, our children have come forward, responding to the cause of peace, giving interviews, delivering speeches around the world and at home, invoking their father's words, carrying on his legacy. How horribly sad and sadly ironic that Yitzhak cannot see his children now. How proud he would have been.

Every Friday afternoon since Yitzhak's death, a crowd has gathered at the site of the murder among the candles and the flowers. At first it was small, fifty or so people coming to pay their respects before Shabbat. But over the months, these vigils have grown to include hundreds of people. I have always felt it was my place to be with them every possible Friday. These people congregate not just to mourn, but to reflect, to meditate, and ultimately to act. And, indeed, these gatherings have given birth to a movement.

My son, Yuval, is one of a group of young people who have begun an outreach organization called Dor Shalom—"the generation of peace"—which seeks to build bridges of understanding and tolerance, to ease the polarization of our country, to embrace every sector of our society, religious and secular alike.

This note of reconciliation was sounded just days after Yitzhak was killed, in a stirring article by Joseph Aaron that appeared in *The News,* a conservative Jewish newspaper in Chicago. "An educated Jew, a learned Jew, a religious Jew, killed the prime minister of the state of Israel," Aaron wrote. "It is a stain that can only begin to be removed if we recognize that we must learn anew how to disagree, must reawaken the spirit of Hillel and Shammai, must debate each other without hating each other, must recognize that a democracy must be respected even if your man is not in power. . . ."

Let us never forget that we are all of one people. In a speech delivered at Yad Vashem in 1995, Yitzhak recalled the course of adversity we have faced throughout history and the cause of peace and harmony as a lasting, governing rite of Jewish tradition. They are words well worth remembering today.

"He who maketh peace in heaven, may he make peace on us and on all Israel. . . ."

Almost from the dawning of our days as a nation, our prayers have fluctuated between the content of Kaddish—the prayer that sanctifies Him who sits on high and expresses the Jewish people's deep belief—and "He who maketh peace in heaven." Our rejoicing is always permeated with sorrow. The wedding canopy and the broken glass beneath it, the housewarming with its exposed plaster in memory of the destruction of the Temple, the Passover seder and its bitter herbs. In Israel, the tears of Remembrance Day splash the circles of dancers on Independence Day.

The Jewish people have known many harsh days throughout their history, hours of weakening spirits, moments of helplessness, on the verge of despair. . . .

We have known bereavement and holocaust—and we have emerged from them all victorious.

We have done so with the power of our faith. . . . Man lives by his faith. Man dies by his faith. We bear the dreams of generations. We shall not cast it off now.

We today celebrate, together with the whole of the free world, the joy of victory—yet we do not rejoice. . . . The blow to the Jewish people was too heavy for us to bear. The sparkling eyes were doused—but nothing doused the spark of life and faith. And it is this faith that guides us into the future—to days of remembrance and benevolence, to the days of peace.

Let us, the Jewish people, make these days ones of "remembrance and benevolence." Let us begin with tolerance and understanding and pray that it leads our nation to healing.

Eighteen thousand graves in the cemeteries of Israel contain the remains of young Israelis who were willing to pay the highest price to defend our country since the founding of the state. "The Generation of the Candles," named after a tragedy, have come to know too soon bereavement and were schooled in the lessons of the Holocaust—and they wish to emerge from it victorious. They are willing to speak out for peace, to claim their rights to a secure future. We must listen and lend our voices. We must cherish and love this generation as Yitzhak did. For they bear the dreams of generations.

∞ And God commanded Abraham to slay his son in sacrifice:

Take now thy son, thine only son Yitzhak, whom thou
lovest . . .

God tested Abraham. But God showed mercy and gave Abraham a ram instead, so as to save his son.

This time there was no ram. Hate robbed us of the heart of my heart . . . and the heart of this nation.

Are we willing to let this sacrifice be in vain? We cannot undo what was done to Yitzhak, but we must not betray his lifetime of commitment to his people. "He walked a lonely road," Henry Kissinger noted in an interview with CNN on the day of Yitzhak's funeral. "But if what he did is to have meaning, it cannot depend on him alone."

Where, oh where, are there others like that man?

As great a challenge as it may be, our greatest duty is to find them, to nurture them, and to support the men and women who will carry Yitzhak's vision forward and breathe life into his legacy. And we ourselves must have the courage to seek the peace of the brave.

INDEX

INDEX

INDEX

INDEX

INDEX

INDEX

Photo Credits

Photos not credited are from the author's collection.
Page numbers refer to those in photo insert.

PAGE 7: *top:* Courtesy of The White House
    bottom: Courtesy of Israel Government Press Office
PAGE 8: Courtesy of The White House
PAGE 10: *top left:* Courtesy of The White House
    upper right and bottom: Courtesy of Israel Government Press Office
PAGE 11: *top:* © Dalda Photography, Madrid
    middle: Courtesy of The White House
    bottom: Courtesy of Israel Government Press Office
PAGE 12: *top:* Courtesy of Israel Government Press Office
    bottom: © *Der Spiegel,* photograph by Mark Darchinger, Bonn
PAGE 13: Courtesy of Israel Government Press Office
PAGE 14: *top:* © Noam Wind
    bottom: © Israel Defense Forces, photograph by Dan Erlich
PAGE 15: *lower left:* © Dan Ilan—Israel, Hamenachem 5, Hod-Hasharon
    45263, tel.: 972-9-7429810/fax: 972-9-7455123
    lower right: © AP/Worldwide Photos
PAGE 16: © Amir Weinberg